(19)

Labour Law and Industrial Relations

LABOUR LAW
AND INDUSTRIAL
RELATIONS:
BUILDING
ON KAHN-FREUND

Edited by

LORD WEDDERBURN OF CHARLTON MA, LLB, FBA
(Cassel Professor of Commercial Law in the
University of London at the London School of Economics;
Barrister, Middle Temple)

ROY LEWIS LLB, M Sc (Econ)
(Senior Research Fellow, SSRC Industrial
Relations Research Unit, University of Warwick)

JON CLARK BA, Dr Phil
(Lecturer in Industrial Relations,
Department of Sociology and Social Administration,
University of Southampton)

CLARENDON PRESS·OXFORD
1983

Oxford University Press, Walton Street, Oxford OX2 6DP
London Glasgow New York Toronto
Delhi Bombay Calcutta Madras Karachi
Kuala Lumpur Singapore Hong Kong Tokyo
Nairobi Dar es Salaam Cape Town
Melbourne Auckland

and associates in
Beirut Berlin Ibadan Mexico City Nicosia

Oxford is a trade mark of Oxford University Press

Published in the United States by
Oxford University Press, New York

British Library Cataloguing in Publication Data
Labour law and industrial relations.
1. Labor economics   2. Labor law and legislation
I. Wedderburn of Charlton, Kenneth William
Wedderburn, Baron   II. Lewis, Roy
III. Clark, Jon
342.4'1'0924   HD4901
ISBN 0-19-825393-1
ISBN 0-19-825482-2 Pbk

Set by Oxprint Ltd (Oxford)
Printed in Great Britain
at the University Press, Oxford
by Eric Buckley
Printer to the University

Preface

When Otto Kahn-Freund died in 1979 we were among the many who felt not only grief at the loss of a friend and mentor but a new determination to learn from his life of scholarship. Indeed the months following his death saw a notable increase in the frequency with which scholars in the field of labour law met one another. They were drawn together from all over the world by his very absence. For most of them it was the first time they had joined in an international gathering on labour law and industrial relations without his participation; but always—as he would have applauded—their attention moved through him to his work and through that work to the urgent problems of industrial relations and the law.

We were privileged to participate in two such conferences. The first took place in Siena in December 1980 on the theme of 'Otto Kahn-Freund and the Evolution of Labour Law'. A book based upon the proceedings of that conference will be published in 1982 as *Kahn-Freund e l'evoluzione del diritto del lavoro*, edited by Professors Guido Balandi and Silvana Sciarra. Then, in February 1981, we were invited by Professor Spiros Simitis to discuss similar themes at the University of Frankfurt with a number of our West German colleagues; this gathering took place on the day following the delivery of the Sixth Hugo Sinzheimer Memorial Lecture, the text of which forms Chapter 3 of this book. (A book by our German colleagues will appear in the near future as *Arbeitsrecht—Theoriegeschichte und Rechtsvergleichung—Otto Kahn-Freund zum Gedächtnis*.) Chapters 4 and 5 of this book are also based upon papers given at the Siena and Frankfurt conferences.

To understand Kahn-Freund it is necessary to cross boundaries, both national boundaries for comparative inquiry into the laws and practices of other countries, and disciplinary boundaries to set the law in the crucible of society and to see it in action. But, as he always insisted, comparative research cannot have as its objective, and only rarely will have as its reward, the direct importation of foreign laws for the solution of domestic problems. The comparative scholar must rest content with a

wider understanding leading, if he is lucky, to new insights and
questions as well as to new ways of looking at problems that
await him at home. So too the sociologist cannot provide the
answer to legal problems. But the lawyer who ignores the
insights into the problems of industrial relations offered by
colleagues in the social sciences will never make, by the standards which Kahn-Freund set, a labour lawyer worthy of the
name.

Many students of labour law and industrial relations in
Britain now take these precepts almost for granted; yet they
represent an enormous leap when compared with the character
and climate of teaching and research in British industrial
relations and labour law only three decades ago. During this
post-war period Kahn-Freund became the foremost labour
lawyer on both the national and international stage. However,
shortly before his death, it was becoming increasingly clear that
the decade which was to follow would bring with it, both in
Britain and in the world, problems of a kind scarcely imagined
even in 1979. In 1982 one of the most significant questions for
the future is the place and the function of law in industrial
relations, and the wider relationship between labour law and
society as a whole.

These are the origins of this book. The first chapter is a
translation of one of Kahn-Freund's last pieces, the special
introduction which he wrote in 1978 to the German translation
of the second English edition of his book *Labour and the Law*.
Professor Hugh Clegg's chapter provides the perspective of one
of his colleagues on the Donovan Commission. It is well known
that they were both highly influential in shaping large parts of
the Commission's Report, and all subsequent work in the field
of industrial relations and labour law owes many debts to both
of them.

The theme of the book—'Building on Kahn-Freund'—high-
lights the use which we have attempted to make of Kahn-
Freund's insights, analysis, and method in the pages that
follow. Nevertheless it would be no tribute to him to turn his
work into a monument rather than a foundation. Events of the
last three years have themselves rendered it necessary to
venture beyond even his last tentative conclusions. Few in 1979
foresaw that within three years Britain would contain three
million people who were unemployed. Few could have pre-

dicted that Poland would experience the rise and repression of an independent trade union movement. Such events inevitably challenge one's interpretation of the function and meaning of independent trade unionism.

It is indeed no accident that one of our chapters stems originally from research into the works of Kahn-Freund in the final period of the Weimar Republic; and that another discusses the role of ideology in Kahn-Freund's work. The politicization of labour law at a time of economic and social crisis is not just a theme of the past few years in Britain, but a persistent theme of twentieth-century history. In Britain in the eighties there is a need to reassess the role of the law, not of law in the abstract, but of Parliament, courts, practitioners and legal advisers, the civil service and magistrates. We must examine anew the place of the law in the fabric of industrial relations and describe more clearly the different patterns likely to be fashioned by the threads of various policies offered for its renovation. Above all, these are the laws which directly affect ordinary people. They concern them at the point where most of them spend the major part of their lives—at work. Kahn-Freund always insisted that this simple truth should never be forgotten. The reality of the transaction through which men and women are 'employed' was constantly before his mind. That is cause enough to build further research on labour law and industrial relations upon his work.

This is an appropriate place to acknowledge with thanks the permission of Elisabeth Kahn-Freund and Professor Michael Kittner of the Otto Brenner Stiftung to publish the translation of Kahn-Freund's introduction to the German edition of *Labour and the Law*. For their help and encouragement in the preparation and writing of this book we also wish to record our deep thanks to Elisabeth Kahn-Freund, Frances Wedderburn, Annette Benda, Jenny Pardington, Spiros Simitis, Bob Simpson, Norma Griffiths, Catherine Swarbrick, Angela White, Jonathan Wedderburn, Guido Balandi, Silvana Sciarra, Mariolina Freeth and Gino Giugni, and to our publishers the Oxford University Press.

London   W.
1 February 1982*   R.L.
     J.C.

* References in Chapter 6 have been amended to include the Employment Act 1982.

Table of Contents

Chapter 1

Labour Law and Industrial Relations in Great Britain and West Germany*

Otto Kahn-Freund

This book, whose first English edition appeared in 1972 and whose second edition appeared in 1977, arose from a series of public lectures which were directed not only at lawyers but also at a general audience. They formed the twenty-fourth series of the Hamlyn Lectures, which are intended to provide a bridge between the lawyer's view of the world and the interest of a broader public.

The problems of collective labour law discussed here—the system of collective bargaining, trade unions, industrial disputes—are of general interest. The part played by the law in the regulation of relations between employers and their organizations on the one hand and trade unions on the other is problematical everywhere. The problems of industrial relations and collective labour law in the developed capitalist countries of Western Europe are, however, similar everywhere, although of course the solutions are often different. This means, though, that the knowledge of these solutions in one of these countries is of much more than theoretical interest to every other country. For instance, it is important for the Federal Republic of Germany to see how the problems are seen and formulated in other countries, above all in other member countries of the EEC. Naturally one must always seek to distinguish between the effects of those economic, social, and also political factors which are broadly common to all Western European countries, and the influence of national traditions, customs, convictions, and prejudices. Differences in formulations should not mislead us into failing to recognize common problems, nor should the

* This is a translation by Jon Clark of the 'Preface' written in 1978 by Otto Kahn-Freund especially for the German edition of *Labour and the Law* (*Arbeit und Recht*, Cologne and Frankfurt, 1979). The title and footnotes have been supplied by the editors. Editorial additions to the text are in square brackets.

deceptive semblance of similarities mislead us into a blurring of contrasts.

This book places greater emphasis on problems than on solutions. The general problem of the distribution of power in the relations between capital and labour, which is a prominent theme of the book, may differ in certain details in the Federal Republic and in Great Britain, but in its basic structure it revolves around the same problem. The sources of the regulation of these relations are—if we disregard exceptions such as the German works agreement—essentially the same, but the balance between the different types of regulation is different. There is much talk in the Federal Republic about 'bargaining autonomy' (*Tarifautonomie*)—the expression is virtually untranslatable into English and has in Britain no juridically construable meaning. Nevertheless a German reader of this book will probably gain the impression that in social reality the autonomy of the collective bargaining parties forms the core of industrial relations in Britain. Many Germans will ask themselves whether in the reality of things this autonomy does not go further than in the Federal Republic—and very many Britons ask themselves whether it does not go too far. This autonomous regulation of collective and also individual industrial relations takes place traditionally in Britain outside the sphere of state-established and state-enforced law. This is still largely the case today, even if—and this is one of the main themes of the book—the law has a far greater significance today than it did even twenty years ago. The explanation of the extra-legal nature of such a large part of industrial relations can be found partly in the third chapter [on purposes and methods of collective bargaining]—to give a more adequate explanation it would be necessary to write a history of British industrial relations. Above all it would be necessary to show the significance of the fact that the Industrial Revolution (roughly between 1770 and 1850) took place at a time when the working class did not yet have the right to vote, which it obtained only through the suffrage laws of 1867 and 1884. It would be necessary to explain that in large parts of industry, particularly amongst skilled workers and in mining, the trade unions already possessed great power at a time when their members were still without any political influence. The development of the British trade union movement preceded the political labour movement by at least half a century—the Labour Party developed ultimately largely out of the trade unions. With a degree of simplification one could say that the reverse was true for Germany (as well as for France)—first came the political, then the trade union movement—one needs only to think of the role of Lassalle.[1] This is crucial for the attitude towards 'autonomy' and the law. By nature trade unions are everywhere and at all times conservative in a non-party-political sense: a way of behaving and thinking created by external circumstances easily becomes a tradition. The tradition of extra-legal autonomy may owe its origin to the historical factors we have touched upon and moreover also reflect the heritage of the 'guild system' which plays such a large role in the whole of British society, particularly in England. It may have much to do with a reaction of the working class to the anti-trade union attitude of the courts, especially in the nineteenth and early twentieth century. Whatever its origin may be—the fact that the law stands aside, the tendency (of the employers as well) to get by with a minimum of law, is unmistakable, even if, as we have said, it is nowhere near as clear today as it still was shortly after the Second World War.

In this special edition for German readers this must be particularly stressed because of the peculiarities of German industrial relations and German labour law, which are just as difficult to understand for a British observer as the corresponding British phenomena are for a German observer. For what is characteristic in this area for Germany is the opposite of the British situation, namely the hypertrophy of legal thinking, the central importance of the law for the relations between capital and labour. If this was already extensive at the time of the Weimar Republic, is it not still more extensive in the Federal Republic? How many problems must the Basic Constitutional Law (*Grundgesetz*) solve? How many things are read into and read out of the text of the statute by representatives of employers and employees, and above all by professors? Seen in the light of day is not this notion of a gigantic corpus of legal norms, hidden from view and needing to be dug out like buried treasure by a series of laborious intellectual operations, much more incomprehensible than 'custom and practice', which admittedly is difficult for lawyers to grasp (does that matter?), but not for those people, whether employers or employees, who have grown up in it.

Here, in the nature of the sources of regulation, lies the great difference between industrial relations in the two countries. What is more, the practice of the courts has until recently played a subordinate role in the regulation of individual (as opposed to collective) industrial relations. The reasons are touched upon in the first part of the second chapter [on the sources of regulation]: this needed explaining to the British reader, who is accustomed to the dominant role of judicial decisions in contract and commercial law in particular. German readers need only to be reminded that institutions similar to the German labour tribunals were established as late as 1964 and only became really important at the beginning of the 1970s. The role of judicial decisions in the development of British labour law is therefore now in a process of rapid change. It must also be realized that in general—but this is also changing—British laws do not have a systematic, codifying character, but are intended to deal with abuses. This is a crude generalization, but what is said in the second chapter about the changing character of legislation must be understood in this light.

In the chapters concerned with the system of collective bargaining the reader will repeatedly come across comparative legal references, among others to German law. If the collective bargaining law of the Federal Republic is to be explained to a British specialist, then it is necessary above all to show that, and why, in the Federal Republic of today the content of Chapter IV [promoting negotiation] plays no role, the content of Chapter V [promoting agreement] a modest role, and the content of Chapter VI [observance of agreements] a central role. The world has learnt since 1935 from the United States, that is since Franklin Roosevelt's New Deal, that the problem of achieving a willingness to bargain is part of collective bargaining law (the willingness to bargain is something quite different from the willingness to agree). This is now also understood in Great Britain, and the problem of 'recognition' stands in the centre of things since the beginning of the rapid growth of white-collar trade unions. That the problems of arbitration have a special character in Germany will be understood by everyone who knows of the extent to which compulsory arbitration in the Weimar Republic prepared the way for the national-socialist destruction of the collective bargaining system.[2] It is not only in Britain that the power of the past over the present is great. This must be felt by everyone concerned with the enforcement of collective agreements: the German reader must appreciate how far the obligatory effect of collective agreements is a German (and also a Scandinavian) phenomenon, even though it does find a counterpart in quite different circumstances on the other side of the Atlantic (but not on the other side of the North Sea).

Without any doubt it is the complete absence of a statutorily regulated system of employee representation at plant and company level [the so-called 'works constitution'] which represents the most fundamental difference between British and German industrial relations. Seen in a European context, the absence of any kind of legislation on works councils in Great Britain is an almost unique phenomenon. What is still more remarkable, and at first sight more difficult to understand, is the fact that the British trade unions not only do not demand the introduction of a statutory system of works councils but categorically reject it. If there are any serious aspirations in this direction at all, then they exist in employer circles. In the present book, which was originally intended for British readers, there is no detailed discussion of the causes of these developments, which diverge so strongly from continental reality; but some intimations are given in Chapter III, especially in the context of the 'level' of bargaining. In large and continually expanding areas of the British economy there is extensive trade union organization at plant level, and to a lesser but growing extent at company level. This means that the trade unions have their plant representatives, members of the work-force, elected by the trade-union organized employees of the plant (often by acclamation) and accredited by the trade union leadership. These shop stewards play a central role in working life. Above all, and the German reader must constantly keep this in mind, a very large part of what is called 'collective bargaining' takes place at plant level, where the trade unions are represented by the shop stewards, even if at the same time they can also be represented by full-time officers.

It must be appreciated that the trade unions are obviously afraid that the shop stewards would be weakened by the introduction of a statutory system of works councils, perhaps on the pattern of the German Works Constitution Act. In trade union circles it is emphasized, not without reason if at times a little exaggeratedly, that the function of the German works councils is fully carried out by the shop stewards without—from the British point of view—the oppressively gigantic legal apparatus of the works council system. Seen from Britain, the choice between the shop steward and the works council is the dilemma of choice between democracy and bureaucracy. Of course this is also an exaggeration, but at bottom it has some justification. The German system of works councils, with its systematic organization of election procedures regulated down to the finest details, and its clear definition (subject to the strictest legal control) of the rights and duties of the works councillors, is perhaps the supreme example of that hypertrophy of the law and of the influence of lawyers and bureaucracy which, seen from outside, is the central characteristic of German industrial relations. On the other hand, though, this bureaucratization and 'juridification' has great advantages: it offers certain guarantees of a regulated conduct of day-to-day affairs and leads to the avoidance of frictions. In other words: it has all the advantages and all the disadvantages of administrative routine.

In Britain there is a tendency (particularly in trade union circles) grossly to overestimate this feature of the German system of works councils and moreover to ignore the extent to which the works councils are the 'extended arm' of the trade unions. Likewise, though, there is a tendency in Germany to overrate the 'anarchic' element in shop steward organization. In general it functions on the basis of a routine, not laid down by law, but nevertheless now supported by certain obligations on the employer which help to facilitate the activities of shop stewards and to protect them against discrimination, particularly against discriminatory dismissal. It is also often not realized (largely because of the nature of reporting in the mass media) that very frequently shop stewards promote industrial peace rather than industrial conflict, even though naturally the opposite can also happen. Nevertheless shop steward organization has quite obvious disadvantages compared with the German 'works constitution'. Only organized employees are represented by the shop stewards and, more seriously, a shop steward represents only his union. Since there is no systematic structure of industrial unions it is usual for the work-force of a particular plant to belong to two, three or even more unions; in a chemical factory, for example, the fitters belong to the Metal Workers' Union and not to the Chemical Workers' Union, and the typesetters in a printing works are not members of the same union as the bookbinders. To a certain, and indeed ever-increasing, extent this evil is overcome by the creation of joint shop steward committees. Nevertheless it remains ultimately ineradicable.

However there are good, if usually not articulated, reasons why, in spite of all these disadvantages, there is scarcely a thinking trade unionist who would advocate the introduction of works councils on the German pattern in place of (or alongside) the shop stewards. The inestimable advantage of the system of shop stewards is that they counteract the 'alienation' between the trade union and its members, or (which amounts to the same thing) that they are, in Rudolf Smend's sense, an 'integration factor'.[3] The big unions (the Transport and General Workers' Union has two million members) are mass organizations; from the standpoint of the individual member the trade union leadership is extremely remote, and even the local branch leadership may frequently appear to the individual to be in an exalted position far removed from the shop-floor. But shop stewards are 'on the spot'. You see them every day, you can confide in them, and (this is very important) you can swear at them. In spite of all so-called 'trade union democracy' the bureaucratic element must prevail in the day-to-day administration of large and medium-size unions and even in the formation of their basic decisions. Whether offices are filled by election or appointment is of secondary importance. It is of fundamental importance, though, that an element of 'senior lay administration' (or, to use Max Weber's terminology, *Honoratiorenverwaltung*)[4] is carried into the bureaucracy of trade union organization by the shop stewards, and that the full-time trade union bureaucracy is constantly forced to come to terms with this 'lay' element. If British trade unions perhaps provide better guarantees against ossification than the unions of many other countries, then this may be due to a considerable extent to the existence of shop stewards. In a nutshell, shop stewards are today a mainstay of democracy in trade unions, and any attempt to place them on a 'legal' footing could be detrimental to this their most crucial function. The German reader of this book, who is acquainted to some extent with the history of Germany over the last half century, will not need to be reminded of the immense general political significance of the maintenance of internally active trade unions.

Perhaps the German reader will now understand why there is hardly any mention of 'co-determination' in this book. Whereas co-determination in the German sense relates to those things which are in the domain of the works councils, it has its British equivalent largely in the functions of the shop stewards, which are based on 'custom and practice'. This means that it is not guaranteed by law or not remotely to the extent of the Federal Republic. Consequently co-determination is not an 'achievement' which you possess in black and white and can safely take home with you, but something which must be fought for and secured by daily vigilance and activity. Vigilance, runs an English proverb, is the eternal price of freedom. *Jura vigilantibus scripta sunt*, it was once said, and 'jura' does not only mean rights in the legal sense. Trade union 'co-determination', though, comes about to a large extent through the making of collective agreements and the supervision of their administration. It takes place, even when there is no question of a formal collective agreement, through negotiation. But as a negotiating partner of the employer, the trade union remains outside the enterprise. This applies, for example, to questions of rationalization and its consequences, to extensions, reductions and transfers of plant, changes in methods of production and distribution, and so on. The statutory provisions concerning the obligations of the employer to disclose information to trade unions on matters of importance to collective bargaining are relevant in this context, however imperfect they may be. The same applies to the regulations based on EEC Directive No. 75/129, which requires employers to consult with the recognized trade unions in advance of any dismissal caused by a reduction in plant, irrespective of whether the employees concerned are members of these unions.

All these are minimum standards. There are, perhaps to an increasing extent, companies in the private sector which, quite voluntarily and often as a result of an understanding with the trade unions, establish joint consultative committees in order to promote mutual understanding and co-operation. They have an extra-legal basis, and obviously have nothing to do with the statutory corporate organs established under company law. In the public sector, on the other hand, for instance in the steel industry and in the Post Office, there are the beginnings of the participation of trade union representatives, partly established by law and partly by administrative practice, in the strategic organs of public corporations.[5]

But the question of the representation of the trade unions (or of employees) in the organs of private companies is hotly disputed, and by no means only between the employers' and the employees' side. On this issue neither the trade unions nor the employers are of one view—on both sides the differences of opinion are great, but above all inside the trade unions. Moreover the problem is a matter of top-level party politics. Following the publication in May 1978 of the White Paper *Industrial Democracy* (Cmnd. 7231), it is highly unlikely that there will even be a parliamentary Bill, and it is clear that such a Bill would not contemplate the introduction of 'parity co-determination' in the foreseeable future. The most fundamental parts of the *Report of the Committee of Inquiry on Industrial Democracy*, published in January 1977, the so-called 'Bullock Report', will clearly not be put into practice. Whatever happens, I think no one can avoid the impression that this problem does not remotely play the role accorded to it in the Federal Republic.

In contrast there is another problem in Britain which has been almost completely overcome in Germany, namely the problem of trade union structure. Industrial trade unions of the kind which have existed in the Federal Republic since the Second World War are not unknown in Great Britain: the prime example is the National Union of Mineworkers. Thus there are industrial unions, but alongside these there are still also numerous craft unions (e.g. in the textile industry) and above all 'general unions', which cover many branches of industry and many categories of employee. The three largest unions are the Transport and General Workers, the General and Municipal Workers, and the Amalgamated Union of Engineering Workers (which originally developed out of the craft union of skilled metal workers). In addition there are in both the public and private sectors a number of white-collar unions whose significance has grown extraordinarily quickly and which play a major role today. (Neither in Britain nor in the USA is there a special category of 'civil servants' (*Beamte*)[6]—in Germany they are a legacy from the absolutist period.) To give one example: in the railway industry there are three unions, the 'general' National Union of Railwaymen (NUR), the 'specialized' Associated Society of Locomotive Engineers and Firemen (ASLEF), and the white-collar Transport Salaried Staffs' Association (TSSA). It goes without saying that this situation must lead to complications. In spite of this the British trade unions cope with this problem, provided that the many different unions represent different categories of employee. The real difficulties arise when they try to recruit the same employees—as is often the case today with the extension of the trade union movement to commercial and technical white-collar staffs. This partly explains what is said in Chapter IV on trade union recognition.

In Great Britain, and particularly in the USA, the questions of union democracy and the protection of the individual against arbitrary exclusion from, or termination of, membership play a large role. This is partly, but only partly, connected with the question of the 'closed shop', *de facto* compulsory union membership, which ties access to the labour market or the retention of a job to membership of the union. It is true that these things are not nearly as important in practice as the arbitrary termination of the contract of employment by the employer and the resultant necessity of statutory protection against unfair dismissal (which since 1971 now exists in Britain as well). Nevertheless we are concerned in all these cases—protection of freedom of association against arbitrary refusal of admittance to, and expulsion from, a trade union, and also protection against discrimination inside a trade union—with practical problems. It is interesting to note that these problems, which are vigorously discussed in America, Great Britain, and other English-speaking countries, play only a minor role in the countries of continental Europe including the Federal Republic. We are dealing here with the repercussive effect of differences in trade union character on the formation and scope of legal norms.

In practice, compulsory union membership—the closed shop—plays a considerable, and probably an increasing, role. The attempt made in the Industrial Relations Act (1971) to suppress it by a series of legal sanctions was a complete failure. The Act was repealed in 1974. For the sociologist of law this is, as it were, a classic example of the limited social effectiveness of state-established law when confronted with very deeply rooted customs, practices, and attitudes. Anyone who has ever engaged in legal comparisons will recognize this phenomenon: we know, for example, that there are very clear limits to the 'reception' of the legal codes of highly-developed countries in less-developed, particularly in predominantly agricultural, countries. It would also be wrong to believe that the attempt to ban the closed shop failed because of the trade union bureaucracy: it failed because of the employees at plant level. Moreover, while it should be appreciated that the attitude of state-established law towards the external compulsion to join a trade union is fundamentally different in comparable countries—in the USA it is legal in one form but illegal in another, in Canada it is legal, in Australia it is also legal in one particular form, it is largely legal in the Netherlands and illegal in Belgium—nevertheless outside totalitarian dictatorships the legal norm is naturally powerless as regards the actual behaviour of employees at plant level. If you do not intend to lock up every tenth person in a concentration camp, then you cannot force any work-force in the world to tolerate in their midst a fellow employee who is either not organized or organized in a different union. The observer of developments in, for example, the Federal Republic asks himself—without expecting an answer which no one knows anyway—how far the extended academic discussion about the 'negative freedom of association' has any practical significance at all. We must assume that it is not only in Britain that the role of state-established law in relation to such social phenomena is very modest.

In saying this we make no judgment about the desirability of compulsory union membership. It has its advantages and disadvantages from the perspective of the 'common weal' (*salus publica*), but legal policy is, like all politics, the art of the possible. A closed shop agreed with—or, which in practice amounts to the same thing, tolerated by—the employer strengthens the trade union; internal trade union discipline can be achieved (so to speak) with the heavy artillery of the threat of the loss of the job. It also spares the trade union the trouble of recruitment and in this sense strengthens it externally. But these very things are also a danger for the union. Compulsory union membership makes life too easy for it. It weakens internal integration. Many trade unionists know this and are not enthusiastic about the closed shop. But on the other hand there can be no doubt that many an employer, large, medium, and small, knows very well that the closed shop prevents frictions in the workplace and promotes industrial peace. The Donovan Commission had clear proof of this attitude amongst not a few, if by no means all, employers in the public and the private sector of the economy, and it is mentioned in the Report of 1968. If further proof were needed then it was provided by the experiences under the Act of 1971. Is it so different on the Rhine from on the Thames?

The question of the strength of the trade unions, or more accurately of the full-time trade union bureaucracy, is today perhaps the most crucial problem of industrial relations, particularly of the so-called law of industrial conflict. British trade unions share with the German, Scandinavian, and American unions a not unimportant characteristic: they have substantial assets. Consequently it 'pays' to create a law of collective bargaining or law of civil liabilities, to make trade unions as such liable, or to impose on them the moral obligation to accept financial responsibility for their members if the latter are liable. This is the explanation for a large part of the history of the law of industrial conflict in large parts of the European continent (including Germany) and in English-speaking countries. It is necessary to take a look at the financial situation of the French and Italian trade unions in order to understand why things are quite different—also in purely legal terms—in these Latin countries. The financial strength of British trade unions—which can be partly explained by the fact that they developed out of the craft unions of relatively well-paid, highly-qualified workers from about 1850—exposes them to the danger of extensive legal liability. Seen like this their strength was also their weakness, although it was offset from the beginning of this century by the political influence of the working class and the legislation which resulted from it. This very complicated historical development is one of the main themes of the last chapter.

But the question of the strength of the trade unions has yet one more, and probably more important, aspect. British trade unions represent today a great political force—under every government (their party-political colour is not unimportant, but by no means crucial). Without the active participation of the trade unions and employers' associations (both represented by their central confederations) the anti-inflation policy of the government would be unworkable. This is a commonplace and does not hold only for Great Britain. But what is characteristic of Britain today is that the trade unions—or rather some trade unions—lack internal strength. I spoke above of the 'integratory' role (in a democratic sense) of the shop stewards. This coin has its reverse side. We are concerned here with the question of 'direct democracy', with democracy which is, like Renan's nation, 'un plébiscite de tous les jours'. In a certain respect it is a national factor of the first order that the trade unions are internally active, that the element of 'organization' does not suppress 'spontaneity'. Magnificent, but very dangerous. This relates by no means only to wildcat strikes, whose significance is perhaps at times exaggerated. It relates also to the much more dangerous clinging to traditional restrictive practices of different kinds, to the insufficient utilization of increasingly capital-intensive plant, to that link between direct democracy and fundamental conservatism which political science knows so well. This, and not labour law, is the subject of concern for those who care in their hearts about the well-being of the country.

1. Ferdinand Lassalle (1825–64), lawyer and politician, was the first President of the General German Workers' Association, founded in 1863. He is generally held to be the founder of German social democracy.
2. See O. Kahn-Freund, *Labour Law and Politics in the Weimar Republic*, Oxford, 1981, esp. pp. 41, 85–6, 173–6, 182–5.
3. The concept of 'integration' was central to Rudolf Smend's theoretical studies of constitutional law published in the 1920s when he was Professor of Public Law at Berlin University. For Smend, institutions such as the state exist as real entities only through a process of continual daily renewal and self-constitution. He described this basic process as 'integration'. This conception is very close to Renan's famous characterization of the nation, quoted by Kahn-Freund above (p. 13), as 'un plébiscite de tous les jours'. See R. Smend, *Verfassung und Verfassungsrecht*, Münich and Leipzig, 1928, pp. 18–74.
4. *Honoratiores* means in Latin literally 'those of higher honour'. In 1954 Kahn-Freund described *Honoratiorenverwaltung* as 'the fulfilment of public functions as a spare-time activity without substantial remuneration by persons enjoying social prestige'. See O. Kahn-Freund, *Selected Writings*, London, 1978, pp. 69–70.
5. The two-year experiment in the Post Office was ended in 1980 by the Conservative government with the support of the management and against the wishes of the unions. The steel experiment was seriously undermined by the decision of the government in 1981 not to accept the new board nominees of the main steel union, the ISTC.
6. For a discussion of the role of the German civil servant see T. Ramm's chapter in C. Rehmus (ed.), *Public Employment Labor Relations*, Michigan, 1975, pp. 101–24.

Chapter 2

Otto Kahn-Freund and British Industrial Relations

Hugh Armstrong Clegg*

That Otto Kahn-Freund fell in love with British industrial relations during his first twenty years in Britain is readily understood. Virtually every fault that he had seen in the industrial relations of the Weimar Republic[1] could be matched by a virtue in the British system. Whereas German unions had become enmeshed in a web of laws and regulations, British unions enjoyed the 'voluntary system' of industrial relations which he was later to analyse so brilliantly, showing that the law for the most part abstained from intervention, and, when it intervened, did so to support and extend collective bargaining, not to weaken or diminish it.[2] Even in the great depression of 1929–33, when compulsory arbitration had largely taken over from collective bargaining in Germany, differences between British employers and unions were, with few exceptions, settled by collective bargaining without outside intervention. Even when conciliators or arbitrators were called in, their recommendations or awards had none but moral sanctions behind them, and applied only to the extent that the parties accepted them. By 1933 the German unions were apathetic and hidebound, while the British unions were confident and flexible in their approach despite the depression years which they had been through. They had brought down Ramsay Macdonald's Labour government when he insisted on heavy cuts in benefits for the unemployed; and they had found ways of applying pressure on the 'national' government which came next that were beginning to yield results. Despite unemployment their membership had fallen by no more than 10 per cent between 1929 and 1933, or from 25.7 per cent of the labour force to 22.6 per cent. By 1934 employment and membership were rising again. Over the following years it was the unions that forced the

* Leverhulme Research Fellow and Titular Professor at the University of Warwick.

Labour Party to take a realistic approach to Fascism and the ways in which it could be resisted; and, during the war, successes on the home front, in the organization of production, in the avoidance of serious industrial conflict, and in actual improvements in the living standards of at least lower-paid workers owed almost as much to Ernest Bevin as Minister of Labour as the successful prosecution of the war owed to Churchill.

In an essay published in 1954,[3] Kahn-Freund compared the British system of collective bargaining with those of continental Europe and the United States. In Britain, he said, emphasis was on creating 'permanent joint institutions charged with the function of formulating standards and of adapting them to changed circumstances and demands' (p. 202) whereas in Europe and the United States the emphasis was on the periodic 'contracts' between the parties which directly determined standards. The British method 'might be described as collective administration rather than as collective contracting' (p. 203) and he saw it as closely related to the voluntary nature of British collective bargaining, for its 'obligations and liabilities defy verbal definition' and 'do not lend themselves to enforcement by state-created legal machinery' (p. 204). The parties in Britain did not bother with the distinction, so important elsewhere, between conflicts of right and of interest in industrial relations; and often differences about setting new standards (conflicts of interest) were dealt with by the same bodies as handled differences over interpreting the standards (conflicts of right). Similarly in Britain there was no need to distinguish conflicts between the unions and employers' organizations from conflicts between individuals represented by those organizations.

The terms which Kahn-Freund chose to describe the two methods are significant. The British method was 'dynamic' and reliance on periodic contracts was 'static' (p. 202). These words would hardly have been chosen if he had no intention of implying a value-judgment, and his preference for the British method is made explicit elsewhere in the article. In dealing with British voluntarism he said that 'legal norms and sanctions are blunt instruments for the shaping of intergroup relations which have developed into a higher community' (p. 202). At other points in his argument he referred to 'the maturity of collective industrial relations in Britain' (p. 212) and to 'the most highly developed forms of labour-management relations' (p. 205).

What did Kahn-Freund see as the main structural features of the system of collective bargaining in Britain? In contrast to the United States, Britain shared with continental Europe industrial relations which were 'normally genuine "inter-group" relations, that is, . . . unions bargain with employers' associations and not with individual firms' (p. 200). He admitted that, with the growth of monopolies, bargaining between unions and individual enterprises was to some extent supplementing intergroup bargaining, but the only examples of enterprise bargaining which he gave were nationalized industries, the Coal Board and the Railways Board. These exceptions apart, intergroup agreements established the standards regulating terms and conditions of employment, or the 'laws of the trade' as he called them (p. 211). There was no mention of plant bargaining, and the only reference to shop stewards did not touch on their functions. It contrasted the methods by which they were selected and recognized with those applying under the statutory systems of workplace representation in France and Germany. The importance of custom and practice arrangements in British industrial relations was acknowledged as 'the informality of intergroup standards, or what one may call the principle of imperfect codification' (p. 204). However, the customs he had in mind were mainly those dealing with 'the conditions of entry into industry and the reservation of jobs to categories of workers' (p. 204). He said nothing about the customs which boosted overtime and piece-work earnings or which limited effective working hours (such as 'welting' or 'job and finish').

There is no reason to suppose that Kahn-Freund's perception of British industrial relations changed radically over the next ten years. He must have noted with regret the increasingly frequent attacks on the incompetence and backwardness of British trade unions, and their apparent inability to prevent or control the unofficial strikes which were attracting more and more attention and coverage from the media; but probably his conclusion was that the British system was perhaps a little less admirable than he had supposed, rather than that its structure was diverging from the model he had in mind. The awakening came through his membership of the Donovan Commission,[4] as it did for nearly everyone else who had accepted the invitation to serve on that body.

What changed their perception? The evidence of one or two of the many witnesses stands out. Allan Flanders, then Senior Lecturer in Industrial Relations at Oxford, and the outstanding British theorist of industrial relations, had been rethinking his whole approach to British industrial relations as a consequence of his study of the productivity agreements at the Esso Refinery at Fawley, and in particular the painful struggles of the management there to come to terms with their shop stewards.[5] His new approach was set out in his evidence, subsequently published as *Collective Bargaining: Prescription for Change*.[6] Les Cannon, having hacked his way out of the jungle of Marxist beliefs and the web of confusion spun by the former Communist leaders of the Electrical Trades Union to win control of the union from them, was now, as its President, prepared to cut his way through the obfuscation of national agreements and procedures in the engineering industry to what was happening on the shop-floor, and to show the Commission what he found there. The series of research papers prepared for the Commission was also influential, most of all the first of them, *The Role of Shop Stewards in British Industrial Relations*,[7] by the Commission's research director, Bill (now Lord) McCarthy. Solid confirmation for the notions that were now forming in the minds of Kahn-Freund and some of his colleagues came from the series of private sessions at which managers, union officers, and shop stewards from three major car plants gave evidence in camera on the conduct of industrial relations within those plants.

What was the new perception? Firstly, in manufacturing industry the system of industrial relations was not only, in many instances not primarily, a matter of intergroup relations, nor was it a matter of dealings between the trade union and a company or the board of a nationalized industry. It was also, and in some instances primarily, a matter of relations between workplace trade union representatives and plant managers. These dealings also established standards, which applied in addition to, and sometimes instead of, the intergroup standards. Informality was a marked feature of many of these dealings, and codification was far from perfect, but it was informality of plant, and not intergroup, relations. In many instances they regulated entry and the reservation of jobs to particular groups, but for the plant and not for the industry; and they also regulated overtime, piece-work, and other elements of the pay packet to such an extent that in many instances pay in the plant depended more on plant than on industry negotiations. Many shop stewards held credentials from their trade unions, but they were elected by, and primarily responsible to, their members in the shop; and in a fair number of instances they were multi-union stewards representing the members of two or more unions. The notion that their functions and powers were derived from a delegation of power from trade-union national, regional, or district offices was untenable.

This view of plant relations led direct to a new interpretation of unofficial and unconstitutional strikes. They were not necessarily a malfunction of the system, the manifestation of a disease. Since the unions did not control negotiations in the plant, it was unreasonable to expect them to exercise effective control over the use of strikes or other sanctions in those negotiations. Equally it was not surprising that strikes in breach of the procedure for handling disputes negotiated between the employers' association and the trade union occurred over issues which the workers and their shop stewards regarded as concerning no one except themselves and their plant managers, or the company for which they worked.

Unofficial and unconstitutional strikes were therefore a natural and inevitable consequence of the system of industrial relations in manufacturing industry as it then existed. That did not make them desirable, but it did point towards the means of reducing their incidence. The first step was to recognize the existence and importance of plant negotiations, and to bring them out into the open; the second was to settle regular procedures for the conduct of these negotiations, and for the interpretation and application of the agreements which would be their outcome; and the third was to embody the agreements in clearly written documents instead of relying on customs and practices, oral agreements, informal understandings, and nods and winks. When that was done it would be reasonable to expect that the agreements would be observed and upheld until proposals for change had been considered through the plant procedures.

There was also another undesirable consequence of the

British system of collective bargaining—the inefficient use of manpower. Overmanning was even then being recognized as a widespread and damaging characteristic of British industries and services. Because they had little control over what happened at plant level, at least in manufacturing industry, industry-wide agreements could not provide a means of improving manpower utilization; and the informal system of industrial relations in the plant, relying so heavily on customs and understandings, provided an ideal environment for the development of restrictive practices. Accordingly the proposals of the Commission were in its view 'fundamental to the improved use of manpower'. The reform of collective bargaining at plant level would put in the hands of management an instrument 'which, properly used, can contribute to much higher productivity'.[8]

It remained for the Commission to devise ways by which the changes it proposed could be brought about as quickly as possible. Its members were agreed that the educational value of their report should be considerable; that a Commission on Industrial Relations (as it was subsequently called) should be established to encourage change by inquiry and advice; and that a requirement on companies to register their agreements, or the fact that they had none, should act as a spur to reform. Beyond that, however, there were important differences. To understand them it is necessary to appreciate the situation in which the Commission was preparing its report during the early months of 1968.

About that time there were several unusually large and damaging unofficial strikes, especially in vehicle manufacture and related industries. The Press was running a virulent campaign against unofficial strikers. The Labour government was coming to believe that such strikes were undermining the incomes policy which it had instituted three years earlier; many ministers thought that drastic action must be taken, and also that a legislative prohibition on unofficial strikes would be highly popular with the electorate. Their views were not unknown to the Commissioners.

The Commissioners themselves were divided between those on the one hand who believed that unofficial strikes were the main problem with which they had to deal and that the proposals which they had to make so far, though useful, were not sufficient, in particular because they did nothing to cope with this problem during the period when the reforms were being carried out; and those on the other hand who believed that improvement in manpower utilization was as important as, or more important than, curtailing unofficial strikes, and that any attempt to legislate against unofficial strikes was bound to fail in the current state of plant industrial relations.

The most popular proposal for imposing legal sanctions against unofficial strikers was to make collective agreements, which were understood to be binding in honour only, into legal contracts. Then the obligation to follow the disputes procedure of the industry concerned before calling a strike would become legally binding on strikers and their leaders. Since almost all unofficial strikes were over issues which had not 'been through the procedure', whereas trade unions rarely called official strikes in breach of procedure, the enforcement of agreements would in practice apply to unofficial strikers and their leaders. The supporters of this proposal could point to the majority of developed democratic countries overseas in which collective agreements were legally binding, and which did not appear to have a problem of unofficial strikes to anything like the same extent as Britain. Its opponents replied that to suggest that the enforcement of existing industry-wide procedures could diminish unofficial strikes without a reform of plant industrial relations was in flat contradiction to the argument of the report as drafted so far. It would do nothing to remove the causes of such strikes.

For two or three weeks the issue hung in the balance. The Chairman, Lord Donovan, had not come down on either side. Then he told his colleagues of his reluctant decision (later elaborated in an 'Addendum' to the Report) that, at least in current circumstances, there was no likelihood of making the legal enforcement of collective agreements effective in practice. He had been convinced by the arguments of Kahn-Freund for whose knowledge of the law, especially of labour law and of its application, he had developed an immense respect.

Now that the majority opinion of the Commission was no longer in doubt, the task of drafting its conclusions was naturally entrusted to Kahn-Freund. The draft became Chapter 8, 'The Enforcement of Collective Agreements'. It is a classic statement. On rereading, I find only two points for hesitation. The first is that one or two passages, taken in isolation, might give the impression that the underlying cause of unofficial strikes lay in the lack of clearly-drafted plant procedure agreements, from which it might be inferred that the Commission believed that agreement on a written plant procedure could in the space of a few days remove the main cause of unofficial strikes from that plant. Further reading makes clear that Kahn-Freund had in mind a thoroughgoing overhaul of the methods of conducting industrial relations in the plant (including agreement on plant procedures), but perhaps he gave some excuse to those who jumped to the conclusion that if the problem of unofficial strikes had not disappeared within a year or so the Donovan Commission could be written off as a failure. Indeed, several members of the Commission had extremely optimistic expectations of the time it would take to reform industrial relations on the lines proposed by their report.

The second hesitation is over the final section of the chapter dealing with the situation which would follow the reform of plant industrial relations. The argument up to that point was that the enforcement of collective agreements would be useless or worse so long as the root causes of unofficial strikes were left untouched. But when these causes had been removed by the proposed reforms, what then? On two points the opponents of immediate enforcement were in agreement. Firstly, there was no objection in principle to the enforcement of collective agreements, including procedure agreements, as contracts. Agreements were legally enforceable in a number of other countries where the consequences were not disastrous, and might even be argued to be beneficial. Secondly, it was impossible to foresee whether enforcement would be advantageous or not in a Britain whose plant industrial relations had been reformed. It would be necessary to wait and see.

Some members of the Commission, certainly George Woodcock and myself, would have been content to leave it at that; but not Kahn-Freund, for two reasons. Firstly, he was anxious that, if enforcement was to be used at a later stage, it should not be employed where it was not needed, nor where it was likely to be ineffective. He therefore wished to propose a system of selective enforcement which was set out at the end of the chapter. Secondly, the text of the chapter makes it clear that, although he was convinced that the cause of Britain's unofficial strike problem lay in the system of collective bargaining, nevertheless strikes in breach of agreement were for him morally reprehensible. He repeatedly referred to strikes in breach of agreement as an 'evil' (paras. 475–6 esp.). If part of the evil remained after the reform of collective bargaining, then it would be right to look for other means to eradicate the remainder, and it would then 'be possible to identify the situations in which it would be neither unjust nor futile to apply legal sanctions' (para. 509).

The relevant passages have often been read as meaning that if the proposed reform of collective bargaining failed to deal with the problem of unofficial strikes, then resort should be had to the enforcement of collective agreements. This interpretation is incorrect. If the reform of collective bargaining proposed by the Donovan Commission failed to bring about a substantial diminution in unofficial strikes, then the whole analysis of the report was wrong, and no valid conclusions of any kind could be deduced from it. What Kahn-Freund said was: 'We are confident therefore that the size of the problem will be greatly reduced once our recommendations for the reform of the collective bargaining system have been implemented, but we cannot be certain that the problem will disappear altogether' (para. 509). Thus the question of further action might or might not arise at that stage; but it could only be justified on Kahn-Freund's argument provided the reform of collective bargaining had clearly produced substantial results. There was nothing in all this to which any of his colleagues on the Commission could object, unless they were among the minority who held that collective agreements should be made legally enforceable forthwith, or unless they could find some objection in principle to collective agreements acquiring the status of contracts.

There were other aspects of industrial relations concerning which Kahn-Freund, and other Commissioners, were prepared to advocate the intervention of the law without qualification. There was general agreement that the law should provide a means whereby a union denied recognition by an employer should be able to establish its case that recognition was justified. If it succeeded and the employer still refused recognition, the union should have the right to invoke arbitration over claims for improvements in terms and conditions of employment. Kahn-Freund also drafted Chapter 9 on 'Safeguards for Employees against Unfair Dismissal', and Chapter 10 proposing the establishment of labour tribunals to handle this and other issues.

Kahn-Freund's perception of British industrial relations had undoubtedly undergone radical change by the time the Donovan Report was written. He had looked below the surface and become aware that intergroup relations counted for much less than he had supposed in 1954. The 'permanent joint institutions' at industry level were less influential in formulating and adapting standards than he had supposed. They did not deserve the description 'mature' so much as 'decaying', undermined by the development of uncontrolled workplace bargaining which bred unofficial strikes. His choice of the adjective 'dynamic' to distinguish the British system of industrial relations now rang less true in view of what had been revealed about the obstacles to greater efficiency erected through custom and practice in the workplace. In a number of respects British industrial relations now appeared to contrast adversely with overseas experience; and British voluntarism was not necessarily a feature of the 'most highly developed forms of labour-management relations'. In several respects legal intervention might effect improvements. It was a reasonable inference from his part in the Donovan Commission that Kahn-Freund had fallen out of love with the British system of industrial relations.

Readers of his account of the British voluntary system of industrial relations in his chapter in *The System of Industrial Relations in Great Britain* might have supposed that the non-contractual status of collective agreements was for him one of its essential elements, and that this would have led him to object on principle even to selective enforcement of procedures. When dealing in that chapter with the unreality of the assumption by the law that the 'workshop community' is governed by 'a series of individual contracts', he asserted that the 'voluntary principle is sufficiently valuable to be purchased at the price of lack of realism in the law'.[9] Why should it not also be worth a relatively high rate of unofficial strikes, especially when the Donovan Commission believed that it had shown how that rate could be substantially reduced? However, when he brought his account of the legal framework of British industrial relations up to date in *Labour and the Law*,[10] he made it quite clear that he did

not believe the proposal for selective enforcement of procedures
involved an issue of principle: it 'is a question of expediency and
nothing more' (p. 130).

In the second edition of *Labour and the Law*, Kahn-Freund
commented on mass picketing as a defect of current British
industrial relations which had not attracted the attention of the
Donovan Commission; and one which was already clearly
illegal. Otherwise he did not take his analysis of British industrial relations beyond the Donovan Report until he gave his
final reflections on them in the Thank-Offering to Britain Fund
Lectures for 1978 which were published by Oxford University
Press as *Labour Relations: Heritage and Adjustment* in 1979, shortly
before he died. In 'Intergroup Conflicts and their Settlement'[11]
he had followed, perhaps a little too readily, the generally-
accepted account of the working of British collective bargaining
at that time in order to draw his illuminating comparisons with
systems of collective bargaining overseas. Subsequently he had
radically revised his perception of British industrial relations as
a result of the evidence offered to, the research conducted for,
and the discussions within the Donovan Commission; but these
new views had also been derived from others, mainly from Allan
Flanders and other members of the 'Oxford School'. His particular contribution was to draw out their consequences for
labour law. *Heritage*, by contrast, embodied his own personal
reflections on British industrial relations.

His affection for British methods and British trade unions
once more showed through as clearly as in his 1954 article, but it
was a far from uncritical affection. Faults were given as much
attention as virtues, indeed more, for his concern in these
lectures was to analyse the faults in order to discover ways in
which they might be put right without destroying what was
good.

He began with the findings of the Donovan Commission. The
most important of them, he thought, was the shift in pay
determination 'to the enterprise or plant level' (*Heritage*, p. 7),
together with the change of dramatis personae: 'the shop
stewards and their committees and convenors have in many
important industries become bargaining agents as important as
the permanent union officials, or even supplanted them' (p. 10).
He suggested that 'one of the principal aspects of this decentral-
isation . . . is that is can make collective bargaining more

comprehensive and give it richer content' (p. 8), for many issues can be settled by agreement in the plant which could not easily be regulated by agreements between trade unions and employers' associations. He went on, however, beyond the Donovan Report to explore the relations between this decentralization of collective bargaining and a characteristic of British industrial relations which, 'though by no means unknown abroad', occupied 'a position of special importance' here. This was 'direct democracy, that is that traditionally important trade union decisions are in many sectors of British industry made by the membership itself rather than by elected representatives, and this mainly at the workplace' (p. 3).

Kahn-Freund pointed out that decentralization of trade union decision-making does not necessarily strengthen direct democracy, instancing German works councils and contract bargaining in the United States. Nevertheless the link between the two had proved to be very close in recent British history, especially through the 'permanent and dominant accountability' of shop stewards 'to the rank and file' (p. 13). He noted the formalization and crystallization of workplace bargaining and shop-steward organization over the previous decade— 'precisely what the Donovan Commission had recommended' (p. 15)—which had to some extent substituted representative workplace institutions for direct democracy. Accountability to the rank and file, however, ensured that 'direct democracy, shop-floor democracy continues to flourish, and strong elements of direct democracy will presumably always survive' (p. 15). Because of it, trade unionism in Britain remained more of a movement than elsewhere; and the advantages of this feature of British unions 'should be obvious to anyone who, like myself, has consciously lived through the dying days of [the] Weimar Republic and witnessed the moral and political collapse of the gigantic German unions' (p. 20)—a comment straight from the heart.

Nevertheless, there was a price to be paid. 'The very depth of the roots which the unions . . . have struck in this country may endanger or even preclude those fundamental changes which are now needed' (p. 34). Kahn-Freund saw a close relationship between direct democracy and 'the regulation of the volume of output, the allocation and distribution of work among workers and categories of workers, and the closely-linked regulations of the supply in the labour market and of access to jobs' (p. 35). It would be a mistake, he thought, to ascribe to deliberate union policy restrictions which were 'so often an ingrained custom of the union members' (p. 38) and therefore an expression of direct democracy. Regulation of this kind was not only characteristic of union members, but of British society as a whole. To support this assertion, he turned again to personal experience. The visitor from the Continent, he wrote, and perhaps also from America, 'is puzzled beyond words by the careful and rigid division of professional and commercial activities in Britain. This, he feels, must be a nation riddled with demarcation lines, and with professional taboos and rituals' (p. 48).

Kahn-Freund offered no solution which would preserve the advantages of direct democracy without the defect of restrictive practices. Instead he emphasized the difficulty of the problem. Restrictions were in many instances 'founded on a rational defence of economic self-interest' (p. 51). They 'may be damaging and beneficial at the same time, they are all part of a national heritage, they may all be a danger to efficiency and conducive to waste of resources' (pp. 51–2). What was not in doubt, however, was their association with 'the ideology of conservatism', with 'the spirit of: "this is the way we have always done it, why change?"' (p. 52). Perhaps he thought that, if we saw our cherished customs in this light, we should be more disposed to modify them.

To the student of the Donovan Report it comes as a surprise that there is only one mention of unofficial strikes, and then not by name, nor as a unique and pressing British problem. They are 'sudden and spontaneous strikes . . . not nearly as frequent as they were some ten or fifteen years ago' which 'continue to be a characteristic of British as of some foreign, e.g. French and Italian industrial relations' (p. 15). He referred to them as further evidence of direct democracy, not least because they 'may be a revolt against the shop steward himself', thus revealing a fluidity in workplace organization which 'will presumably for a long time remain one of the chief characteristics of British labour relations' (p. 16).

In *Heritage* the main problem of the strike is that its target has changed from the employer to the consumer. 'The centralisation not only of the supply of services, but also of some essential goods means that any stoppage or delay or slowing down is

likely to expose to serious hardship masses of people who do not
have the slightest influence on the outcome of the dispute' (p.
76), and 'the victim of this change in the target and nature of
many strikes is to an appreciable extent the working class itself'
(p. 77). Consequently traditional collective bargaining in in-
flationary conditions begins to acquire an internecine
character, with stronger sections of the trade union movement
protecting their position at the expense of the weak.

Kahn-Freund hastened to assert that the strike remains 'the
necessary ultimate sanction, without which collective bargaining cannot exist' (p. 77), and that law can make no contribution
to the solution of the problem. However, he warned that the
freedom to strike may nevertheless be in great peril unless the
unions find some solution for themselves.

This revision of Kahn-Freund's perception of the problem of
strikes reflects a substantial shift in the British pattern of strikes.
Compared with the period up to 1970, the strike record of the
last twelve years has been dominated by large-scale, official,
set-piece stoppages, most of them in the public sector, in which
the government rather than the employer has been the target,
although it is through hardship inflicted on the consumer that
the strikers seek to influence the government.

On this issue Kahn-Freund proceeded from diagnosis at least
in the direction of prescription. 'Somehow—however academic
such groping in the dark may be—one tries to find an institutional expression of this simple fact that the settlement of wages
(and also of other conditions) has lately become an act of policy-
making in which . . . the union movement as a whole must have
the decisive share' (p. 88). There is need, he suggested, for
curbing 'that spontaneity which in other respects is so positive a
feature of labour relations in this country' (p. 81). This should
be done by means of centralizing authority in the trade union
movement and developing central negotiations between the
Trades Union Congress and the Confederation of British
Industry so that they could set the global increase in labour
costs, along with guidance on the distribution of pay increases,
'so as to do justice to the lower paid categories' (p. 85).

Many others have suggested that Britain should seek to
imitate Sweden's centralized industrial relations. The advantages of doing so are obvious, but so are the obstacles to success.
Over the last twenty years the Trades Union Congress has on

several occasions revealed an impressive moral authority over British trade unions, going well beyond its constitutional powers; and it is perhaps possible to imagine that Congress could extend its authority to fill something like the role of the Swedish LO. But the Swedish system of industrial relations relies as much, or more, on the centralization of power in the employer's confederation, the SAF; and the Confederation of British Industry gives little sign of wanting to play such a part in British industrial relations, and none at all of the capacity to do so. The most compelling thing that can be said for Kahn-Freund's proposal to put an end to the anarchy at the centre of Britain's wage determination is: 'Who can think of a better?'. But no matter, for what Kahn-Freund offered in *Heritage* was understanding, not prescriptions. He pointed to the central paradox of British industrial relations, that its chief virtue is but the opposite side of its outstanding vices. Through its direct democracy and its system of workplace representation by shop stewards it has given workers more power—far more power— over their working lives than any other country's industrial relations arrangements; but the other face of this achievement is the 'British disease'. our low rate of economic growth and our high rate of inflation—at least to the extent that the causes of these things are to be found in our conduct of industrial relations. The superhuman task which faces us is to find a way of correcting those defects without destroying direct democracy.

1. See O. Kahn-Freund, *Labour Law and Politics in the Weimar Republic*, edited and introduced by R. Lewis and J. Clark, Oxford, 1981.
2. This analysis is set out in Kahn-Freund's chapter 'Legal Framework', in A. Flanders and H. A. Clegg (eds.), *The System of Industrial Relations in Great Britain*, Oxford, 1954.
3. 'Intergroup Conflicts and their Settlement' (1954) 5 *British Journal of Sociology* 193 (*Selected Writings*, London, 1978, Chap. 2).
4. *Royal Commission on Trade Unions and Employer's Associations 1965–68, Report*, London, Cmnd. 3623, 1968.
5. See A. Flanders, *The Fawley Productivity Agreements*, London, 1964.
6. London, 1967 (reprinted in *Management and Unions*, London, 1970).
7. Donovan Research Paper, No. 1, 1966.
8. Donovan Report, para. 329.
9. *System* (1954), pp. 50–1.
10. London, 1972; 2nd edn. 1977.
11. See above, n. 3.

Chapter 3

Otto Kahn-Freund and British Labour Law*

Lord Wedderburn

Between 1933 (when he and his wife and partner Liesel arrived in England) and his death in 1979, Otto Kahn-Freund revolutionized the study, the teaching, and the very character of labour law in Britain. His remarkable achievement falls naturally into four periods. First, his considered analysis of British law as it related to industrial relations (culminating in two brilliant papers of 1954 and 1959);[1] second, his contribution to the debate in the 1960s about the 'reform' of industrial relations (especially as a member of the Royal Commission on Trade Unions and Employers' Associations chaired by Lord Donovan which produced the Donovan Report of 1968);[2] third, the short but revealing period of the Industrial Relations Act 1971; and fourth, the years after the repeal of that statute in 1974.

Britain after the War–Legal Scholarship and Labour Law

It is impossible to judge the monumental achievements of Kahn-Freund without appreciating the sad state in which legal studies and legal education still languished in the Britain of the 1940s. Most university Faculties of Law adopted what Professor Robson (of the London School of Economics, from whom Kahn-Freund took over the teaching of labour law) dubbed the 'trade school' approach. Kahn-Freud insisted in a famous lecture on legal education that a lawyer could not understand, let alone be an educated lawyer, unless he learnt

* The Sixth Hugo Sinzheimer Memorial Lecture delivered in honour of Hugo Sinzheimer and Otto Kahn-Freund in the University of Frankfurt on 2 February 1981. I am grateful to Spiros Simitis, Gino Giugni, Jon Clark, and Roy Lewis for helpful suggestions in preparing this Lecture, and especially to Jon Clark for his translation and delivery of it in German.

the law 'in the frame of a *universitas literarum* or *scientiarum*, that is in conjunction with other disciplines; and this can only be done in a university'. The lawyer must go 'through' the law, 'not around it'; but *not* 'get stuck' in it; and then go on to study the other social sciences.[3]

Such an insistence on a liberal and functional approach to law (to be added to a firm grasp of legal technique) was then the view of only a small minority. Most social scientists saw their colleagues, who were lawyers in the universities, as Laski had in 1929: 'a very inferior set of people who mainly teach because they cannot make a success at the bar' 'as practitioners'.[4] As late as 1966, a senior judge, Lord Diplock (whom we shall meet again), told the assembled conference of univeristy law teachers: 'I do not regard law as a fit medium of liberal education'. What is more, he went on, the law student taught law 'sociologically' or 'philosophically' would need to 'unlearn' all that he knew when he went into practice.[5] No one even laughed.

The state of the literature was little better. When Kahn-Freund was arguing that a lawyer needed *both* his 'dogmatic' technique *and* the social context and functions of law, students were still recommended books on jurisprudence which (to select one at random) devoted four pages to 'sociological jurisprudence'—'a comparatively modern' addition to the subject.[6] Justice Brandeis is reputed to have said that 'a lawyer who has not studied economics and sociology is very apt to become a public enemy'. If that be so, the legal profession in post-war Britain was little less than a national catastrophe.

Gradually Kahn-Freund became known (especially to younger lawyers) as a standard-bearer of the functional approach. In 1949, he wrote extensive notes and an intro-duction to the first translation of Karl Renner's *The Institutions of Private Law and their Social Functions*. (Sinzheimer has never been similarly translated; but happily my colleagues Jon Clark and Roy Lewis are publishing a translation of Kahn-Freund's German writings which will provide a window upon Sinzheimer for the English reader.[7]) In the introduction to Renner, Kahn-Freund noted how, in the light of Weber's work (another strong influence upon him of course), one was com-pelled to understand the 'thought processes of the common law' as the 'outcome of the needs and habits of a legal profession organized in gilds [*sic*] and preserving the structure and the power of a medieval vocational body'.[8] He found England explicable only if to the concepts of power, class, and bureaucracy one added the legacies of pre-capitalist guilds.

As for labour law in Britain, Kahn-Freund remarked shortly before his death that immediately after the war: 'Labour Law was the contract of employment and a bit about protective legislation.' A leading textbook on industrial law contained 'not a word about collective bargaining or collective agreements'.[9] The Webbs had published a short section on law and collective bargaining in 1902,[10] but even in the 1960s the English tradition continued in legal books: the 1962 edition of the same textbook now contained just two pages on collective agreements; a major book on 'Master and Servant Law' devoted not one of its six hundred pages to the subject.[11] And all this in the very motherland of collective bargaining!

In 1947, there were only two British universities offering a course to students in 'Labour Law' in a modern form (relating the subject to collective bargaining). One such course had been taught at the London School of Economics since the astonishingly early date of 1903—one of the legacies of its founders, Sidney and Beatrice Webb. Surely it was a historic miracle that Otto Kahn-Freund came to teach, for most of his career in Britain, at the London School of Economics—the only university which offered a foundation for the developments of the subject which he was to pioneer.[12] By 1966 over half the university Law Faculties taught 'Labour Law'; and the last bastion fell in 1980 when first degree students were permitted to study it at Oxford. The Donovan Report commented in 1968 that lawyers needed training in labour law, with 'at least an elementary knowledge of industrial relations'.[13] The subject even received royal approval in 1976 when a knighthood was bestowed on Otto Kahn-Freund 'for services to labour law'. Today, textbooks abound; the subject is accepted; labour law decisions of the courts are even reported in specialized series of law reports.

Clearing the Ground

To ask whether this revolution would have taken the same course without the presence of Otto Kahn-Freund at the London School of Economics is rather like asking whether the

Russian revolution would have taken the same course without
Lenin's arrival at the Finland station of Petrograd in April
1917. For he brought to bear on the relationship between
industrial relations and English law a breadth of knowledge and
a range of scholarly methods of which English lawyers were for
the most part deprived. His first task was to use his sociological
approach to explain the mystifications imposed by the law upon
industrial relationships. He had to begin by revealing an
elementary fact of life—that the individual 'contract' of
employment mystified the true nature of the 'subordination'
inherent in the worker's social status. The employment contract was the 'indispensable figment of the legal mind'. This was
a very shocking analysis to most English lawyers years ago—
and it still is to many even today.

Few of my own colleagues when I began to teach at
Cambridge University approved of my putting before students
such 'political' propositions as:

> In industrial capitalism ... [the contract of employment] is a command
> under the guise of an agreement. The employer by exercising his power to
> command fills in the blank and that power rests in him by virtue of his
> *dominium*, his ownership of the means of production.[14]

Nor did they feel happy about someone who could explain
English developments in the tort doctrine of a master's
'vicarious' liability for acts of his servant, drawing closer to the
French test of '*subordination*' or the German 'dependence'
(*Eingliederung*), as another example of 'a similarity of
developments in common law and "civil law" systems which
are simply forced by the irresistible power of economic necessities'.[15]

To suggest that English Law Faculties at this time lacked
scholarship would be untrue. The best were strong both in the
techniques of legal analysis and in positivist and historical
jurisprudence. But a sociological approach was felt to be
dangerously 'political'—except at a few places such as the
London School of Economics, where Kahn-Freund's qualities
as a cultivated comparative lawyer were also appreciated. The
average law student might have heard of Gierke (largely
through Maitland's introduction to a translation of passages of
his work);[16] of Ehrlich or Ihering; possibly of Weber, at least
after the presentation by Shils and Rheinstein in 1954; certainly

not of Sinzheimer; and if he had heard of Marx's work, it was usually better he did not refer to it in his seminars.

Of all the attributes brought by Kahn-Freund to England perhaps none was more important than his sociological perception of 'pluralism'. In a sense, the examination of his relationship to Britain and its labour law is an examination of his understanding of that concept, especially in the light of his later statement—in a footnote—in 1977: 'I consider "pluralism" as a method of explaining what happens in a non-totalitarian society—not as an "ideology".'[17] 'Pluralist' was, of course, a description which he had once applied to Sinzheimer.[18]

A comprehensive investigation cannot be adequately attempted here. For it involves Otto Kahn-Freund the whole man; his infectious enthusiasm, his piercing intelligence and curiosity. He brought to his study of English law an unparalleled combination of qualities: not only a dominance of legal and sociological technique, but also an understanding of class, of class conflict, and collectivism; an analysis of *norms* made effective by the autonomous social action of trade unions and employers—'social rights' as against 'legal rights';[19] a comparative approach which covered many different legal systems; a refusal to be bound by traditional categories of 'public' and 'private' law; an awareness of social 'equilibrium' to which the law contributed only as a secondary phenomenon—'the law', he insisted, is not the principal source of social power';[20] an insistence that law made by statute was, for ordinary working people, as important as—if not more important than—judge-made 'case law' by which the English lawyer is so often mesmerized—above all in labour law which is (he always reminded us) 'the legal basis on which the very large majority of the people earn their living';[21] a keen sense of injustice and heartfelt concern for ordinary men and women; the insistence that workers run grave risks if they allow their trade unions to be 'integrated' into the apparatus of the state. Much of this was foreign to the average English lawyer. Some of it—alas!—still is. Yet, the England of 1947 was in many respects an ideal society into which Kahn-Freund could be, as it were, reborn; a society in which a German social democrat, already experienced both as a brilliant legal analyst and scholar, and as a judge in the German Labour Court, could, after the final defeat of Fascism, spread his talents and imagination afresh. This was the first phase.

The First Period—The General Analysis

Kahn-Freund's circumstances after the war provided us with a miraculous coincidence—or, in that phrase of Montesquieu of which he was so fond: *'un grand hazard'*.[22] In the Britain of 1947 questions he had asked in the Germany of 1932 seemed to be rather irrelevant. Take, for instance, his question in 1932 in 'The Changing Function of Labour Law':[23] 'Can the State recognise the idea of class and yet remain "neutral"? Must not the conflict eventually break up the legal system or the legal system suppress the conflict?' No such issue seemed to arise. The British trade unions were independent and powerful. Yet Britain in 1947 was about to become the first modern Welfare State. Class conflict remained; but its continuance seemed unlikely to break up the legal system. The Labour Party held effective governmental power for the first time. Basic service industries were being nationalized. The free National Health Service was about to be created. The 'State' was being harnessed to social democracy. In 1959, Kahn-Freund expressed a universal sentiment of the time when he wrote: 'Since the *White Paper* on Employment Policy of 1944, all parties and all governments have been committed to a policy to maintain a high level of employment'[24]—a statement less easily accepted in Britain today. Trade unions appeared to face little danger of integration into statist machinery. In his study of the British system of industrial relations, Kahn-Freund had become more and more impressed with the singular character of its relationship to law. For, as his colleague Professor Phelps Brown put it: 'When British industrial relations are compared with those of the other democracies, they stand out because they are so little regulated by law.'[25] The 'legal system' seemed to be little concerned with conflict in the industrial arena—and the conflict between classes showed no sign of fragmenting a deeply-rooted legal system.

Moreover, the system of employment law did not distract the scholar with side issues, paradoxically because of its almost antiquarian attachment to the supremacy of the *individual* employment relationship. The individual contract of employment was—and in many ways still is—supreme; certainly no norm created by collective bargaining can *automatically* displace its conditions—a 'unique feature of British industrial

relations'[26] although of course, today the contract of employment normally incorporates the collectively agreed conditions.
It is true that the question remains uncertain whether an
employee of the Crown or 'civil servant' has an enforceable
'contract' of employment (because of the principle—largely of
theoretical interest—that the Crown can dismiss 'at
pleasure').[27] But both labour legislation and common law
employment principles have been applied equally to Crown
employees;[28] and, except for a period of partial disability
between 1927 and 1946, civil servants (other than the police
and the armed forces) have been free to organize and to strike,
and recently have been among the more militant trade unionists.[29] Kahn-Freund was happy to find that he need not discuss
the 'doctrinal and other difficulties encountered e.g. in the
United States and in Germany'[30] arising from the status of an
'arbitrarily designated group of public employees' such as the
fonctionnaire or *Beamte*.[31] The strange historical relationship
between the Crown and the common law which deprived
England for so long of an understanding of administrative law
gave to the modern English labour lawyer that immense
advantage of which even his American cousin was deprived.[32]
The same history facilitated the rejection of any rigid boundary
between 'public' and 'private' law.

As in all comparable societies, the British individual
employment relationship is now subject to a wide range of
employment protection legislation. This began with the
statutes of the nineteenth century, above all with the Factories
Acts originating in 1833. Since 1960, we have witnessed an
explosion of protection laws creating a 'floor of rights' for
workers, sometimes (as with equal pay for women) operating
through obligatory terms in the contract of employment,[33] but
more commonly merely by fixing statutory standards (for
example, on payment of wages in cash, health and safety standards, employment hours of women and young persons, race or
sex discrimination, maternity rights, 'redundancy' of workers,
unfair dismissal, and minimum periods of notice to terminate
employment).[34] The curious British practice of *not* incorporating most of the employment protection rights into the individual worker's contract of employment could, Kahn-Freund
pertinently observed, give rise to absurd results.[35] In general,
though, such protective legislation was 'an attempt to infuse

law into a relation of command and subordination'.[36] At first he said that the history of British protective legislation had pro- ceeeded gradually by 'trial and error',[37] an attribution to our social history of the virtues of British pragmatism which he later retracted in favour of the phrase that such laws developed by 'the hazard of pressures and counter-pressures'.[38] But the development of those laws never achieved extensive regulation of the terms and conditions of adult male workers; nor did they set out to regulate collective bargaining.

Such laws normally were not even the consolidation of norms already created socially by collective bargaining, as happens in other countries.[39] On the contrary, British protective legis- lation frequently just fills in a gap and even permits the trade union and the employer to take a group of workers outside the application of its standards, if certain conditions are met, and to place them under a regime of 'voluntary' but superior con- ditions. By so doing the law itself recognizes what Kahn- Freund often referred to as the 'primacy' of collective bargain- ing.[40] So, too, we have no general minimum wage legislation; some four million low-paid workers fall under tripartite Wages Councils, bodies set up under statute which fix their employ- ment conditions by Order. But since these bodies were first created in 1909, as soon as trade union organization is strong enough the minister will abolish the Wages Council for that sector of employment in favour of autonomous collective bargaining. Similarly, whilst there are complex laws especially in 'factories' restricting the hours or conditions for which women and young persons are employed[41] (groups for whom historically statute provided protection in the nineteenth century before modern collective bargaining, and for whom voluntary arrangements are thought not to provide adequate cover), the hours of work of adult male workers are determined normally by the sacrosanct method of collective bargaining. Even in an era where trade unions are likely to become desper- ate in their demands for 'work-sharing' in the face of new technology and higher unemployment, this seems so far unlikely to change. Anything like the regulatory laws and administrative provisions closely controlling overtime in France, would traditionally be regarded as anathema.[42]

Why then did British employment law come to assert this 'primacy' of voluntary collective bargaining? Kahn-Freund at first responded, as no scholar had before: 'The difference between the legal developments in Britain, on the one hand, and say in France, in Germany or in Austria on the other, reflects the histories of the working class movements.'[43]

The primary reason lay not in the law but in society. The unique character of British labour relations reflected—and reflects still—the unique development of the British labour movement. Comparable labour movements in Western Europe and in North America faced the same problem and were compelled to emerge from parallel illegalities imposed naturally upon them by systems of law that applied concepts of property and contract and sometimes feudal or statist prohibitions. But the organic relationship between law and labour relations in the 'formative period' in Britain (that is 1850 to 1906) was unique because of a combination of three circumstances found in no other comparable labour movement in the 'formative' period of its labour laws.[44] This caused a unique legal solution to the common problem of trade union illegality, a unique quality of British labour which, I have suggested, permeates even the modern law.[45]

First, the labour movement was relatively strong. Trade unions achieved bargaining status without legal assistance at a relatively early stage. Secondly, this was achieved without the aid of a working-class political party. Pressure was applied on the bourgeois parties in Parliament. The Labour Party was born only in 1906. Thirdly, the basic trade union laws were established before universal male franchise. What is more, this development occurred in a society deeply involved with the philosophy of *laissez faire*. British trade unions thus achieved legality and collective bargaining without the aid of any positive constitutional guarantees or legal rights.

The specific legal quality which this history bestowed was the achievement by the labour movement of its 'social rights'—to associate, to organize, or to strike—without equivalent legal rights. No such legal rights exist even today. Instead the legal form of collective trade union rights in Britain is still largely that of 'negative statutory protections' or 'immunities'.

By 1871, trade unionists were sufficiently well organized to demand an end to the illegal status of their unions by reason of the common law doctrine of 'restraint of trade'. In 1871 Parliament enacted that this doctrine should no longer apply to

trade unions—and that law is still the basis of workers' right to
associate.[46] Strikes were illegal under the criminal law and in
civil law, for example, because they induced workers to break
their employment contracts; and in civil law that is still the
common law position. Statutes of 1875 and 1906 decreed (as the
Acts of 1974 and 1977 decree today) that such liabilities based
upon combination, economic pressure, and consequent interference with contracts shall not apply to acts done 'in contemplation or furtherance of a trade dispute', the golden formula of
British labour law.[47] It can immediately be appreciated that
rights to strike or to associate formulated as 'immunities' from
judge-made liabilities may be subject to 'erosion' if judges
enlarge the ambit of the common law.[48] Moreover, those who
do not understand the history of their development may believe
that the 'immunities' are 'privileges', as a judge of our Court of
Appeal recently declared, deciding that these protections from
the 'ordinary common law' of the land must be strictly interpreted: '. . . when Parliament granted immunities to the leaders
of trade unions it did not give them any *rights*'.[49] Yet it was on
this legal base that collective bargaining had emerged in all its
complexities in Britain. Each industry, indeed each factory,
followed its own 'custom and practice' in bargaining patterns;
the law did not intervene. Government had, after the reports of
the Whitley Committee in 1917, promoted consultation and,
thereby, negotiation in 'public' employment; conciliation and
arbitration had (except in wartime) traditionally been
voluntary not compulsory; no general legal system operated for
the 'extension' of the norms of collective agreements; and
'procedures' were dominant in bargaining arrangements which
paid scant attention to the 'distinction' (as Allan Flanders said)
'between conflicts of interests and conflicts of rights, which is
fundamental in European labour law'. Kahn-Freund agreed:
there was no *need* to keep 'rights' in such 'watertight com-
partments' when they were enforced 'by social and not by legal
sanctions'.[50]

A Conceptual Framework

In analysing—or rationalizing—this strange picture, Kahn-
Freund gave to us a feat of genius. His industry between 1933
and 1949 had led him to examine not only the law and its social
history but also the modern practices and agreements which

permeated our industrial relations system. The result, I suggested in the year of his retirement, was 'a conceptual framework which began to make sense of the pattern of British labour law', an 'analytical edifice' which had housed all scholars of British labour law since he built it.[51]

This study impressed upon him the vigour of the 'social rights' enjoyed by trade unions in Britain. First, he noted in 1943: 'The proud edifice of collective labour regulation was built up *without the assistance* of the law. . . . No Wagner Act, no Weimar Constitution, no Front Populaire legislation'.[52] Moreover, when legislation played a role, it was largely 'auxiliary', even 'marginal, sporadic and does not affect the normal processes of collective bargaining at all', an 'absolutely dominant feature of British labour law'.[53] Then in 1954, he wrote: 'All British labour legislation is, in a sense, a gloss or a footnote to collective bargaining.'[54] In 1959, commenting on the absence of a legal 'right to bargain' for trade unions (an important focus for his analysis):

Does not the unwillingness of the unions to invoke the help of the law . . . demonstrate how much the aversion against state intervention in industrial relations, how much in particular union preference for industrial rather than political or legislative action, dominates the impact of public opinion on the development of labour law in our time?[55]

'Public opinion' was an important concept for him. It was not founded upon a class analysis—if he wanted to do that he would speak of the opinion of the 'middle class' (to which he openly related the anti-union attitudes of nineteenth-century judges). The opinion of the interests of the 'public' represented, I believe, for him that central area of *consensus*, the core of an 'equilibrium' in British society which existed despite its manifest class divisions. Indeed, as time went on he was to place more and more emphasis upon the survival of that equilibrium.

To this system of law and industrial relations the concept of 'pluralism' was obviously most relevant. In their deep conflict of interest, management and labour had an interest in common: the regulation of conflict 'from time to time by reasonably predictable procedures' (which does not exclude 'ultimate resort' to social sanctions).[56] They normally fulfilled the common interest by bargaining. Indeed, it was a Law Lord who adapted the civil law of conspiracy to pluralist *laissez faire* values in labour relations in 1942 by declaring not only that the 'right to strike' was, for workers, an essential element in collective bargaining, but also that 'apart from these differences in interest, both employers and workmen have a common interest in the prosperity of their industry though the interest of one side may be in profits and the other in wages'.[57] Kahn-Freund was categorical in dismissing any overarching 'pre-established harmony'; for 'conflict between capital and labour is inherent in an industrial society'.[58] Yet, it was hardly possible for a pupil of Sinzheimer *not* to apply to this industrial relations system the concept of 'State abstention' as the basis of this apparently stable system. 'We have' (he concluded his first major survey of labour law in Britain) 'found that generally speaking the attitude of the law is one of abstention and neutrality.'[59] Moreover, he discovered 'this neutrality of the state towards trade disputes' even in social welfare legislation—a proposition never quite so widely accepted.[60] As he refined the analysis, Kahn-Freund tended to use the concept 'abstention of the law' less frequently. Some of us dared to criticize that phrase as 'metaphysical'—'a momentary semantic victory of Hegel over Marx or Weber?'[61] We did not then know of his own criticism of Sinzheimer for writing about the state as if it were a kind of *corpus mysticum* (one of many invaluable passages which the translation of his German writings opens up for us).[62]

By 1959 Kahn-Freund had gone further. He described the policy of the law as 'non-intervention'. But the sharpest flash of insight came when he (with characteristic hesitance) described the root principle of British labour law as: 'if you like, collective *laissez faire*'.[63]

The leap forward in the phrase 'collective *laissez faire*', as against 'abstention', lay in its implications. It was so clearly a deliberate rationalization of the historical process whereby unions had successfully influenced the legislature to exclude legal liabilities and where the autonomous collective industrial forces had continued thereafter to govern industrial relations mainly by the 'method of Collective Bargaining', as the Webbs had called it,[64] where the spirit of *laissez faire* continued to inform 'an eternal dialectic of spontaneity and organization'.[65] This analysis has been said to be 'permeated by the pluralist assumptions of equilibrium, consensus and State neutrality'.[66] Kahn-Freund himself wrote: 'The line between "State" and "society" has been blurred, very deliberately.'[67]

If the phrase 'collective *laissez faire*' (or 'abstention' or 'non-intervention' of the law) was primarily descriptive of a historical process and its bequest to a particular era (in our case, the Britain of 1930 to 1960), it was not only that. What was a description was surely also a prescription. 'There exists', he wrote in 1954, 'something like an *inverse correlation* between the practical significance of legal sanctions and the degree to which industrial relations have reached a state of maturity.' In no major country of the world had law played a *less* significant role in the shaping of industrial relations:

Reliance on legislation and on legal sanctions for the enforcement of rights and duties between employers and employees may be a symptom of an actual or impending breakdown and, especially on the side of the unions, frequently a sign of weakness, *certainly* not a sign of strength.[68]

There were few, if any, scholars at the time in Britain who could catch the echo—as you will hear it—of the Kahn-Freund of 1931 and 1932 in *The Social Ideal of the Reich Labour Court* and 'The Changing Function of Labour Law'. He was not content that this British society be seen as in a transitional social phase of 'collective *laissez faire*'. The social arrangement was, in itself, desirable; a 'mature' society in which such 'controversial' elements as trade unions gradually become 'parts of the accepted patterns of life'.[69] Is it not all summed up—his own perception of Weimar and of England; his own faith in autonomous industrial liberty for employers and for organized workers—in the ringing declaration in his lecture of 1959? '*What the State has not given, the State cannot take away.*'[70]

It is of interest to note that in the same period of the middle 1950s industrial sociologists and economists in Britain and elsewhere were, quite independently, using similar language in their commentaries. Dahrendorf wrote: 'By collective bargaining the frozen fronts of industrial conflict are thawed . . . [and thereby] socially regulated'.[71] American writers took up similar themes. When employers and unions support one another's objectives the system is frequently referred to as 'mature collective bargaining';[72] and yet again: 'We have thus built in the institutional practice of collective bargaining a social device for bringing conflict to a successful resolution.'[73] But only Kahn-Freund in his classic, idiosyncratic analysis used such concepts to identify and praise the peculiar British legal structures. He was, however, too good a lawyer not to identify specific *legal* obstacles in the path of his analysis. For example, those very 'immunities' which had given so much colour to 'non-intervention' rested (and still rest) in great measure on the definition of acts immune from civil liability because they are done in contemplation or furtherance of a '*trade dispute*'—an 'industrial', or 'economic' dispute, as against a 'political' dispute.[74] That definition, he wrote in 1954, 'rests on a theory of society and of politics which, even in 1906, was open to grave doubt and which today is plainly untenable'.[75] In painting the broad pattern he refused to pass over the detail which did not quite fit. Much more important, though, was Kahn-Freund's contribution to the British understanding of the central feature, the Queen of the industrial chess-board, the collective agreement itself.[76]

The Collective Agreement

Before 1954 no jurist had ever considered in a comprehensive, scholarly manner British collective agreements. By 1943, Kahn-Freund felt he had read a sufficient number of them to begin. Much of what he wrote then was concerned with wartime regulation; but he quite naturally applied to such agreements at least part of the analysis derived from Sinzheimer. Collective agreements possessed a double function: the 'normative' effect, which expressed itself in Britain by terms being incorporated into the individual employment contract;[77] and the 'contractual' effect, obligations—especially 'peace' obligations—which the collective parties undertook. The individual contract could draw to itself the collective norms either expressly or impliedly (by 'crystallized custom'); but, he always insisted, 'no-strike' or 'peace' obligations could not be normative so as to bind the individual employee[78]— despite clear English judicial and legislative authority to the contrary.[79]

More important, in 1943 it was natural for him to speak of the obligations placed upon the collective parties by the second function as 'contractual'. But close contact with colleagues in other social sciences had made him rethink his approach to British collective bargaining.[80] People had told him, 'There isn't any collective labour law'; but that is why it interested him. *Why* was there no litigation involving the collective agreement directly? What was the 'true reason for the complete absence of any attempts legally to enforce the mutual obligations created by collective agreements',[81] and especially, of course, no enforcement in the courts by employers of the 'peace obligation'?

By 1949, he had the answer. He later said that he had 'a crisis' in his thinking on the matter 'towards the end of the war'.[82] An agreement is an enforceable contract in English law only if the parties are taken to have that intention. Where there is no intention to create legal relations, there is no contract. In an obscure footnote to the translation of Rennner he wrote that the collective agreement in Britain 'remained an "unenforceable" "gentleman's agreement"' as against the 'legal enforceability' of such agreements on 'the Continent'.[83] By 1954, he was ready to launch the explanation on the flood tide. By now 'labour law' was, you will recall, beginning to be discovered in Britain. Suddenly, in the first modern survey of labour law and its industrial context, the English lawyer was faced with the assertion that collective agreements:

are intended to yield 'rights' and 'duties' but not in the legal sense; they are intended, as it is sometimes put, to be 'binding in honour only' or (which amounts to very much the same thing) to be enforceable through social sanctions but not through legal sanctions.[84]

The very style and character of British collective agreements (with their emphasis on 'procedure'; with the British employer and union establishing 'negotiating machinery' where 'the Americans and most Continental Europeans talk about "contracting"')[85] showed that their creators did not *intend* to make contracts enforceable in courts of law. This was all part of 'collective *laissez faire*' or legal 'abstention'. At collective level they could be, but were usually not intended to be, contracts in the legal sense.

This light in the dark places of collective labour law did more than anything else to stir controversy where before there had been silence.[86] Few of those who went into battle considered the relationship of Kahn-Freund's thinking to the work of Ehrlich and of Sinzheimer. They were, like good English lawyers, looking for a judicial precedent. Indeed, the voyage of the new doctrine was characteristically English.

Kahn-Freund was, with Professor Clegg, a leading figure on

the 'Donovan' Royal Commission; its Report in 1968 in a central chapter informed Britain that:

In this country collective agreements are not legally binding contracts . . . [because of] the intention of the parties themselves . . . one of the characteristic features which distinguishes [our system of industrial relations] from other comparable systems.[87]

The proposition now carried the authority of a Law Lord, Lord Donovan, the Chairman; and the Report rejected by reasoned, pragmatic argument all the many proposals made by the conventional wisdom of the day to turn collective agrreements by law into binding contracts.[88]

By an irony of fate in an unprecedented initiative, an employer, the *Ford Motor Company*, just one year later in 1969 sought an interlocutory injunction against Britain's two largest trade unions, alleging that a collective agreement had been broken by the unions in supporting their members' strike in breach of the agreement's procedural clauses. This, of course, is what the 'contractual' status of the agreement is all about; the *only* issue involved in reality is whether the employer can obtain a 'labour injunction'. It is necessary to say at this point that until relatively recently judges in the English High Court would not listen to arguments derived from the works of academic jurists (unless they were *dead*, when they were sometimes regarded as legal 'authorities'). I was myself one of the counsel for a trade union defendant in the *Ford* case. We decided to ask the judge to consider the views both of the Donovan Commission's *Report* and of Professor Kahn-Freund in 1954. Counsel for the company objected; but the judge decided to look at those (and other extra-judicial) sources in order to decide what was the 'general state of opinion' at the time the collective agreements were made and in order to ascertain objectively the common intention to be attributed to the parties. By this means Kahn-Freund's reasoning of 1954 and the views of the *Report* were incorporated into the judgment, leading the court to the conclusion that: 'Without clear and express provisions making them amenable to legal action [the collective agreements] remain in the realm of undertakings binding in honour.'[89] The Ford Motor Company did not take the case to the Court of Appeal.

There can be few jurists in England who have ever done what

Kahn-Freund had done to collective agreements. He analysed the social and legal practice; he clarified the problem; he proposed an answer; he convinced a Royal Commission that the answer was correct; and he was (without doubt) a major reason why the common law was declared to be what he had first asserted it was!

What is more the wisdom of his answer was endorsed by subsequent history. By 1969, he referred caustically to the way 'legal enforcement of collective agreements has become a political slogan'. Few who used it understood the functions of such agreements; but the 'headlines of the daily press' had taken up the cause, isolating the issue from its 'historic context' and current problems.[90]

The Industrial Relations Act 1971 tried to wipe out his answer and reversed the legal presumption; collective agreements were presumed to be contractual *unless* the parties expressly declared otherwise. A declaration to that effect was inserted in so many collective agreements that this part of the Act was 'rendered almost entirely invalid'.[91] Some shop stewards acquired rubber stamps with the words 'This is not a legally enforceable agreement' with which they marked each new agreement without objection by management. In 1974 Parliament restored the Kahn-Freund doctrine.[92]

This first phase of Kahn-Freund's work in Britain held a mirror to the face of British labour law in which it could at least recognize its character. It was a scholarly feat of genius. His analysis of 'collective *laissez faire*' was confirmed by so many other facets of past and present British industrial relations. For example, the courts in the 1960s extended *common law* liabilities in tort so as to outflank the trade union 'immunities'. Kahn-Freund drew the obvious analogy with the pendulum which between 1871 and 1906 had swung between extensions of trade union liability by the judges and in reply a series of legislative amendments of the industrial 'immunities' by Parliament. In effect, the judges of the 1960s were creating new liabilities in 'tort' against which the existing statutory 'immunities' gave workers no protection. Speaking in terms rather closer to a class analysis, he commented in 1964 that one such decision by the Law Lords (in the House of Lords) was a 'frontal attack on the right to strike', adding 'One is under the impression that the repressive tendencies of the courts which in the 19th and early

20th centuries had to be repeatedly counteracted by Parliament, are on the point of being revived.'[93]

So too, wartime legal restrictions on workers' rights were not repealed until 1951, when misguided attempts by the government to enforce them met with a hostile reception by public opinion. Kahn-Freund commented: 'In peacetime the power to interfere with freedom to strike was tolerated only as long as it was not used.'[94] The wartime exceptions proved the normal peacetime rule that the law did not directly regulate such matters by allowing for government intervention. But these two examples also carried a question. Could this labour law system survive if state intervention in the economy increased? As usual, Kahn-Freund was already ahead of us, writing in 1959: 'The strong public opinion in favour of industrial autonomy may perhaps ultimately prove a national weakness. It would seem to frustrate any idea of planning in the area of industrial relations.'[95]

Even before the end of this phase, the question had indeed arisen: would the strength which industrial relations drew from collective *laissez faire* prove to be a weakness to the modern Welfare State? Others—rather later—put different questions. In 1972, I ventured to suggest that 'non-intervention' as a 'traditional framework of British labour law really rested upon a middle-class acquiescence in the current balance of industrial power'.[96] Before the Second World War the unions were acceptably weak; during the war they were needed; in the 1950s perhaps tolerated. In those decades, judges and legislature practised 'non-intervention'—except for wartime regulation which was seen to prove the peacetime rule. But by the 1960s middle-class opinion had changed in the face of a new balance of power in which with full employment the unions appeared to be too strong for comfort. 'Non-intervention' grew from the history of social forces no less than from the legal 'immunities'.

Kahn-Freund did not see it quite in that way. But as we turn to the other phases of his work, the issue of 'balance', 'order', or 'equilibrium' becomes even more central, and with that a concern for its survival. 'We have learned' (he said in 1968) 'that, contrary to a Marxist assumption, the "industrial reserve army" is not a pre-established fact of any economic system, capitalist or socialist, no more than is equilibrium.'[97] Nothing is immune from change; πάντα ῥεῖ, as one early Hegelian,

Heracleitos, insisted. In the comment that 'equilibrium' too is
at risk of change, we surely hear a distant echo of Weimar, of
his statement in 'The Changing Function of Labour Law' in
1932, when he wrote:

> Perhaps it was a mistake to believe that it was possible to realise a collectivist
> system in a capitalist economy without recognising that the economic con-
> ditions of capitalism allow this system to function only under quite specific
> circumstances.[98]

But in the British analysis this theme had become a footnote—if that. 'Collective *laissez faire*', as he called it, was such a
deeply-rooted reality in British labour relations that it
dominated the text. And in 1954—or even twenty years later—
the phrase encapsulated a brilliant and compelling intellectual
judgment.

The Second and Third Periods

The important second phase—in which Kahn-Freund gave his
aid to efforts to reform and save the British system of industrial
relations—and the third (in which he opposed a misguided
attempt by government to replace it) may be dealt with more
shortly together.

From 1965 to 1968 Kahn-Freund served on the Royal
Commission under Lord Donovan, the most recent in a long
line of numerous such Royal Commissions since that of 1867.
He and Professor Clegg were the dominant intellectuals, and
both were 'pluralists' (though of different origins, for Clegg was
rooted in the school of English pragmatism which—not always
unprofitably—rather scorns 'ideology'). Kahn-Freund had
come to share some of the accepted criticisms of the British
industrial scene—such as the prevalence of 'unofficial' (or
'wildcat') strikes. But he and Clegg convinced the majority of
the Commission's members that direct legal regulation was not
the correct answer to such 'problems'. For instance, two
chapters of the Commission's Report in 1968 are still the *locus
classicus* of the argument against invoking the teeth of statute to
repress unofficial strikes or to enforce collective agreements as
contracts in Britain.[99] The Report did propose an increase in
'auxiliary' law to help produce more orderly bargaining
arrangements; a small limitation of the 'immunities' (on one

aspect of which Clegg and Kahn-Freund were in a minority);[100] an increase in employment protection law; and an extended jurisdiction for a new tribunal to review trade union decisions to exclude a person from membership (though that tribunal should not be resorted to until voluntary conciliation had failed—'a kind of long stop' as he later described it).[101] This last was without doubt part of his own reassessment of the position of trade unions in society. In 1970 he wrote that the opposition of trade unions to further legal intervention in their internal affairs (including admission of members) was 'understandable' but represented a 'dead hand of history . . . at a time when their power in society was not comparable to what it is now'; now it was time to remove that 'dead hand', albeit 'with caution and a realisation that the distrust of the unions against the courts and the lawyers is well grounded in the hostility' shown towards them by both.[102] Here he had moved appreciably, however cautiously, from his stance a decade earlier when he saw no need 'in a very homogeneous society' for the courts to control admissions to the unions.[103]

Similar changes occurred in his presentation of labour law—not surprisingly, for we all change with the years, and he would change his mind rapidly whenever he saw good reason. His experience on the Donovan Commission clearly encouraged him, for example, to present labour law not only as 'a counter-vailing force to counteract the inequality which is inherent and must be inherent in the employment relationship'. Now he added, 'The principal purpose of labour law . . . is to regulate, to support and to restrain the power of management *and* the power of organised labour.'[104] The need to bring 'order' back to the trade unions—not primarily by legal teeth, but by invoking legal sanction cautiously where required—was one of the themes of the Donovan Report.[105]

There was, however, one development at this time on which Kahn-Freund spoke eloquently by what he did *not* say. In 1964 statute had established the 'Industrial Tribunals', tripartite, informal, regional courts which the civil service saw as 'the nucleus of a system of labour courts'.[106] The Donovan Report proposed that these tribunals should have jurisdiction over all individual employment disputes between a worker and his employer (rather like the French *conseils de prud'hommes*), but emphatically *not* over collective disputes—a prohibition which is ignored by the 1980 Employment Act which Kahn-Freund did not live to see. By 1978 the tribunals had acquired jurisdiction over disputes connected with most *statutory* rights in protective legislation; in 1975, moreover, an Employment Appeal Tribunal was established, similarly tripartite—a judge as chairman, one 'wingman' from employers, and one from the unions.[107] Kahn-Freund strongly supported this development both on the Commission and later; he strongly supported the proposal to make individual employment law 'a little more accessible by enlarging the jurisdiction of the existing industrial tribunals'.[108]

Critics had begun to question the role of the tribunals, as they do now: they have become 'legalistic'; the line between 'individual' and 'collective' employment rights cannot, it is said, be held; the ideology of the tribunals and judges is that of 'progressive' management, even at times a 'unitary' ideology.[109] What matters here is not whether such views are correct, but that Kahn-Freund did not answer any such criticisms most of which were freely heard in the second and third periods. His two major essays on the Weimar labour courts explained the judges' 'petty bourgeois ideal of individual peace'.[110] But no fear of integration of the unions ever led him to ask at what point *British* trade unions should question the presence of their nominees as 'wingmen' on the industrial tribunals or whether they were caught up in administering laws that incorporated their members into a social system based on such an ideology. I believe this silence was deliberate, not only because Kahn-Freund perceived that the Britain of the 1960s was very different from the Weimar of 1930; but, more important, because he saw in it a society which accommodated conflict. The 'divergency of interests' of 'management' and 'labour', he insisted to the end, must be 'recognised and articulated' because it is 'sheer utopia to postulate a common interest in the substance of labour relations'.[111] British trade union structures he saw as almost unalterably powerful and strongly representative of worker's interests, above all at 'grass roots' (the shop stewards') level. He seemed to assume that the British trade union movement was immune to statist incorporation—an assumption which may have to be re-examined in the 1980s. Indeed, often he took its strength for granted.

He wrote relatively little about the period of the 1930s when the labour movement, defeated in the General Strike of 1926, was weak. And he did not live to see the movement weakened by crushing unemployment, which rose in Britain from 1.2 million workers at the time of his death to over 2.0 million by the end of 1980.

Indeed, his understanding of the strength of collective workers' institutions in Britain was one of the factors which led him to join in the diagnosis and the remedy proposed by the Donovan Report in 1968. It would be true to say that the Royal Commission accepted the conventional wisdom of that era as to the 'problems' besetting British industrial relations; but rejected many of the remedies proposed by the conventional critics. Both are illustrated by the paragraph stating:

What is needed first of all is a change in the nature of British collective bargaining and a more orderly method for workers and their representatives to exercise their influence in the factory, and for this to be accomplished if possible, without destroying the British tradition of keeping industrial relations out of the courts.[112]

British collective bargaining, said the Donovan Report, was beset by a problem of 'disorder' in factory and workshop relations and, especially, in pay structures. The 'formal' system (industry-wide, official bargaining) and the 'informal' system (local management and factory work groups led by shop stewards) were in a state of 'tension' and 'conflict'; the informal system 'undermines the regulative effect of industry-wide agreements'. The commonest illustration of this 'problem' was the 'unofficial' strike by spontaneous work groups. 'Consequently the remedy must seek to introduce greater order into factory and workshop relationship.'[113] But the 'two systems' could not be made more orderly 'by forcing the informal system to comply with the assumptions of the formal system. Reality cannot be forced to comply with pretences.'[114]

The Report thus combined description with prescription in the manner of the pragmatic pluralists. New, more formal factory agreements should be devised; shop stewards should be brought into improved 'procedures'; a new Industrial Relations Commission should be set up to investigate difficulties and help find solutions. Allan Flanders (whose evidence was greatly prized by the Commission) spelt out the message to management which now 'faced a rival authority on the shop floor':

The paradox whose truth managements have found it so difficult to accept is that they can only regain control by sharing it. . . . Co-operation in the workplace . . . demands first and foremost the progressive fusing of two systems of unilateral control . . . into a common system of joint control on agreed objectives. Such agreement can only be reached through compromise.[115]

Such was the overall design. Kahn-Freund added the legal section with the skill of a master and a believer. Emphatically, however, he asserted the limited role which law could play. The problem of undue 'spontaneity' was familiar to him, for he had long condemned the 'relapse into more primitive forms of conduct' as against strong and orderly collective arrangements that made for 'peace', and he described 'the growth beneath the surface of the institutional guarantees of collective bargaining, of something like a code of industrial morality demanding mutual group recognition on both sides.'[116]

Law had a function (even if a secondary function): for example, in enforcing payments to dismissed workers to promote labour mobility, a problem which Kahn-Freund saw as critical in a European perspective in both social and industrial terms.[117] But the arguments for legal compulsion to make collective agreements into contracts; for imposing Draconian legal sanctions upon strikers, especially 'unofficial' (wildcat) strikers; for compulsory strike-ballots or 'cooling-off' periods; or for outlawing the 'closed shop'—all these were rejected with devastating skill. On the other hand, the 'auxiliary' role of the law in, for example, establishing the Commission or even helping to enforce reformed orderly procedures; legal intervention to extend individual employment protection (above all, for unfair dismissal); and the registration of trade unions and a cautious increase in legal control of trade union rules—these were proposed in a manner not inconsistent with the traditional British 'voluntary' system. One member of the Commission dissented; but his proposals for a legally 'regulated' system rested upon the layman's belief that a system of 'legal abstention' meant that there was total 'absence' of law, that collective bargaining was conducted 'outside the law'.[118] He had no Kahn-Freund to help him.

The Industrial Relations Act 1971

Yet it was to the objective of a legally-regulated system that the next Conservative government turned with the project that became the ill-fated Industrial Relations Act 1971. The failure of that legislation is well documented.[119] It was legislation which attempted to reform the entire system of industrial relations, using the law (the government put it) as the 'main instrument'.[120] As such it was hardly to Kahn-Freund's taste. It offended basic principles. To believe that the reform (for example) of trade union practices which impeded efficiency 'can be achieved through the creation of a "legal framework" is as realistic as the idea that the common law could by a stroke of the legislative pen be transformed into a codified system'.[121]

The Act was a 'radical breach with the tradition of free voluntary collective bargaining' and liable to bring *the law* itself into discredit.[122] Regulatory provisions weakening trade unions had no 'relevance' to such problems as spontaneous unofficial strikes, the role of the special National Industrial Relations Court was unlikely to help 'stability' in labour relations in the face of trade union opposition. In the event, that opposition, which perceived the new Court as an instrument of class justice, led the second largest trade union in Britain to defy the Court, even to the sequestration of its property—an event which from personal contact I recall evoking mixed feelings in Otto Kahn-Freund. For while he shared in the opposition to the Act, he was clearly concerned about the long-term effect upon the British social structure if the unions felt themselves compelled to pit industrial strength against the law and the courts—even this law and this Court.

He concluded his masterly survey *Labour and the Law* of 1972:

The law has now—to some extent—abandoned the previous policy. We shall see whether this change will help or hinder the reform of industrial relations, the need for which cannot be in doubt. . . . I regard it as possible or even probable that, sooner or later, the law will have to return to that policy of self-restraint which in the past served British society so well.[123]

Three comments serve to illustrate his thinking in this period. The law of 1971 imported from the Taft-Hartley Act in the United States the power for the government to obtain an order from the Court compelling a ballot of workers about to strike if there was a 'national emergency'. He wrote:

[In] individual labour relations . . . transplantation is comparatively easy . . . (though) even here deeply ingrained legal ideologies may set a limit to transplanation. . . . The bulk of the Act, however, is about unions and their relations with employers, about collective agreements and strikes. . . . It would indeed be a remarkable '*hazard*', an unexpected coincidence, if substantive rules wrenched out of their American constitutional, political and industrial context could successfully be made to fit the needs of a country with institutions so different from those of the United States.[124]

Secondly, the 1971 Act launched an attack upon the legality of the 'closed shop'. He stated: 'The case for the closed shop can only be made in terms of the need for an equilibrium of power. It cannot be attacked or defended in terms of general ethical sentiments but only in terms of social expediency.'[125] His opposition to the Act in this respect was based far more on its likely ineffectiveness than upon its quality as an attack upon workers' collective strength.

Thirdly, commenting upon one of a number of judgments which enforced an individual worker's new rights to the serious detriment of a trade union, its members, and the collective bargaining structure, he commented that judges 'should sympathise with the small against the big'. One such decision by the new Court was legally 'correct'; but 'from the point of view of *orderly* industrial relations, in which the country is vitally interested, the consequences of the decision are unwelcome, perhaps quite intolerable'.[126] His comments on the 1971 Act repeatedly reasserted the dangers both of expecting too much from the law and of smashing the precious British equilibrium. That danger to equilibrium was renewed in the last phase, the five years after 1974.

The Fourth Phase: 1974–1979

The Act of 1971 was, I thought and still think, an attack upon free and autonomous trade unionism in Britain. But also, in a sense the period of its operation was an irrelevance—a dream or a nightmare (according to your point of view) when everyone could enthuse for or against the Act and scarcely have time or energy for the real world. And it must be admitted that the statute did have a plan and a vision, however wrong-headed and myopic, something lacking in the present government's Employment Act of 1980. The 1980 Act is a much more naked attempt to reduce the bargaining strength of trade unions, largely by narrowing the ambit of the 'immunities' (in some cases to an area smaller than the liberties won in 1906)[127] without any pretence about using law to 'reform' the industrial relations system.

In 1974, the legislators awoke from this curious episode of the 1971 Act and repealed it. Who could blame Parliament for deciding to return to the legal structures of traditional 'voluntarism' and invoke the principle of 'collective *laissez faire*' alongside the other policies of the new social-democratic government? Indeed, I would say to the critics: 'Where else was there to go?'. No doubt it had to be 'voluntarism' with a difference; with a vastly expanded 'floor of rights', for example, in individual protection employment laws.[128] Indeed, that great expansion led some commentators to suggest that the new scope of such laws (on unfair dismissal, 'redundancy', maternity rights, racial and sexual discrimination) not only put a new colour on the 'voluntary' system within the framework of the revivified 'immunities',[129] but also represented a 'fundamental and irreversible trend' towards 'legal regulation of the British *system* of industrial relations'.[130] Kahn-Freund accepted the trend as regards 'individual' regulatory legislation, but not as regards collective labour law and auxiliary legislation 'where the description might be misleading'.[131]

There was, however, one major attempt to 'regulate' part of the system. The Employment Protection Act 1975 provided that the Advisory Conciliation and Arbitration Service (ACAS)—which operates on the basis of voluntary persuasion—should have the exceptional power to oblige an employer to 'recognise' and bargain with a union representing some or all of his employees.[132] Thinking in some trade union circles had changed since 1959 when Kahn-Freund noted the 'unwillingness of the unions to invoke the help of the law' on this matter.[133] The absence of such an obligation had a prominent place in his analysis of 'non-intervention'. Some hopes ran high for this unusual element of regulation in *collective* labour relations;[134] regulation which stopped short of direct sanction, however, since the remedy for refusal to bargain was an arbitration award of new employment conditions (a route which Kahn-Freund had advocated because 'all legal development must be along a diagonal in a parallelogram of forces' where one line formulated policy to a goal, the other what is 'practicable in a society in the light of traditions, habits and available means').[135] Even Kahn-Freund, who stressed the tripartite character of the ACAS Council (unions, employers, and 'independents') 'the traditional pattern of British self-governing institutions in the field of labour relations',[136] was optimistic about this new departure. But the courts soon showed themselves ready in classical English judicial style to control the discretion which Parliament seemed to have bestowed exclusively upon ACAS;[137] unions gradually reverted to their belief that 'recognition' was best obtained from employers by industrial strength, not by the use of the law;[138] and in 1979 the Chairman of ACAS effectively invited the new Conservative government to repeal this part of the 1975 Act, which it did in 1980.[139] It turned out to be astonishing but true that 'even this small degree of intervention may be too strong a burden for the traditionally "voluntary" system of collective labour law to bear'.[140]

More generally, Kahn-Freund took the opportunity in his second edition of *Labour and the Law* in 1977 to paint a panoramic picture of the newly-restored legal system of 'collective *laissez faire*'. The old framework had been restored, but the structure of the 'immunities' in trade disputes had been adjusted by Parliament to take account of judicial expansions in the common law of tort in previous decades. This led to a further 'politicisation' of labour law itself. Some observers—even some judges—alleged that the legislation of 1974 to 1976 had 'extended the privileges' of trade unions. One judge even suggested that this had been done because Parliament 'felt so confident that trade unions could be relied upon always to act "responsibly" in trade disputes' and found the privileges of trade unions to 'stick in judicial gorges'.[141] It was Lord Diplock who, we recall, mistrusted the teaching of law as a liberal education. Indeed in a number of judgments, most of the judiciary reverted to the habits of the 1960s interpreting the 'immunities' in a novel, restrictive manner and made it clear that they did not welcome these statutes.[142] But their legal effect was accurately summarized by one Law Lord when he remarked in 1979, 'The law now is back to what Parliament intended when it enacted the Act of 1906—but stronger and clearer than it was then.'[143]

It was in this phase that Kahn-Freund's truly remarkable powers of comparative assessment were displayed comprehensively in the sustained exposition of British law, in the context both of general legal concepts and of the labour law systems of European and American countries. The reader is referred on one line to subsections (4) and (5) of section 18 of the British Act of 1974, only to be swept along gently a few lines later to comparisons with Articles of the French *Code du Travail* (and their origins in 1919) and to the relevant laws in Germany, Switzerland, the Netherlands, and Belgium. He modestly called this in his 'Conclusion' a work on some of the 'essential characteristics' of our law and comparisons with 'analogous features of some foreign systems'. But this time the conclusion of the book ended differently. No longer had British labour law 'abandoned the previous policy' of self-restraint. The failure of the 1971 Act had 'reinforced our insight that neither the legislature nor the courts should attempt to burden the law with tasks which it cannot fulfil'. Despite a growth in the scope of labour law, it was now again in Britain 'the policy of the law to allow the two sides by agreement and practice to develop their own norms and their own sanctions, and it abstains from legal compulsion in their collective relationship. In this respect the law has returned to a road from which it departed between 1971 and 1974.' In future, economic necessities 'may compel both sides of industry to adopt policies of adjustment and of restraint'. In context, in 1977, that plainly referred to 'planning the economy', 'incomes policy', and 'wage restraint'. Kahn-Freund concluded: 'To these however the *law* can make no significant contribution.'[144] Even so, one felt he had not forgotten his warning in 1959, that in terms of 'planning' industrial relations, autonomy might be a 'national weakness'.

There can be no doubt about the influence of this book. If in 1971 some had felt that we had seen the end of 'legal abstention' which might have been valid for only those decades when the balance of social forces allowed, this reconstitution of the pluralist package was hard to resist. Kahn-Freund made it make sense not only in Britain but also now in an international setting. It was true that 'middle class opinion'—and with it the judiciary—was more hostile to trade unions than at any time since 1926; and that hostility increased as the 'Social Contract' between the Labour government and the trade unions began to crumble in 1977.[145] But Kahn-Freund in the last years of his life did not regard that as the central problem. His later works contain scant mention of the 'repressive tendencies' of the judiciary. Nor was he disposed to spend his energies—still extraordinarily powerful—upon such issues as whether British labour law should jettison 'immunities' and enact 'rights' (a current issue by then already aired).[146]

It was, he wrote, 'a commonplace' that the 'scope and force of law is circumscribed by national boundaries which bear no relation to the international scope of economic activities'; and that labour law 'designed to promote an equilibrium of power of management and organised labour' inevitably failed internationally when the transnational enterprise faced unions unable to organize 'effective international co-operation'. But while noting that the updated British 'immunities' allowed for 'international solidarity' among workers (by the new definition of 'trade disputes') he concluded: 'The law can do little to promote [such co-operation].'[147] Moreover, he doubted whether, even if national laws presented no obstacles, a countervailing union power could confront the transnational enterprise. What is more, these 'empires more powerful than nation states' brought welcome investment to some workers and deprived others, thereby creating an actual or potential conflict of interests *between* workers in, for example, 'the developed and . . the developing countries'.[148]

The Threat to Equilibrium

But it was the state of that 'equilibrium' in Britain itself that preoccupied him in 1978, and this gave rise to his last work, three lectures published in 1979 as *Labour Relations: Heritage and Adjustment*. By now he had made explicit one major concern and one renewed rejection. The concern related to what he saw as a threat to social balance from trade unions themselves or spontaneous work groups. While 'the heritage' of trade union direct democracy might be a political asset, it was also a 'serious and continuing liability' when adjusting labour relations to social and economic change because of 'the omnipresent danger of irrationally motivated action'.[149] In a sense, this was little more than a more intense return to the anxieties of Donovan.

No one who knew him through these years, however, could fail to notice that he became increasingly alarmed about aspects of industrial conflict, especially 'picketing'. This had always been an area of concern to him; but whereas in 1972 he felt that

the law placed 'serious limitation' on picketing, by 1977 (after
mass picketing by coal miners in 1972 and 1974 both at their
own pits and outside electricity power stations to cut off both
coal and oil supplies to them) he became more alarmed. He felt
it was permissible to picket the pits and thereby put pressure on
the employers; but the miners' disruption of oil supplies to the
stations, albeit in furtherance of their dispute, was 'pressure
brought to bear on the *consumer*' and certainly 'not "picketing"
as this word was understood until fairly recently'.[150]

This was an appeal to the history of the concept which he did
not justify and which may not, indeed, be justifiable. But
protracted official stoppages had begun to replace short
spontaneous strikes in the pattern of British industrial action.
In his view, the miners' picketing to starve power stations of all
supplies—including oil—was not only not true picketing; it was
'outside industrial relations'. All 'mass picketing' was obstruction (as indeed legally it may well be) and not picketing 'in
the proper sense'. Wilful obstruction of the highway was and is
a crime which has long limited the right of 'peaceful picketing'.[151] The conviction of a union official who obstructed a lorry
for a few minutes in a trade dispute was sustained by the Law
Lords in 1974.[152] But Kahn-Freund's fierce condemnation of
the miners' extension of their industrial action in 1972 was
important. After all, if the oil-tanker lorry drivers had declared
a strike in sympathy with the miners' claims, one would con-
fidently have expected him to have supported their traditional
right in Britain to take such solidarity action. There was,
therefore, something strangely formal about his definition of
'proper' picketing. Of course, the image that 'mass picketing'
necessarily involves violence or obstruction has been assiduously
cultivated by the media, leading one Chief Constable of Police
to say in 1980 that, with large numbers of pickets, frequently 'all
is peaceful. . . . They are sometimes there for comradeship and
solidarity. . . . You sometimes get a very jaundiced picture from
the news media who tend to highlight the occasions when things
go wrong.'[153] But one could detect a note of fear in Kahn-
Freund when he saw what he believed to be an increase of
unacceptable 'picketing' as a symptom of renewed disorder that
might threaten British society. Why else should he write as
early as 1974:

It seems that there is a spreading belief that the law cannot put any limits to any action taken in the course of industrial disputes. The complete confusion in the use of the work 'picketing' by the Press at the time of the coal strike in early 1972 is only a symptom of a very great danger. Perhaps those who have with so much justification always argued against legal intervention beyond the point of absolute necessity should now consider the need for emphasising the role which the law still has and will always have to play in industrial relations.[154]

In his last publication in 1979 his critical reassessment of British trade unions led him to allege without spelling out the evidence an increasing use of 'force' in picketing.[155] More generally, 'direct democracy' inside the unions (which he analysed on the basis of the important new findings from research completed at Warwick University)[156] was now a liability in modern British society, for it could lead to 'suicidal industrial action'. Unless the unions themselves found a solution to this problem—an 'almost super-human' task; but it must be the unions; the law could *not* solve it—then 'the freedom to strike' (that necessary sanction without which neither collective bargaining nor the unions can exist—on that he remained adamant) 'may' he warned 'one day be in mortal danger'.[157] One year later the Employment Act 1980 was enacted. 'Sympathetic' or 'solidarity' strikes were severely curtailed (as 'secondary action') by savage new restrictions on 'immunities' in trade disputes; and 'secondary picketing' away from a worker's place of work was subjected to civil liability. He would not, of course, have approved of this statute. But the danger he foresaw. What was his prescription to avert it?

Industrial Democracy

Before we examine that, it is necessary to touch upon the avenue of reform which he rejected. In this decade a debate about 'industrial democracy' by way of workers' representation on the boards of employing bodies, public corporations or private companies, which had gone underground in Britain in 1932, gushed forth afresh.[158] The Trades Union Congress in 1974 reversed traditional policies and proposed workers' representation through trade unions on the boards of large companies to the extent of 50 per cent (and no less). This was to be a supplement to traditional collective bargaining which finds it difficult—as both Swedish and Italian experience particularly illustrates—to reach such strategic corporate decisions as investment or closures. In 1977 the Bullock Committee of Inquiry proposed equal representation for trade unionists and for shareholders in the company boardroom—plus a number of 'eleventh' men to hold the balance,[159] a proposal which sent British management into a paroxysm of alarm and anger.[160] Kahn-Freund also rejected this road, despite the longstanding Draft Fifth Directive of the European Economic Community (an institution to which he was in general completely committed).[161] One had to choose between building 'industrial democracy' either 'in the land of collective bargaining on the pluralistic pattern or in the land of company law on the unitary pattern'.[162]

He would brook no compromise on this. He rejected what some of us called the 'conflictual partnership' of the Bullock Committee's proposals in which workers could participate on the board *without* 'reification' (as he put it) of the 'best interests of the company'—a danger which was of course a direct echo of his views about the direction of labour law in the Weimar Republic. Paul Davies and I made the suggestion that the new 'land of industrial democracy' might turn out to be 'one where the old maps of "unitary" and "pluralist" models are inadequate'.[163] The attempt to give workers a real voice (at least, in this transition of our society) in the 'joint regulation' of industrial issues central to their lives which are still in the unilateral control of their employers despite decades of collective bargaining might, we thought, demand also an attempt to break free from the 'pluralist', 'corporatist', 'syndicalist', and 'unitary' concepts now fading on the charts of industrial sociology. Such a new direction need not diminish and indeed could complement political democracy.

But Kahn-Freund was adamant. He did not see 'industrial democracy' in this form as any transition to a desirable new social order. He made no secret that his scepticism derived partly from his experience of Weimar.[164] He disapproved of *board* representation, but was rather more attracted by works councils in the substructure of the enterprise. On this topic he reserved his sharpest criticism for those (perhaps German) 'trade union leaders anxious to blur the line between labour and management . . . elevating "codetermination" almost to the level of religious belief . . . the "unitary" approach to labour relations ... [which] should be firmly rejected'.[165] But he seemed quite unwilling to regard the British shop steward as a satisfactory alternative to a works council. He tried to read the Bullock Report 'with an open mind'; but 'I was doing my best to find the road to Damascus and to turn from a sceptic into a believer. It is my painful duty to confess that I did not succeed.'[166]

Whatever the merits of 'industrial democracy', Kahn-Freund lived to see it removed from the agenda in Britain. Some union leaders reinforced their objections to 'participation' when they realized what Professor Simitis has insisted can be the price of 'participation', that is, the increasingly question-able validity of strike action.[167] But, more significantly, by 1979 the accelerating recession and rising unemployment killed any interest there was for 'industrial democracy' in the hearts of trade union leaders; they were, and are, understandably more concerned for the moment to defend the jobs of their members. Today, however, the question remains for us all: if 'democracy' is to be given an 'industrial' dimension, what *are* the models for tomorrow? How can the formal democracy of the ballot box, through which society might control its economic destiny by centralized machinery, be complemented by decentralized participation at the place of work where working people can share in fellowship the shaping of their own lives?

Beyond Pluralism?: The Need for a New Analysis?

The debate about 'industrial democracy' suggested again, however, that Kahn-Freund did not espouse 'pluralism' *only* 'as a method of explaining what happens' (as he claimed in 1977)[168]—at least not always. By this time, 'pluralism' had also been the subject of attack by sociologists, such as Fox and Goldthorpe, who offered what has come to be called the 'radical critique' of pluralism. For conventional pluralism, wrote Fox, 'conflict above a certain level is felt to be evidence that the ground rules need changing'. Otherwise its motto is 'live-and-let-live' and tolerance of collectivism, subject to the observance of 'honourably negotiated agreements'.[169] To the Marxist critique which alleged that pluralism only covered or even sanctified class inequalities of power,[170] these writers offered an alternative critique which also concentrated upon the im-balance of power, and on the strengthening of *managerial* power brought about by institutions in the pluralist frame, including collective bargaining. 'Pluralism', wrote Fox, 'could be presented, in fact, as the far-seeing manager's ideology.'[171] Workers' collective organizations may mitigate the imbalance; but the imbalance remains. In bargaining, trade unions do not attack the 'basic principles' of private property, hierarchical structures at work, massive inequalities, and extreme division of labour.[172] In the same period, other writers began to describe the British developments in yet another way: as 'corporatist' (or, in Crouch's phrase, 'bargained corporatism').[173] The participation by trade unions at various levels of social government in *'tripartite'* structures accelerated the popularity of this analysis with all the monitory nuances that 'corporatist' conveyed.

But Kahn-Freund adopted none of these alternatives to 'pluralism'.[174] Instead, he devoted what proved to be his final publication to a renewed investigation of British trade unions: their special heritage of both spontaneous action and direct democracy; their unusual concentration upon 'control of the job'; their special responsibility; and the place of the worker himself in the midst of great economic and social change.[175]

Distinguishing British unions from those in other European countries, he stressed again their emergence in the absence of a working-class political party, and the critical importance of the decentralization of power to the rank and file. He now placed added emphasis, however, upon the 'long persistence of the influence of craft unionism'.[176] Of course, he accepted that, in other European countries too, skilled crafts were the 'cradle of unions'. But in Britain, craft attitudes and methods remained 'dominant'— and there survived 'the very deep-seated pre-capitalist guild spirit'. This, he thought, begat a special attitude towards 'job control'—control of access to the job and control over membership of the union. Whereas German legal debate, therefore, was about the validity of privileges bargained for union members only, in Britain the equivalent issue was the law about the 'closed shop'. The difference was social not legal in origin—witness the wholly unsuccessful attempt by the Industrial Relations Act 1971 to outlaw the closed shop.[177] But the 'guild spirit' was a critical British element.[178]

The responses of British trade unions, especially to 'control of the job', are, I would suggest, equally referable in *modern* times to the dramatic effects upon the labour market of technological change; huge concentrations of capital; new mechanisms of subordination and alienation of the worker; the deepening crises and contradictions of both the capitalist 'mixed economy' and the world economic order; the development of gigantic national and transnational engines of power in the modern world. When a tradition impedes progress, one must ask whose progress is being impeded. Even a Luddite had a case—at any rate if he could mature into a Chartist. But Kahn-Freund insisted that the 'pre-capitalist basis of contemporary British society' engendered 'conservatism' and in the unions, through the craft tradition, 'job control'.[179]

It is often forgotten how strongly the Donovan Report also criticized the legacies of the 'craft' tradition.[180] For Kahn-Freund, this tradition only impaired 'working class solidarity'; now, with the predominance of 'restrictive practices' and 'demarcation', it obstructed progress—just as it did (he took the opportunity to repeat) in the legal profession.[181] Almost despairingly he asserted:

This *damnosa hereditas* of British society and of the British economy can, I submit, be only understood as an element of the general history of this country and—more than that—it is a legacy inherited not only by the working class or by the trade unions but by the entire nation ... a nation riddled with demarcation lines, and with professional rituals and taboos.[182]

The thesis that the conservative 'craft' traditions of British trade unionism are a central obstacle to working-class solidarity is surely doubtful. As Eric Hobsbawm has recently pointed out, current trade union action certainly is 'economic in the narrowest sense' in *all* types of union and is indeed riddled with 'sectionalism'; yet paradoxically 'this militancy unquestionably reflects a notable assertion of class consciousness and class power'.[183] Unless one defined 'progress' by reference only to managerial interests, it would surely be difficult to sustain the thesis that the 'craft' tradition in unions was its dominant obstacle. Indeed, it is not clear exactly which meaning of 'craft' is here being used.[184] Kahn-Freund accepted that there was not necessarily any *historical* link with the old 'guild spirit';[185] that much seems likely from the work of the labour historians;[186] and although the British movement has full experience of an 'aristocracy of labour',[187] the emergence of a 'class spirit as against a guild spirit'[188] is a notable feature of its nature at various historical moments.

Details of disagreement on such matters pale into insignificance, however, beside what Kahn-Freund had to say in his third chapter—the last chapter he ever wrote. Analysing once more the special evolution of British labour law as changes overtook the labour force (especially in the service sector) he turned to his most urgent theme: 'the growing conflict between the interests of the worker as a producer and his interests as a consumer'.[189] The very social function of industrial action had, he declared, changed. Centralization of the supply of services, the gradual disappearance of competition and manifold other changes in the economy meant that:

socially (but by no means legally) speaking, the employer is in such a situation no more than the agent of the consumer, the instrument of the public (in the sense of the amorphous mass of the consumers) for maintaining or regaining the supplies and the services on which they depend.

The employer as the 'instrument of the mass of the consumers' was indeed a radical change in analysis.

Moreover, he claimed,

Since . . . something of the order of 80 to 90 per cent of the consumers are workers the victim of this change in the target and the nature of many strikes is to an appreciable extent the working class itself.

By this time the old analysis is fast crumbling, only to be dealt another telling blow:

In this sense the strike as a social institution—once considered as the supreme example of working class solidarity—may have been dialectically transmuted into its opposite: groups of workers seeking advantages at the expense of others . . . [leading to] false consciousness . . . a heritage impeding adjustment.

Already in 1972, Kahn-Freund had presented the divergency of interest in society as the desire to increase the rate of consumption *versus* the desire to increase the rate of investment.[190] But the new allegation that we must replace our 'nineteenth century ideology' about strikes with the concept that they represent a working-class civil war was novel and provoking. Had the damage caused to other workers by those on strike really changed qualitatively by reason of the new technology? Is 'co-exploitation' a new phenomenon?[191]

Kahn-Freund insisted that the freedom to strike must be preserved. On that he never compromised. But now, he declared, it remained in 'permanent political danger' unless 'the helpless consumer' could be protected. These propositions could not, of course, sit easily together. Against whom could workers be allowed to strike if their employers were the instrument of 'the public'? And if 'false consciousness' were a problem, what role did other institutions play in moulding our consciousness? Why did Kahn-Freund ignore the mass media, drowning the mass 'workers' and 'consumers' in its values?

To these questions Kahn-Freund would certainly have returned. In 1979, trying to formulate a new analysis on a broad canvas, he concentrated upon trade unions, not upon their weakness against the gigantic forces to which they are so obviously a pitiful 'countervailing power', but upon the new role which he felt they must play in society. For to the solution of the new problems 'the law', he insisted, 'can make no contribution'. The law cannot alter basic social mores. The solution must come from 'the trade-union movement itself'. Moreover there was a further twist in the tangled skein of the internecine warfare of competing work groups in traditional collective bargaining. Kahn-Freund identified (in another very controversial assessment) a major cause of inflation as wage push: wage increases transformed into price increases which then fell upon the worker-consumer. Here again the law was no remedy; every attempt to enforce a wages policy by statute had eventually failed. Back in 1943 he had forecast in connection with 'the planning of wages by the State', that 'the traditional British method of trade union negotiation can be reconciled with state planning, but the terms of the compromise will have to be carefully considered by trade unionists and employers'.[192]

But now all had changed. To the 'crucial and fearful dilemma' confronting the use of their freedom to strike by workers who might thereby commit economic suicide, he added the bitter footnote that through inflation they would take their families down with them. But to his readers who had come, over thirty years, to expect copious footnotes, this time he offered almost none to support a structure of new assertions about the nature of modern British society.

'Groping in the Dark'

If neither 'traditional' collective bargaining nor the law could solve such problems, where might the answer be found? Kahn-Freund proposed 'with some diffidence' that it might be in 'a new type of collective bargaining . . . if you like, legislation in scope and in substance, but collective bargaining in form'.[193] (One is reminded of: 'If you like "collective *laissez faire*"'.) Towards that end the trade union movement must direct its efforts. Concretely, he proposed that we should attempt a new type of tripartite arrangement, involving the TUC, CBI, and government—something like their 'present political negotiations', but 'more regular and more regulated'. Could we not learn from what had happened in Sweden and in Germany?[194] This would, no doubt, offend the 'organizational autonomy to which the *damnosa hereditas* of the British guild tradition' gave such emotional overtones. But should it not be tried—even if we were only, he said, 'groping in the dark'?[195] Centralized collective bargaining, brought about not by legislation but by voluntary means, stood a chance of having at least an educational and psychological effect. Individual trade unions and employers could not be left in today's world to fix wages irrespective of the damage to others.

When he conceived this idea in 1978, the remains of the 'Social Contract' between the TUC and the Labour government could still be detected sufficiently for him to believe that it might be reconstructed in some such form. But even behind those rosy spectacles of 1978, why should it be said that the major part of this task must fall to the trade unions? Why was it to them that Kahn-Freund wished to bequeath the Herculean task of saving the pluralist society? It was not the trade union movement which had invested abroad rather than in British industry; nor had it centralized the nation's investment funds in a fashion which failed to protect both production and employment.[196]

It is impossible to believe that Otto Kahn-Freund would have maintained this prescription in the 1980s. Today the idea that the trade unions can save society by an offer to engage in centralized bargaining has become not so much Utopian as laughable. A government has emerged whose economic doctrines scarcely allow for their existence. Few could have predicted in 1978 the volcanic changes which have overcome British society and the shattering blows dealt to its 'equilibrium', its 'consensus', and even its order.

Even so, it is interesting to inquire what might be the nature of Kahn-Freund's proposed change in the habits of collective bargaining. Was it likely that labour law and even 'collective bargaining' could survive in anything like the old forms in which we in Britain have known them? On the last page he wrote, Kahn-Freund resolutely began on an answer to that obvious question: 'That which on previous occasions I have called "collective *laissez faire*" may be in need of adjustment more than any other part of the British heritage.'[197]

He was prepared to start afresh. These lectures were a prelude to a new—possibly despondent—analysis which he did not live to complete. It is a tragedy not to have him amongst us now, when new social crises and new technologies are prompting even greater changes in the labour market than those which he described—creating a high and growing rate of unemployment which leaves organized workers at their weakest for decades; a need for training and re-training of perhaps millions of workers (especially young workers trying to enter the privileged sector of employment); new needs among women workers (especially in dual-worker families); increased problems of health and safety in a nuclear society; a new world of robots, microprocessors and information systems able to control not only production but also people. Insistent attacks by the mass media upon trade unions will aim to sharpen the crisis of confidence among workers in their own collective defence against subordination. The implications of the North–South debate exposed in the Brandt Report will be less apparent to these workers than the visible crumbling of many older industries in the heartland of Western Europe, as new industrial societies emerge elsewhere (with no trade union movements as we know them—in Korea and Singapore, for example). What would have been Kahn-Freund's priorities in this seemingly endless list of dramatic economic and social change? And what of his 'consumer-workers'? Caught in the web of old societies amid new technology, they will see ever deeper social contradictions: on the one hand, unparalleled opportunities for the development of human personality, the level and the quality of life; on the other, new avenues for authoritarian suppression, enforced idleness, poverty, even enslavement. It will be hard to adapt the labour law we have now to that world; and it is only a few years away.

These were the questions with which Kahn-Freund was about to grapple in 1979. Is it not characteristic of the man that he left us, on the very final page, as he put it 'groping in the dark'? Seeking new answers to very new questions? It cannot be of prime importance to compress the tentative answers which he adumbrated at the end of his life into one or other of the orthodox moulds; to assess his call for new methods of central-ized and tripartite bargaining in Britain as 'corporatist' or 'unitary'; to leap to the conclusion that his much-prized 'pluralism' is dead. Even more than in the debate about 'industrial democracy', those old charts may be inadequate guides to a clear perception of the new reality.

Moreover, the old categories have never been very precisely defined. 'Pluralism' surely carried with it fundamental value-judgments. Even though—in a footnote—Kahn-Freund claimed, as we saw, to use 'pluralism' only as a description, in the same breath he claimed that it was 'a method of explaining what happens in a non-totalitarian society'.[198] Pluralism was—and is—more than a description. In 1979, his new 'description' of the role of the employer as defender of the consumer, even of the nation, left little place for the right to strike. His insistence that it must be retained stemmed from his values. *Values* obviously lay behind Kahn-Freund's panegyric of the 'mature' British system of 'collective *laissez faire*' in 1954. Those same democratic values led him still to insist in 1979 that the law not only could not be the means to the social leap forward he desired, but should not be used to destroy workers' trade unions or their industrial rights.

Starting from very different neo-Marxist positions, various British authors have made a related claim of central importance. Thompson has stressed 'the obvious point, which some modern Marxists have overlooked, that there is a difference between arbitrary power and the rule of law';[199] and he felt in 1979 even a sense of despair that Britain might now be 'in the final year or two of its own Weimar', leading to 'a very foul, policed and managed authoritarian state'.[200] Miliband, commenting on what he sees as 'the failure of social democracy', has stressed the 'profound weaknesses' of many parties offering an alternative to it, of which the 'gravest is their lack of genuine internal democracy'.[201] Indeed, some commentators critical of 'Corporatism' seem to overlook more readily than their neo-Marxist colleagues 'the vital distinction . . . between state power and class power'.[202] Distintegration of the state is not necessarily in the interests of the working class at a given moment of social transition. Conversely, the consideration that what the state does not give the state cannot take away is not necessarily decisive for trade unions who are offered the opportunity to negotiate joint regulation with a government whose policies they detest but whose actions they can influence. The vital question is whether there has been an 'accommodation' with the state or an 'imposition' of its will.[203]

By 1979, Kahn-Freund saw that if 'pluralism' was indeed only a transition, the next stage of our society might well be nothing like the democratic socialism in which he had once trusted. In his last pages one feels a pressing urgency to find new maps to guide us through hitherto uncharted economic and social change. In Britain this need is perhaps the most pressing; for it may be the case that the home of the first industrial revolution is to be the first to enter the unknown. We simply do not know what happens to a geriatric capitalist society which permits (or insists upon) massive de-industralization in a context of social and racial discrimination.

If, therefore, we reject aspects of Kahn-Freund's last tentative analysis—as it is easy to do with hindsight—I suspect that few of us can with honesty do more than join him 'groping in the dark'. As for the past, even if history proves that Kahn-Freund's analysis of 'non-intervention' was, as a description, a brilliant rationalization of just six decades of British industrial and legal life, his bequest will still have many other treasures. Not the least of these is a passionate belief in democratic values, alongside a clear vision of the subordination and injustice to which the worker is committed by the very act of selling his labour. From that very subordination springs the moral right of ordinary men and women to associate together, to speak freely, and to act collectively. And it is because of this special character of the employment relationship that labour law 'is a place where law, politics and social assumptions meet in a man'.[204]

But now we must navigate without Kahn-Freund. It is perhaps prudent and proper, when one has lost a giant among scholars, to pause awhile before offering judgment upon his own unfinished reassessment of our social condition. Nor do we offer a fitting tribute to him unless we commit ourselves to the 'unity of politics and scholarship' which he so admired in Sinzheimer.[205] We are not worthy recipients of his rich gifts if we fail, in the shadow of his courage, constantly to reconsider the assumptions which we have taken for granted; resolutely to pursue the path of free inquiry so precious to him; ceaselessly to re-examine the place of law not only abstractly in society, but also concretely in the lives of the millions of working men and women to whom the name of Otto Kahn-Freund is unknown but to whom he nevertheless devoted his scholarship and his life.

1. For brevity the main works of Kahn-Freund will be referred to below as follows: Ch. II, 'Legal Framework', in A. Flanders and H. Clegg (eds.), *The System of Industrial Relations in Great Britain,* Oxford, 1954: *System* (1954); 'Intergroup Conflicts and their Settlement' (1954) 5 *British Journal of Sociology* 193 (*Selected Writings,* 1978, Ch. 2): 'Intergroup Conflicts'; 'Labour Law' in M. Ginsberg (ed.), *Law and Opinion in England in the 20th Century,* London 1959 (reprinted as Ch. 1 of *Selected Writings, 1978*): *Ginsberg* (1959); *Labour Law: Old Traditions and New Developments,* Toronto, 1968: *Traditions* (1968); 'Industrial Relations and the Law—Retrospect and Prospect' (1969) 7 *British Journal of Industrial Relations* 301: 'Retrospect and Prospect' (1969); *Labour and the Law,* London, 1st ed. 1972; 2nd ed. 1977: *Labour* (1972) or (1977); *Labour Relations: Heritage and Adjustment,* London, 1979: *Heritage* (1979). See too below, nn. 9 and 31.
2. Cmnd. 3623, June 1968.
3. (1966) 29 *Modern Law Review* 121, pp. 128–9; *Selected Writings,* Ch. 14, p. 366, 'Reflections on Legal Education'.
4. *The Holmes-Laski Letters* (1952) ed. M. de Wolfe Howe, p. 1156.
5. 'Introduction to a Discussion of the Wilson Report' (1966) IX *Journal of Society of Public Teachers of Law* 193, 194, Lord Justice Diplock (as he then was).
6. Salmond on *Jurisprudence,* ed. G. Williams, London, 14th ed. 1957, p. 14.
7. See now O. Kahn-Freund, *Labour Law and Politics in the Weimar Republic,* ed. R. Lewis and J. Clark, Oxford, 1981.
8. *Renner,* op. cit., Introduction, p. 13. Max Weber's *Law in Economy and Society* (1925) was translated into English only in 1954 (with Introduction and Annotations), ed. Max Rheinstein, 1954, Cambridge, Massachusetts.
9. 'The Study of Labour Law—Some Reflections' (1979) 8 *Industrial Law Journal* 197, 199 (hereafter 'Reflections' (1979)) referring to Mansfield Cooper, *Outlines of Industrial Law* (1947), and Slesser and Baker, *Trade Union Law* (1950). Some writers had begun to relate collective agreements to the law, notably the article by F. Tillyard and W. Robson (1938) 48 *Economic Journal* 15; F. Tillyard, *The Worker and the State,* London, 3rd ed. 1948.
10. S. and B. Webb, *Industrial Democracy,* London, 1902 ed., Appendix I.
11. Mansfield Cooper and Wood, *Outlines of Industrial Law,* London, 4th ed. 1962. Batt, *The Law of Master and Servant,* ed. G. Webber, London, 5th ed. 1967. Even in 1980, the latest students' textbook contains only three pages on collective

bargaining and agreements: Smith and Wood, *Industrial Law*, London, 1980. For different approaches see P. Davies and M. Freedland, *Labour Law: Text and Materials*, London, 1979; K. W. Wedderburn, *The Worker and the Law*, Harmondsworth, 1965; 2nd ed. 1971.

12. Labour law teachers at LSE included R.A. (later Lord) Wright; H. C. Gutteridge; H. Slesser; T. Chorley and A. McNair; see K. W. Wedderburn, National Report: 'The Present State of Law Teaching and of Research into Labour Law', *Sixth International Congress of Labour Law and Social Security*, Stockholm, 1966, Vol. III, p. 26, which is also the source for other academic developments in Britain between 1900 and 1966.

13. Cmnd. 3623, para. 583.

14. *Renner* (1949), p. 28; and *Labour* (1977), p. 6.

15. 'Servants and Independent Contractors' (1951) 14 *Modern Law Review* 504, 508, citing Durand, *Traité de Droit du Travail* Vol. II (1950), p. 223; Hueck and Nipperdey, *Lehrbuch des Arbeitsrechts* (1927), Vol. I, p. 36.

16. See Gierke, *Political Theories of the Middle Ages* (1900), passages from *Genossenschaftsrecht*. *Max Weber on Law in Economy and Society*, translated by E. Shils and M. Rheinstein, Cambridge, Massachusetts, appeared in 1954.

17. *Labour* (1977), p. 15, n. 30.

18. 'Reflections' (1979), p. 197. (The description is criticized by R. Lewis and J. Clark, *Labour Law and Politics in the Weimar Republic*, p. 67, n. 115.)

19. *System* (1954), p. 57.

20. *Labour* (1977), p. 3.

21. Ibid., p. 2.

22. See his lecture 'On Uses and Misuses of Comparative Law' (1974) 37 *Modern Law Review* 1, pp. 6 et seq.; '. . . c'est un grand hazard si celles (les lois) d'une nation peuvent convenir à une autre', *Esprit des Lois*, Bk. I, Ch. 3.

23. In *Labour Law and Politics in the Weimar Republic*, pp. 190–1.

24. *Ginsberg* (1959), p. 257.

25. E.H. Phelps Brown, *The Growth of British Industrial Relations*, London, 1959, p. 355.

26. *Ginsberg* (1959), p. 235.

27. 'In practice those in Crown employment enjoy considerable security of tenure': B. Hepple and P. O'Higgins, *Employment Law*, London, 3rd ed. 1979, p. 65. See too R. Rideout, *Principles of Labour Law*, London, 3rd ed. 1979, p. 16; I. Smith and J. Wood, *Industrial Law* (1980), p. 72; De Smith, *Judicial Review of Administrative Action*, London, 4th ed. J. Evans 1980, pp. 24, 289; T. C. Hartley and J. A. G. Griffith, *Government and Law*, London, 1975, Ch. 5.

28. The best description is still B. Hepple and P. O'Higgins, *Public Employee Trade Unionism in the United Kingdom: The Legal Framework*, Ann Arbor, 1971.

29. See K. W. Wedderburn, 'Industrial Action, the State and the Public Interest', in B. Aaron and K. W. Wedderburn (eds.), *Industrial Conflict—A Comparative Survey*, London, 1972, pp. 364–77.

30. *Labour* (1977), pp. 165–6.

31. O. Kahn-Freund (ed.), *Labour Relations and the Law—A Comparative Study*, London, 1965, pp. 15–16; (hereafter *Study* (1965)). This volume records yet another contribution by Kahn-Freund to scholarship. It contains the papers of the first comparative labour law conference held in Britain after the war, in 1962. From it and from Kahn-Freund's untiring work for the International Society of Labour Law and Social Legislation, comparative labour law reaped untold benefits. (The conference saw the birth of the Comparative Labour Law Group of jurists from six countries, of whom the writer was one, who pursued comparative research together for sixteen years thereafter. Though it has to be in a footnote, this is one appropriate place to record our thanks to him for his stimulation and his help in the Group).

32. See, for example, *United Federation of Postal Clerks* v. *Blount (Postmaster General)* 325 F. Supp. 879 (1971, DDC); and H. Wellington and R. Winter, *The Union and the Cities*, Washington DC, 1971, for unconvincing arguments aimed at limiting the rights of the 'public employee'.

33. Equal Pay Act 1970 (now as amended by the Sex Discrimination Act 1975).

34. For example: the Truck Acts 1831; Payment of Wages Act 1960; Health and Safety at Work Act 1974; Factories Act 1961; Race Relations Act 1976; Sex Discrimination Act 1975. Many other individual employment rights are now consolidated in the Employment Protection (Consolidation) Act 1978. See for interesting assessments: H. Forrest, 'Political Values in Individual Employment Law' (1980) 43 *Modern Law Review* 361; R. Fryer, 'The Myths of the Redundancy Payments Act' (1973) 2 *Industrial Law Journal* 1; L. Dickens, 'Unfair Dismissal and the Industrial Tribunal System' (1978) 9 *Industrial Relations Journal*, No. 4, 4; J. Bowers and A. Clarke, 'Unfair Dismissal and Managerial Prerogative' (1981) 10 *Industrial Law Journal* 34; P. Lewis, 'Employment Protection—A Preliminary Assessment' (1981) 12 *Industrial Relations Journal* No. 2, 19; F. Boothman and D. Denham, 'Industrial Tribunals—An Ideological Background?' (1981) 12 *Industrial Relations Journal*, No. 3, 6.

35. 'Blackstone's Neglected Child; The Contract of Employment' (1977) 93 *Law Quarterly Review* 508, 518–28.

36. *Labour* (1977), p. 7.

37. *Ginsberg* (1959), p. 245.

38. *Labour* (1972), p. 37. See 'Reflections' (1979), p. 201.

39. See, for example, the Swedish Employment Protection Act 1974; and in Italy, Law 604 on Job Security, 14 July 1966. G. F. Mancini, Ch. 1 in *Giusta causa e giustificati motivi nei licenziamenti individuali*, ed. Mazzoni, Milan, 1967.

40. See now on guarantee payments, unfair dismissals, and 'redundancy' ss. 18, 65, 96, and 140, Employment Protection (Consolidation) Act 1978, and s. 107, Employment Protection Act 1975. Frequent use has been made of this right to 'contract out' of the statutory payments only in the case of 'guarantee' payments payable to a worker laid off.

41. See Munkman, *Employer's Liability*, London, 9th ed. 1979; esp., Employment of Women, Young Persons and Children Act 1920, s. 1; Children and Young Persons Act 1933, ss. 18, 19; Factories Act 1961, ss. 73–5; 86–114; and for the history, see Hutchins and Harrison, *A History of Factory Legislation*, London, 1903.

42. See Code du Travail (1979 ed.) Arts. 212–1 to 213–12; J. C. Javillier, *Droit du Travail*, Paris, 1978, p. 357 and *Complement*, Paris, 1979, pp. 224–8; for the origins in the Front Populaire Legislation and le régime des quarante heures, see G. Camerlynck and G. Lyon-Caen, *Droit du Travail*, Paris, 1976, pp. 245–53. (But, astonishingly, in 1981 the British TUC began to discuss a possible demand for legislation on maximum hours in order to promote work-sharing.)

43. *Renner* (1949), p. 172. Later, Kahn-Freund was to retreat somewhat from this unconditional analysis; see *Labour* (1977), pp. 39–40.

44. See S. and B. Webb, *The History of Trade Unionism* first published 1894 (1920 ed.) on which Kahn-Freund greatly relied. His analysis of the development of British labour law and labour movement in *Renner* (1949), p. 172; *Ginsberg* (1959), *passim*; *Traditions* (1968); and *Labour* (1972) and (1977), remains structurally similar though different in emphasis.

45. See Lord Wedderburn, 'Industrial Relations and the Courts' (1980) 9 *Industrial Law Journal* 65. Compare R. Lewis, 'The Historical Development of Labour Law' (1976) XIV *British Journal Industrial Relations* 1.

46. See ss. 2 and 3, Trade Union Act 1871; and now s. 2(5), Trade Union and Labour Relations Acts 1974–6.

47. See ss. 3 and 17, Conspiracy and Protection of Property Act 1875; Trade Disputes

Act 1906; later Trade Union and Labour Relations Acts 1974–6, ss. 13, 15 and 17, and Criminal Law Act 1977, ss. 1, 3, and 5. On the Employment Acts 1980–2 see Clark and Wedderburn below, text to nn. 44, 154, and 328 *et seq.*

48. See the discussion in Davies and Freedland, *Labour Law: Text and Materials*, Ch. 8 and 9; and Wedderburn, *The Worker and the Law* (1971), Ch. 7 and 8.

49. Lord Denning MR, *Express Newspapers Ltd.* v. *McShane* [1979] I.C.R. 210, 218, reversed in the House of Lords [1980] I.C.R. 42 in regard to the point there at issue. But see ibid. the clear demand by some Law Lords that the law should be changed to the disadvantage of trade unions: Wedderburn (1980) *Industrial Law Journal* 65.

50. A. Flanders, *Industrial Relations: What is Wrong with the System?*, London, 1965, p. 28; O. Kahn-Freund, 'Intergroup Conflicts' (1954), p. 205 (*Selected Writings*, p. 57).

51. (1971) *Bulletin of Industrial Law Society*, p. 3.

52. 'Collective Agreements under War Legislation' (1943) 6 *Modern Law Review* 112, 143 (emphasis supplied).

53. *Traditions* (1968), p. 7, summarizing the more extended analysis in *Ginsberg* (1959) and *System* (1954).

54. *System* (1954), p. 66. See, too, *Traditions* (1968), p. 32: 'In Britain, labour legislation is a gloss to collective bargaining', where he acknowledges the debt to Maitland's famous saying that equity was a gloss to the common law.

55. *Ginsberg* (1959), p. 229.

56. *Labour* (1972), p. 19. See the rather different formulation in *Ginsberg* (1959), p. 226 where he lays stress on the 'participation' of labour in legislative, administrative, and even 'judicial' processes. Contrast his attitude to 'participation' in the institutions of the enterprise, see below, text to nn. 162–4.

57. Lord Wright, *Crofter Hand Woven Harris Tweed Ltd.* v. *Veitch* [1942] A.C. 435, 463, 472–9.

58. *Labour* (1972), p. 20. It was only at the very end of his life that he indicated a desire to change the analysis of this conflict, see below, text to n. 174 *et seq.*

59. *System* (1954), p. 123.

60. Ibid., p. 123; see Wedderburn, *The Worker and the Law* (1971), pp. 395–400.

61. K. W. Wedderburn, 'British Labour Law and Otto Kahn-Freund, 1971' (1971) 11 *Bulletin of Industrial Law Society* 2, 3.

62. O. Kahn-Freund, 'Hugo Sinzheimer 1875–1945', the first Sinzheimer Lecture of 1975, in *Labour Law and Politics in the Weimar Republic*, p. 80.

63. *Ginsberg* (1959), p. 224; see too pp. 227–53.

64. *Industrial Democracy* (1902 ed.), Part II, Ch. II.

65. 'Intergroup Conflicts' (1954), p. 196.

66. R. Lewis, 'Kahn-Freund and Labour Law: An Outline Critique' (1979) 8 *Industrial Law Journal* 202, 209.

67. *Ginsberg* (1959), p. 226.

68. *System* (1954), pp. 43 and 44 respectively (emphasis supplied).

69. *Ginsberg* (1959), p. 225–6.

70. *Ginsberg* (1959), p. 244 (emphasis supplied). See too his quotation of Winston Churchill in 1911: 'It is not good for trade unions that they should be brought in contact with the courts, and it is not good for the courts' (ibid., p. 232).

71. R. Dahrendorf, *Class and Class Conflict in Industrial Society*, London, 1959, p. 260.

72. L. Reynolds, *Economics and Labor Relations*, New York, 1956, p. 177.

73. R. Dubin, *Industrial Conflict*, ed. A. Kornhauser, R. Dubin, and A. Ross, New York, 1954, p. 47. Kahn-Freund did not accept the Marxist view that this led to the incorporation of unions into the bourgeois state: cf. R. Hyman, *Marxism and the Sociology of Trade Unionism*, London, 1975.

74. See s. 5, Trade Disputes Act 1906; now s. 29, Trade Union and Labour Relations Acts 1974–6. See now Clark and Wedderburn below, text to n. 137 *et seq.*

75. *System* (1954), p. 127. But surprisingly he did not re-examine such concepts in the later period when he feared for the social equilibrium: see below, text to n. 194 *et seq.*

76. See R. Lewis, 'Collective Agreements: The Kahn-Freund Legacy' (1979) 42 *Modern Law Review* 613.

77. 'Collective Agreements under War Legislation' (1943) 6 *Modern Law Review* 112. For the sparse literature before 1943 see R. Lewis (1979) 42 *Modern Law Review* pp. 614–18.

78. See *Study* (1965), p. 27; *Labour* (1977), pp. 139–40.

79. *Rookes* v. *Barnard* [1964] A.C. 1129 (which he took to be 'quite exceptional' and based on a concession). Section 18(4) of the Trade Union and Labour Relations Act 1974, which he prayed in aid, puts limitations on the incorporation into employment contracts of 'no-strike' or (more usual in Britain) 'procedure' clauses creating 'peace obligations'—limitations which would be pointless if the legislature thought they could *not* be incorporated from the collective agreements into the employment contract, as he insisted. See further Davies and Freedland, *Labour Law: Text and Materials*, pp. 230–1; Wedderburn, *The Worker and the Law* (1971) pp. 193–7; and M. Freedland, *The Contract of Employment*, Oxford, 1976, 'Postscript', pp. 372 ff. But the decision in *British Leyland Ltd.* v. *McQuilken* [1978] I.R.L.R. 245, can be understood as supporting Kahn-Freund's view.

80. (1979) 8 *Industrial Law Journal*, p. 200.

81. *System* (1954), p. 57.

82. (1979) 8 *Industrial Law Journal*, p. 200.

83. *Renner* (1949), p. 172.

84. *System* (1954), p. 57.

85. *Ginsberg* (1959), esp. pp. 232–4, p. 263; and 'Intergroup Conflicts' (1954). By a historical accident, s. 4(4), Trade Union Act 1871 rendered unenforceable contracts between a trade union and other 'trade unions' which by a freak of outmoded legal definition included certain types of employers' *associations*; but it did not apply to an agreement made between a union and *one* company, or other groups of employers. See Wedderburn, *The Worker and the Law* (1971), pp. 179–80. The section was repealed in 1971.

86. See, for example, *contra* Cronin and Grime, *Labour Law*, London, 1970, Ch. 10; N. Selwyn, 'Collective Agreements and the Law' (1969) 32 *Modern Law Review* 377; in favour of Kahn-Freund's view, Wedderburn, *The Worker and the Law* (1965), Ch. 4; R. Lewis (1970) *British Journal of Industrial Relations* 313; and in an intermediate position, B. Hepple (1970) 28 *Cambridge Law Journal* 122. See, too, the discussions in *Study* (1965), Chs. 1 (O. Kahn-Freund) and 2 (J. McCartney).

87. Cmnd. 3623, pp. 125–6.

88. See ibid., Chs. VII and VIII generally.

89. *Ford Motor Co.* v. *A.U.E.F.* [1969] 2 Q.B. 303. The judge rejected the earlier writings in 1943 of Kahn-Freund (which the Company ultimately relied upon) because the *Modern Law Review* was 'unlikely to come into the hands' of the company's managers or the union officers!

90. 'Retrospect and Prospect' (1969), p. 309.

91. B. Weekes, M. Mellish, R. Dickens, and J. Lloyd, *Industrial Relations and the Limits of Law; The Industrial Effects of the Industrial Relations Act 1971*, Oxford, 1975, p. 161; see ss. 34–6, Industrial Relations Act 1971.

92. S. 18, Trade Union and Labour Relations Act 1974.

93. *Federation News* (1964) Vol. 14, pp. 30, 41, commenting on *Rookes* v. *Barnard* [1964] A.C. 1129. For that and other decisions eroding the trade union immunities in the 1960s see Wedderburn, *The Worker and the Law* (1971) Ch. 8. *Rookes* v. *Barnard* itself was answered by the Trades Disputes Act 1965, extending the 'immunities' of those who acted in contemplation or furtherance of a trade dispute to cover the

specifically new element in the decision, a tort of 'intimidation' held (for the first time) to be inherent in a threat to break a contract of employment. On the development of the immunities see Wedderburn (1980) 9 *Industrial Law Journal* 75–82.

94. *Ginsberg* (1959), p. 256.
95. *Ginsberg* (1959), p. 244.
96. K. W. Wedderburn, 'Labour Law and Labour Relations in Britain' (1972) 10 *British Journal of Industrial Relations*, 270, and generally pp. 275–80.
97. *Traditions* (1968), p. 11.
98. 'The Changing Function of Labour Law', in *Labour Law and Politics in the Weimar Republic*, p. 176.
99. Cmnd. 3623, Ch. VII and VIII.
100. Ibid., paras. 800–4; 893–4.
101. 'Trade Unions, the Law and Society' (1970) 33 *Modern Law Review* 241, 254.
102. Ibid., pp. 266–7.
103. *Ginsberg* (1959), p. 260.
104. *Labour* (1972), p. 8 and p. 5; *Labour* (1977), p. 6 and p. 4 (emphasis supplied).
105. Cmnd. 3623, Ch. VI. VII, XI, XII, and XIV. See too Clegg above, text to n. 4 *et seq.*
106. Ministry of Labour, *Evidence to the Royal Commission* (1965), p. 92. See above, n. 34. No politician, employer, or trade union seems to have had such a clear policy before 1965.
107. Employment Protection Act 1975, ss. 87, 88; now Employment Protection (Consolidation) Act 1978, ss. 136, 137 and Schedule 11.
108. 'Retrospect and Prospect' (1969), p. 313, approving the proposal in 'In Place of Strife' (1969), Cmnd. 3888. But the tribunals should *not* hear claims for damages for personal injuries; *Labour* (1977), p. 22. See too ibid pp. 178–80 where he is clearly optimistic about the role of the tribunals in cases involving unfair dismissal; contrast the analyses cited above, n. 34. (See however Clark and Wedderburn below, text to n. 230 *et seq.*)
109. See Lewis (1979) 8 *Industrial Law Journal* 219; W. Daniels and E. Stilgoe, *The Impact of Employment Protection Laws* (1978); Forrest (1980) 43 *Modern Law Review* 361: 'judicial attitudes in some crucial cases still fall back on a unitary position', p. 379; so too Boothman and Denham (1981) 12 *Industrial Relations Journal*, No. 3, pp. 13–14.
110. T. Ramm quotes the phrase in *Labour Courts and Grievance Settlement in Western Europe*, ed. B. Aaron, 1971, p. 86.
111. *Labour* (1972), pp. 18, 19; *Labour* (1977), pp. 15, 16.
112. Cmnd. 3623, pp. 46–7.
113. Ibid., p. 40.
114. Ibid., p. 36.
115. *Collective Bargaining: Prescription for Change* (1967), reprinted in *Management and Unions*, London, 1970, pp. 172–3.
116. 'Intergroup Conflicts and their Settlement' (1954) V *British Journal of Sociology* 193; in *Selected Writings* (1978), Ch. 2, p. 44.
117. 'The problem of geographical mobility of labor in Europe is overshadowed by the housing shortage': in his extensive review 'Labor Law and Social Security', in *American Enterprise in the European Common Market: A Legal Profile*, Michigan, 1960, p. 317; on British mobility of labour see *Traditions* (1968), pp. 37–50.
118. Andrew Shonfield, Donovan Report, pp. 288–302. On this and other legal details in the Report, in particular on trade disputes and strikes, see K. W. Wedderburn (1968) 31 *Modern Law Review* 674: 'Much will depend upon the interpretation put upon the objective' to make the system more 'orderly' and to 'integrate' plant bargainers and shop stewards (p. 682).

119. See Weekes *et al.*, *Industrial Relations and the Limits of Law* (1975); A. Thomson and S. Engleman, *The Industrial Relations Act: A Review and Analysis*, London, 1975; M. Moran, *The Politics of Industrial Relations*, London, 1977.

120. Para. 8, *Industrial Relations Bill: A Consultative Document* (5 October 1970, Department of Employment).

121. *Labour* (1972), p. 66.

122. *Ibid.*, p. 123.

123. *Ibid.*, p. 270.

124. 'Uses and Misuses of Comparative Law' (1974) 37 *Modern Law Review* 1, pp. 26–7.

125. *Labour* (1972), p. 201. For comparative treatments, see *Discrimination in Employment*, ed. F. Schmidt, Stockholm, 1968, Ch. 6; and T. Treu, *Condotta antisindacale e atti discriminatori*, Milan, 1974.

126. 'The Industrial Relations Act—Some Retrospective Reflections' (1974) 3 *Industrial Law Journal* 186, p. 199, commenting on *Post Office* v. *Crouch* [1973] I.C.R. 366 (C.A.); [1974] I.C.R. 378 (H.L.) (emphasis supplied). On this part of the 1971 Act, see K. W. Wedderburn (1972) 10 *British Journal of Industrial Relations* 270, pp. 281–9.

127. See R. Simpson (1981) 44 *Modern Law Review* 188; Lord Wedderburn, 'Industrial Relations and the Courts' (1980) 9 *Industrial Law Journal* 65. See on the Employment Acts 1980 and 1982, Clark and Wedderburn below, text to n. 28 *et seq.*; text to n. 328 *et seq.*

128. Largely in the Trade Union and Labour Relations Acts 1974–6; Employment Protection Act 1975 [of which the protection sections are now codified (with the Contracts of Employment Act 1972 and Redundancy Payments Act 1965) in the Employment Protection (Consolidation) Act 1978]; Sex Discrimination Act 1975; and Race Relations Act 1976.

129. Largely effected by the Trade Union and Labour Relations Acts 1974–6.

130. R. Lewis (1976) 14 *British Journal of Industrial Relations* 1, p. 15 (emphasis supplied); see too R. Lewis (1979) 8 *Industrial Law Journal* 202, pp. 214–15, 218–21.

131. *Labour* (1977), p. 46, n. 55. In the same vein see Wedderburn (1980) 9 *Industrial Law Journal*, pp. 84–5. The enactment of the Employment Act 1980 adds weight to the argument that the 'system' is falling under legalistic control; but it is hardly an inevitable or logical *consequence* of the legislation of 1974–6. To say that the legislation of 1974–6 facilitated the 1980 legislation, hostile to trade unions, mistakes legal for social cause.

132. See ss. 11–16; s. 15(2) in effect created a duty to bargain. The sanction against an employer who refused to bargain was not an order but an award of the Central Arbitration Committee imposing new conditions in his employees' contracts of employment. See Lord Wedderburn, 'The New Structure of Labour Law in Britain' (1978) 13 *Israel Law Review* 435, pp. 452–8.

133. *Ginsberg* (1959), p. 229. See for an early trade union demand for legislation on such issues: C. Jenkins and J. Mortimer, *The Kind of Laws the Unions Ought to Want*, London, 1968, pp. 50–6.

134. It would 'affect the very structure of collective bargaining': R. Lewis (1976) 14 *British Journal of Industrial Relations*, p. 14. In 1979, ACAS dealt with 2,284 conciliation cases but received 227 applications from unions for obligatory recognition (as against 279 in 1978 and 588 in 1977). On the parallel 'right to bargain' in the United States: M. Hart (1978) 7 *Industrial Law Journal* 201.

135. 'Retrospect and Prospect' (1969), p. 308.

136. *Labour* (1977), p. 79. On pages 80–1, he severely underestimated the likelihood of the High Court intervening by 'judicial review' to control the work of ACAS.

137. See the review of R. Simpson, 'Judicial Control of ACAS' (1979) 9 *Industrial Law Journal* 69; esp. on *Grunwick* v. *ACAS* [1978] A.C. 655 (H.L.) and *UKAPE* v. *ACAS* [1979] I.C.R. 303 (C.A.). Ironically after the repeal was proposed of. ss. 11–16,

the House of Lords took a different view and restored greater discretion to ACAS but by then it was too late: see *UKAPE* v. *ACAS* [1980] 1 All E.R. 612; *EMA* v. *ACAS* [1980] 1 All E.R. 896.

138. Especially in the *Grunwick* case (above). See the *Report of a Committee of Inquiry* under Lord Justice Scarman (Cmnd. 6922, 1977) on this explosive dispute which turned a small factory in North London into the national focus of a trade union battle for recognition—which was lost. Also, J. Rogaly, *Grunwick*, Harmondsworth, 1977; G. Ward (the employer in the case), *Fort Grunwick*, London, 1977; and J. Dromey and G. Taylor, *Grunwick: The Workers' Story*, London, 1978.

139. See the Government Working Paper of 24 September 1979 attaching the letter of the Chairman (J. Mortimer—see above n. 133) written on 29 June. Repeal was effected by s. 19(b), Employment Act 1980.

140. Wedderburn (1978) 13 *Israel Law Review*, p. 456.

141. Lord Diplock, *Express Newspapers Ltd.* v. *McShane* [1980] A.C. 672, 686, see Wedderburn (1980) 43 *Modern Law Review* 319, 324. Various other Law Lords attacked the revival of the modern immunities: ibid; see Lord Salmon, p. 690. On Lord Diplock, see above, n. 5.

142. See K. Ewing, 'The Golden Formula: Some Recent Developments' (1979) 8 *Industrial Law Journal* 133; Wedderburn (1980) 9 *Industrial Law Journal* 65, pp. 89–94; *Duport Steels Ltd.* v. *Sirs* [1980] 1 All E.R. 529; R. Simpson (1980) 43 *Modern Law Review* 327.

143. Lord Scarman, *N.W.L.* v. *Woods* [1979] I.C.R. 867, 886; see Simpson (1980) 43 *Modern Law Review* 327. But some commentators still hold that the United Kingdom was in breach of the European Social Charter, Article 6 by not guaranteeing a *right* to strike: P. O'Higgins, *Studies in Labour Law*, ed. J. Carby-Hall, Bradford, 1976, p. 177.

144. *Labour* (1977), p. 276 (emphasis supplied).

145. See the interesting analysis by J. Clark, H. Hartmann, C. Lau, and D. Winchester, *Trade Unions, National Politics and Economic Management*, London and Bonn, 1980, pp. 13–67.

146. See Donovan Report, Cmnd, 3623, pp. 242–3, on a 'right to strike'; CBI *Trade Unions in a Changing World: The Challenge for Management* (1980), p. 22; Wedderburn (1980) 9 *Industrial Law Journal* 65.

147. *Labour* (1977), p. 250.

148. 'A Lawyer's Reflections on Multinational Corporations' (1972) *Journal of Industrial Relations* 351, pp. 359–60.

149. *Heritage* (1979), p. 26.

150. *Labour* (1972), p. 269; *Labour* (1977), pp. 261–2.

151. Established in s. 2, Trade Disputes Act 1906; then s. 15, Trade Union and Labour Relations Act 1974; now severely restricted by ss. 16 and 17 (5), Employment Act 1980: (See B. Bercusson (1980) 9 *Industrial Law Journal* 215; Wedderburn (1981) 10 *Industrial Law Journal* 113.

152. *Broome* v. *D.P.P.* [1974] A.C. 587 (H.L.).

153. J.W. Woodcock, Chief Constable South Wales in *Evidence* to House of Commons Employment Committee, 27 February 1980.

154. (1974) 3 *Industrial Law Journal* 186, p. 200.

155. *Heritage* (1979), p. 73.

156. Chapter 1 of *Heritage* is devoted to a skilful application of their work: see esp. E. Batstone, I, Boraston, and S. Frenkel, *Shop Stewards in Action: The Organization of Workplace Conflict and Accommodation*, Oxford, 1977 and *Social Organization of Strikes*, Oxford, 1978.

157. *Heritage* (1979), p. 81; for the general argument, see pp. 78–81.

158. For an excellent summary of the British developments 1900 to 1932 and 1960 to

1977 see S. Sciarra, *Democrazia politica e democrazia industriale*, Bari, 1978, pp. 7–44. See too J. Elliott, *Conflict or Cooperation: The Growth of Industrial Democracy*, London, 1978.

159. *Report of the Committee of Inquiry on Industrial Democracy* (Chairman Lord Bullock, Cmnd, 6706, 1977). There was a minority report by the employers' representatives proposing one-third representation on supervisory boards. The writer was a majority member of the Committee. The Labour government's paper fell somewhere between the minority and majority 'Bullock' proposals, *Industrial Democracy* (Cmnd. 7231, 1978). The debate about the Bullock Report is described in Elliott, *Conflict or Cooperation* (1978); cf. R. Lewis and J. Clark (1977) 40 *Modern Law Review* 323.

160. See CBI, *In Place of Bullock* (1977); City Company Law Working Party, *A Reply to Bullock* (1977). Even in 1980 the Institute of Directors had not calmed down; see *The Fifth Directive: A Trojan Bullock?* (1980).

161. He welcomed the gradual developments away from the original Draft Fifth Directive in the more flexible Green Paper 'Employee Participation and Company Structure', Bulletin E.C. Supp 8/75. The European Parliament has now proposed an even more flexible structure. He also disapproved of the more attenuated form of workers' representation in the proposed *Societas Europea:* see 'Industrial Democracy' (1977) 6 *Industrial Law Journal* 65, 71–5.

162. (1977) 6 *Industrial Law Journal*, pp. 75–6.

163. See P. Davies and Lord Wedderburn, 'The Land of Industrial Democracy' (1977) 6 *Industrial Law Journal* 197; esp. pp. 198–209, 211. Most authors have, of course, insisted that 'industrial democracy' implies a 'unitary' model; see Elliott (1978), n. 158 above.

164. (1977) 6 *Industrial Law Journal*, p. 83 and p. 72: 'an ineffective system of board representation' under the Works Councils Act 1920. On Kahn-Freund's resistance to unreal legal models based upon a 'unitary' concept of industrial relations, including the reified interests of the 'works' or enterprise, see his German writings of 1931 and 1932 (now Chapters 3 and 4 in *Labour Law and Politics in the Weimar Republic:* esp. pp. 110–26, 133–41, 182–9).

165. *Labour* (1977), p. 17.

166. (1977) 6 *Industrial Law Journal*, p. 84.

167. S. Simitis, 'Workers' Participation in the Enterprise: Transcending Company Law' (1975) 38 *Modern Law Review* 1, pp. 19–22. See the discussion of R. Dahrendorf, *Class and Class Conflict in an Industrial Society*, London, 1959, esp. pp. 241–67, distinguishing 'regulation' which accepts conflict from 'co-determination' which tries to abolish it as an evil.

168. *Labour* (1977), p. 15, n. 30.

169. A. Fox, *Beyond Contract: Work Power and Trust Relations*, London, 1974, pp. 262–3, 265. See too *inter alia* A. Fox, 'Collective Bargaining, Flanders and the Webbs' (1975) 13 *British Journal of Industrial Relations* 151; J. Goldthorpe, 'Industrial Relations in Great Britain: A Critique of Reformism', in *Trade Unions Under Capitalism*, Glasgow, 1977, ed. T. Clark and L. Clements, pp. 184–224; and 'Social Inequality and Social Integration', in *Poverty Inequality and Class Structure*, ed. D. Wedderburn, Cambridge, 1974. On Fox's earlier position see *Industrial Sociology and Industrial Relations* (1966, Donovan Royal Commission Research Paper 3); A. Flanders and A. Fox, 'The Reform of Collective Bargaining, from Donovan to Durkheim' (1969) 7 *British Journal of Industrial Relations* 151.

170. R. Miliband, *The State in Capitalist Society*, London, 1969 (a fascinating critique of 'pluralism') Ch. 6, esp. pp. 155–65; R. Hyman, 'Pluralism, Procedural Consensus and Collective Bargaining' (1978) 16 *British Journal of Industrial Relations* 161; and *Industrial Relations: A Marxist Introduction*, London, 1975. But in considering the 'state', account must be taken of various interests, including the 'state élite': Miliband, *op. cit.*, Ch. I.

171. A. Fox, *Beyond Contract* (1974), p. 282.
172. A. Fox, *Man Mismanagement*, London, 1974, pp. 14–17.
173. See C. Crouch, *Class Conflict and the Industrial Relations Crisis*, London, 1977; L. Panitch, *Social Democracy and Industrial Militancy*, Cambridge, 1976.
174. See *Labour* (1977), p. 15, n. 30 where, however, he insists that it is descriptive not an ideology; but he agrees with H. Clegg's 'counter-critique' of Fox, which is ideological: 'Pluralism in Industrial Relations' (1975) 13 *British Journal of Industrial Relations* 309; see below, n. 180.
175. *Heritage* (1979). These were three lectures delivered in 1978 at the British Academy. It is important to remember that they were written in 1978, and not in the changed economic and social circumstances of 1979 or 1980.
176. For the argument on this matter, see *Heritage*, pp. 38–56.
177. See *Labour* (1977), pp. 202; Weekes *et al.*, *Industrial Relations and the Limits of Law*, Ch. 2.
178. As Ch. II of *Heritage* proceeds, more and more emphasis is placed upon the pre-capitalist 'guild spirit' as an explanation of the special dominance of the 'craft' element in British trade unionism and even British society: see pp. 41–2, 49, 52, 56; and n. 26 for the 'origin' of the *damnosa hereditas*. If (as he acknowledged in the case of the unions) the transmission was not directly historical (p. 41) the question arises as to the *machinery* for transmitting this tradition; see below, text to n. 179 *et seq.*
179. For recent support for the *hitsorical* transmission of 'craft' values, see R. Leeson, *Travelling Brothers*, London, 1980.
180. See Cmnd. 3623, pp. 87–9.
181. *Heritage* (1979), pp. 49–50. See the point made in *Renner*, n. 8 above.
182. *Heritage* (1979), p. 43.
183. E. Hobsbawm, 'Inside Every Worker There Is a Syndicalist Trying to Get Out', *New Society*, 5 April 1979, p. 10.
184. See especially H. A. Turner, *Trade Union Growth Structure and Policy: A Comparative Study of the Cotton Unions*, London, 1962, pp. 233–7. The cotton industry was, of course, central to the first industrial revolution: E. Hobsbawm, *The Age of Revolution*, London, 1962, pp. 27–52, 200–16, who in his authoritative review of 1789–1848 sees below the new 'working-class' tradition the older tradition not of guilds, but 'of riot' (p. 212). (See now the study by R. Undy, V. Ellis. W. E. J. McCarthy, and A. M. Halmos, *Change in Trade Unions*, London, 1981, Ch. 3, 'Areas of Change', and Ch. 7, 'Changes in the Character of Job Regulation', where the different developments of various 'craft' unions illustrate the difficulty of such generalizations about them. See too Wedderburn (1980) 9 *Industrial Law Journal*, pp. 70–4, and sources cited.)
185. *Heritage* (1979), p. 41. But in *Labour* (1977), p. 56 Kahn-Freund regarded it as still 'controversial' whether a historical link existed; see above, n. 179.
186. On the guilds, see S. and B. Webb, *History of Trade Unionism* (1920 ed.), pp. 1–63 (esp. the discussion of L. Brentano, *The History and Development of Guilds and the Origin of Trade Unions* (1870). See E. P. Thompson, *The Making of the English Working Class*, London, 1963, Ch. VIII (the radical attitudes of artisans in the early nineteenth century), XIV, X and XVI (and the 'Postscript' to the Penguin ed., pp. 916–39); E. Hobsbawm, *Labouring Men*, London, 1964, Ch. 4, 10, 15, 16, 17 and 18, and *The Age of Revolution* (1962); T. Tholfsen, *Working Class Radicalism in Mid-Victorian England*, London, 1976. (But see Leeson, *Travelling Brothers*, n. 179 above.)
187. E. Hobsbawm, *Labouring Men*, Ch. 15; whose analysis of 'co-exploitation' is virtually not used by Kahn-Freund. The work of these historians is, in fact, ignored in *Heritage* in favour of the traditional sources, especially S. and B. Webb, *History of Trade Unionism* (1920 ed.) and Phelps Brown, *Growth of British Industrial Relations*.

188. See W. Orton, *Labour in Transition*, London, 1921, p. 95, writing about the rise of the shop stewards' movement. See too the useful description in B. Pribicevic, *The Shop Stewards' Movement and Workers' Control*, London, 1959, p. 85. The 'abolition of capitalism' was one of the 'principal objectives' of the shop stewards' movement in 1915 in opposition to the official trade union movement. As a simile, one might perhaps equally relate the modern shop stewards' movement to an expression of the radical spirit of the 1830s (the early trade unions and the Chartists) or even of the Levellers in 1655. But there is, of course, no historical link as such. It is of interest to note that from France, P. Mantoux, in *The Industrial Revolution in the Eighteenth Century*, London, 1928, perceived that, although British workers appealed to the old regulations of their trades or guilds in the late eighteenth century as a 'protection, real or illusory . . . against economic oppression', the factory system formed the workers into a class (p. 462).

189. *Heritage* (1979), pp. 63, 73–88; and see pp. 76–8 for the quotations which follow.

190. *Labour* (1972), p. 18. This is, of course, a quite different analysis from that advanced in *Heritage* (1979).

191. See, for example, E. Hobsbawm, *Labouring Men*, Ch. 15, esp. pp. 297–303.

192. See (1943) 6 *Modern Law Review*, p. 142.

193. *Heritage* (1979), pp. 82–7.

194. For a negative response see M. Hudson, 'Concerted Action: Wages Policy in West Germany' (1980) 11 *Industrial Relations Journal* 5; cf. Clark *et. al.* n. 145 above; and J. Clark, 'Concerted Action in the Federal Republic of Germany' (1979) 16 *British Journal of Industrial Relations* 242.

195. Ibid, p. 88.

196. See the fascinating analysis by R. Minns, *Pension Funds and British Capitalism*, London, 1980.

197. *Heritage* (1979), p. 88. See also Clark and Wedderburn below, text to n. 328 *et seq.*

198. *Labour* (1977), p. 15, n. 30; see above, text to n. 168 *et seq.* The insistence upon a 'non-totalitarian society' affirms many values, just as it begs many questions.

199. E. P. Thompson, *Whigs and Hunters*, London, 1975, p. 266. See too the radical assessment of the English judiciary by J. A. G. Griffith, *The Politics of the Judiciary*, London, 2nd ed. 1981.

200. E. P. Thompson, *Writing by Candlelight*, London, 1980, p. x. But by 1980 he thought this pessimism 'excessive': ibid.

201. R. Miliband, *The State in Capitalist Society*, p. 274.

202. E. Laclau, *Politics and Ideology in Marxist Theory*, London, 1979 ed., p. 58, discussing the positions of R. Miliband and of N. Poulantzas, *Political Power and Social Class*, London, 1975.

203. Compare Kahn-Freund in *The Social Ideal of the Reich Labour Court:* 'If one starts by making the collective forces into instruments of a fictional state will in the social field, one is preparing the way for the formation of state will in the political arena, not as an accommodation arising out of the conflict between the collective forces in society, but by the imposition of the will of a dictatorial civil service.' (*Labour Law and Politics in the Weimar Republic*, pp. 154–5.)

204. Wedderburn, *The Worker and the Law* (1971), p. 479.

205. The phrase comes from Eugen Loderer, President of I.G. Metall (See Lewis and Clark, Introduction, *Labour Law and Politics in the Weimar Republic*, p. 37, citing *Hugo Sinzheimer: Gedächtnisveranstaltung*, Frankfurt am Main, 1977, p. 19).

Chapter 4

Towards a Sociology of Labour Law: An Analysis of the German Writings of Otto Kahn-Freund*

Jon Clark

Introduction

Over the past decades the 'sociology of law' has been a constant theme for debate amongst British and North American legal scholars. The discussion has focused mainly on general theoretical and methodological questions (the relation between law, values, and human behaviour, between 'positivistic' jurisprudence and sociological approaches to law); but also on the application of the sociological method to specific areas of the law.[1] Surprisingly, though, there has been no attempt to examine systematically the implications of this debate for the study and development of labour law. This is all the more remarkable since the work of probably the leading scholar of British and comparative labour law, Otto Kahn-Freund, was rooted in a number of rich social science traditions, including Austro-German 'sociology of law' (Ehrlich, Ihering, and Renner), Weberian social economics, and Marxian political economy.

The aim of this chapter is to analyse the main German writings of Otto Kahn-Freund,[2] and to develop from this analysis (and from parts of the jurisprudential literature) some hypotheses concerning the sociology of labour law. The German writings have been chosen as the starting point because they contain Kahn-Freund's most explicit and illuminating attempts to elaborate and apply a 'sociology of labour law'. His English writings are full of insights into the social foundations of the employment relationship, but the sociological elements of his analysis are rarely discussed explicitly.[3]

* For helpful comments on first drafts of this chapter I am grateful to Gerald Dworkin, John Hall, Roy Lewis, Howard Rose, David Schiff, and Bill Wedderburn.

The main contention of this chapter is that the function and development of labour law can be comprehended only if 'technical' legal analysis is complemented (and enriched) by sociological understanding. As Kahn-Freund wrote of Hugo Sinzheimer, the founder of German labour law: '[He] was such a great labour lawyer because he was more than a specialist, and in particular because he applied the sociological method to labour law.'[4]

Hugo Sinzheimer and the Development of a Sociological Approach to Law and Labour Law

The overall role of Hugo Sinzheimer (1875–1945) in establishing labour law as a separate academic discipline has been assessed elsewhere.[5] In this analysis of Sinzheimer's work, which is largely based on Otto Kahn-Freund's essay on Sinzheimer of 1976,[6] the main aim is to examine the importance of his sociological understanding and method for the development of labour law, and to discuss the relation between 'legal-positivistic' and 'sociological' approaches to labour law.

In Germany before 1914, the analysis of the law concerning the employment relationship had been confined largely to a technical examination of legal norms contained in the sum total of positive legal provisions. Sinzheimer's writings represented a major break with this approach. In fact, as Kahn-Freund has pointed out, the three fundamental elements of Sinzheimer's conception of labour law[7] (the concepts of work and dependency and the emphasis on legal policy) 'refer us beyond the confines of positive law'.[8] The most crucial extra-legal foundation of his approach to labour law was his sociological understanding of human work as the substratum of the employment relationship under capitalism. For Sinzheimer the social basis of the employment relationship, as distinct from other contractual and property relations, is that human beings exchange not objects but themselves.[9] In exchange for a wage the individual employee is obliged to work under the command of the employer. While property-orientated civil law assumed the contractual equality of the employer and the employee in the exchange relationship, Sinzheimer argued that, under capitalism, the theory of contractual equality was a fiction which reinforced the employer's domination and the employee's subordination.[10] It was therefore necessary to destroy this legal mystification of the worker's actual state of dependency on the employer by explicitly recognizing it in statute law: labour law became by this definition the law of 'dependent labour'.[11]

Sinzheimer's analysis of the contract of employment remains to this day a classic example of the sociology of labour law. He took one of the fundamental concepts of labour law, the contract of employment, and subjected it to an analysis which led him to a concrete examination of one of the central questions of the sociology of law, namely the relation between law and social domination. This analysis was all the more remarkable for the fact that he was able to show the vital importance of a sociological approach to labour law, which not only complemented, but also enriched, the systematic technical-legal analysis of positive law. As Kahn-Freund wrote:

. . . as well as its far-reaching sociological significance, the conception of the employment relationship as one of domination and subordination . . . had direct implications for legal analysis. . . . The idea of the dual nature of the employment relationship as one of subordination and exchange was a corner-stone of Sinzheimer's theoretical system. It was the legal-positivistic correlate of his definitions of work and (in particular) of 'dependency'. . . . The vital point here is the close link between Sinzheimer's sociological insights, the systematic conclusions he drew from them, and the rigorous technical work of the lawyer and advocate.[12]

If Sinzheimer's distinctive conception of labour law resulted from a sociological analysis of the employment relationship in capitalist society, then it was also based on a theory of the sources of law derived from a sociological understanding of the role of extra-legal factors and developments in determining the norms governing industrial relations. The key to this theoretical innovation in labour law was Sinzheimer's analysis of collective labour relations and labour law, particularly his study of the growth and function of collective agreements in Germany in the twenty years before the outbreak of the First World War.

While in the 1890s collective agreements hardly existed in Germany, by 1913 there were around 13,500 in force, covering over two million workers in around 218,000 establishments (about 20 per cent of the total manual work-force). Although collective agreements were not contractually binding on the negotiating parties at this time, they were only rarely breached by the employers. As Professor Däubler has argued: 'the agreements were upheld through the strength of the trade unions and their permanent readiness to take industrial action'.[13] Sinzheimer argued that this development was not only of interest to social scientists and industrial relations practitioners, it also had a direct bearing on the legal norms governing the employment relationship. He therefore proceeded to make a comprehensive study of actual agreements, which was published in two volumes in 1907–8 under the title *The Collective Agreement*.[14]

This work had a number of implications for the study of labour law. Firstly, it extended the scope of traditional legal analysis to cover institutions, such as the collective agreement, which have normative force as 'law' but which (at that time in Germany and still today in Britain) are as such neither legally established nor legally enforceable. This was the beginning of 'labour law' as an independent legal discipline.[15] Secondly, his empirical examination of collective agreements as a means of analysing the legal norms governing the employment relationship was a methodological innovation which broke out of the confines of traditional jurisprudence and suggested the use of new techniques to understand this newly-defined subject.[16] But Sinzheimer's analysis of collective agreements had a third implication concerning the sources of law which had far-reaching consequences for the evaluation of the relation between state and autonomous law-making in industrial relations. As with his study of the contract of employment, Sinzheimer was once again taking one of the fundamental institutions of labour law, here the collective agreement, and subjecting it to an analysis which led him to a concrete examination of one of the central issues of the sociology of law, in this instance the relation between the law and the political structure (the state, legal policy, political parties, etc.). While most of his academic colleagues were unable to grasp the social and legal significance of the growth in collective bargaining before 1914, Sinzheimer located the source of this development in the 'law-creating capacity' of autonomous collective organizations. Trade unions and employers' associations were their own autonomous law-makers in the field of employment through the processes of collective conflict, collective bargaining, and the making and enforcement of collective agreements.

'The collective agreement did not originate in the mind of the jurist',[17] he wrote in 1916. It was a legal institution which had been developed in social reality; it was 'real' or (to use Eugen Ehrlich's phrase) 'living' law.[18]

From this analysis Sinzheimer drew two important practical conclusions for the future development of legal policy in the field of labour law. Firstly, he argued that the state should recognize the growing significance of socially-created law (compared with state-established law and the principles of jurisprudence) in the field of industrial relations, and should actively promote the 'law-creating capacity' of employers and trade unions, assisting them in achieving the primacy of auto-nomous collective bargaining over other (legislative, admini-strative, judicial, unilateral-employer) methods of job regulation. Secondly, he argued that in practice the organized group had primacy over the individual employer or employee in the determination of the rules governing the employment relationship, and that therefore the state should recognize the legal superiority of the collective organizations (employers' associations, trade unions, etc.) if it was not to conflict with legal reality.

Thus Sinzheimer's analysis of collective agreements in Germany not only had consequences for the subject-matter and methodology of labour law, it also had concrete implications for legal policy. His study of the legal framework of industrial relations in Germany also provided a detailed confirmation of one of the basic principles of the sociology of law as spelt out by Eugen Ehrlich in his pioneering work of 1913:

The view that law is created by the state . . will not bear the test of historical analysis. . . . The greater part of legal life goes on in a sphere far removed from the state, the state tribunals and state law. . . . The centre of gravity of legal development . . . from time immemorial has not lain in the activity of the state but in society itself, and must be sought there at the present time. . . . The living law is the law which dominates life itself even though it has not been posited in legal provisions.[19]

We have already seen how two of the fundamental questions of the sociology of law (the relation between law and social domination, and the relation between law and the political structure) were central to Sinzheimer's approach to labour law. However, a third fundamental question, the relation between law and the economy, also assumed central significance in his theory. He formulated this question in terms of the relationship between 'social law' (the law regulating the employment relationship, including social security law) and 'economic law' (the 'legal framework' for the exercise of economic and industrial power, both at government level and at the level of the individual company or plant). Sinzheimer argued that as economic and industrial issues impinge directly and indirectly on labour relations and the employment relationship, labour law should eventually be incorporated into a new kind of economic law. The ultimate purpose of such a development was to establish an integrated legal framework for the exercise of self-government in industry. Practical attempts (and the ultimate failure) to achieve this objective in Weimar Germany through the establishment of economic councils and works councils have been examined elsewhere.[20] In the context of this chapter it is sufficient to note that Sinzheimer regarded the question of the relationship between labour law and the processes of economic and industrial control as one of the central theoretical and practical issues for labour lawyers.

It becomes clear at this point that Sinzheimer had an all-embracing, 'continental-European' conception of sociology. It was the task of the sociologist to build on the work of the other social science disciplines (politics, jurisprudence, economics, etc.) and to explore the relationships between them and how they interact to form society as a whole.[21] In this sense both Sinzheimer and Kahn-Freund stood very much in the tradition of Weberian sociology, even though they were both first and foremost lawyers. It should be remembered that Weber's work on law was part of a major theoretical study entitled *Economy and Society*, which in turn was intended as part of a comprehensive treatise to be called *An Outline of Social Economics*.[22]

It was only after his exile to Holland in 1933 that Sinzheimer developed a comprehensive theory of the sociology of law. In a major study published in 1936,[23] he argued that there were four distinct approaches to the 'discipline': the descriptive, the critical, the historical, and the theoretical. The *descriptive* sociologist of law examines real law in the widest sense, that is, the legal norms regulating the actual behaviour of individuals and groups. This approach was explicitly adopted by Sinzheimer in his study of 1907–8 of actual collective agreements. The *critical* sociologist of law studies the relationship between the formal legal norm (the norm) and the real rule (the normal). This obviously presupposes both a technical analysis of formal law and a descriptive sociological study of real law. The *historical* sociology of law is concerned with an analysis of how legal concepts change as a result of contact with reality; how the social creation of law affects state law; and how the state translates social changes into legal norms. Both the critical and the historical approaches can be found in Renner's study of property in *The Institutions of Private Law and their Social Functions*,[24] Kahn-Freund's analysis of collective agreements and 'collectivism' in 'The Changing Function of Labour Law',[25] and Kahn-Freund's study of judicial decisions in the field of labour law in *The Social Ideal of the Reich Labour Court*.[26] The fourth approach focuses on the fundamental question of the relation between economic and social forces on the one hand, and the world of ideas (including the law) on the other, and was described by Sinzheimer as the *theoretical* sociology of law. Kahn-Freund mentioned an example of such an approach in his monograph on the Reich Labour Court. He argued that it would be an important task to try and explain why the judiciary adopted a particular social ideal in its decisions at a particular historical time. The task of such an analysis would be to 'derive the necessity for the evolution of a particular ideology from the overall economic and social situation in Germany'.[27] Thus all four approaches to the sociology of law were of practical relevance to the sociological study of labour law in Weimar Germany, and provided a useful conceptual framework for the translation of the debates around the sociology of law into the sub-discipline of labour law.

In concluding this section it should be stressed that Sinzheimer's approach to the sociology of law did not involve the rejection of technical-legal analysis. As Kahn-Freund argued in his inaugural lecture at Oxford University in 1965, legal reasoning is necessarily composed of two elements, technical and sociological, 'deductive' and 'teleological'.[28] In other words, legal problems have two distinct reference points: a legal one (what answer can be derived from legal sources such as statute law and judicial decisions?) and an extra-legal one (what is the purpose of the law; what is right, just, expedient, fair, good policy?). Ultimately, though, technical and deductive reasoning were not adequate for what Sinzheimer regarded as the fundamental objective of the study of labour law: to assist in the development of legal policy.

How is legal policy possible? As soon as this question is asked the limited significance of the positivistic legal method is demonstrated. It is indispensable for the understanding of positive law, but unable to assist in the elaboration of new law. . . . In calm periods of history, when a certain degree of equilibrium has been achieved in the relations between the social forces, it is usually simply a matter of formal modifications of the law, for which the positivistic technical method may be sufficient. But in times of sudden change, where the old disappears and the new craves recognition, a purely technical insight into the existing legal order is not sufficient. . . At the very moment when jurisprudential thought advances beyond existing law and wishes to develop new forms of law, it becomes dependent on the sociological method. For only the latter provides the foundations for the tasks of legal policy.[29]

The Social and Political Objectives of Labour Law: Judicial Intervention in Industrial Relations

If Kahn-Freund's article of 1976 on Hugo Sinzheimer was a general review of the problems and issues surrounding the development of labour law and the sociology of labour law, then his monograph of 1931 on the Reich Labour Court[30] and his article of 1932 on 'The Changing Function of Labour Law'[31] were examples of the sociology of labour law in practice. The subject-matter of the monograph, judicial decisions in the field of labour law, was and is one of the recognized areas of traditional jurisprudence. But Kahn-Freund was not concerned simply to provide a technical analysis of these decisions; his aim was to uncover the social ideal, the social and political ideology, underlying the technical reasoning of the judiciary. It was based on quite explicit assumptions about the nature of judicial decision-making derived from the recognition that there was no social consensus on the legal norms governing the employment relationship. Kahn-Freund noted that in a society limited by time and space 'totally opposed legal rules can have normative force at the same time', and that 'the legal principles of employer groups in the field of labour law can be completely different from those of employee groups, which in turn can differ from the principles of the judicial civil service'.[32] He argued, therefore, that judicial decision-making is not simply a logical process of deductive reasoning derived from a given corpus of statutory norms (the judge, in Montesquieu's words, as 'une bouche de la loi'), but a culturally-determined process guided by conceptions originating 'in the judge's own economic, social or moral feelings, in his convictions and inclinations'.[33]

Kahn-Freund's method of analysis differed from the traditional jurisprudential approach in two fundamental ways. Firstly, he treated all the decisions of the Reich Labour Court (the highest appeal court in the field of labour law)[34] as a whole, rather than as the application of the law to a series of disparate individual cases. The aim of this novel approach was to examine whether there was a systematic link between individual decisions by different judges relating to diverse areas of labour law, and, if so, to reveal the ideological interests and social values underlying judicial practice as a whole.[35] Secondly, Kahn-Freund reinforced this systematic, generalizing approach by comparing judicial decisions in Germany with those of Mussolini's Italy. As with the sociology of law, comparative law presupposes a technical understanding of specific legal rules and principles, but ultimately refers beyond purely technical analysis, focusing on fundamental determinants rather than particular details. Here again Kahn-Freund's Oxford inaugural lecture is instructive: 'One of the virtues of legal comparison . . . is that it allows a scholar to place himself outside the labyrinth of minutiae in which legal thinking so easily loses its way and to see the great contours of the law and its dominant characteristics.'[36]

In terms of Sinzheimer's characterization of the different types of sociology of law discussed above, Kahn-Freund's method in *The Social Ideal of the Reich Labour Court* can be described as 'critical'; he combined a systematic analysis of judicial reasoning 'from within' with an examination 'from without' of the general social conceptions and interests served by it. To this end he used one of the basic techniques of social science, the conceptual abstraction or 'ideal type', which helps to link the specific to the general and provides an explicit framework for understanding the often bewildering complexities of concrete reality.[37] He used such abstractions to illuminate the two main substantive focuses of his study, i.e. judicial activity and judicial ideology in the field of labour law. As far as judicial activity was concerned, he outlined and contrasted two basic approaches to the overall role of the judiciary in regulating conflicts in industrial relations. According to the first ideal type the judges refrain from imposing any external criteria on collective or individual conflicts between employers and employees, allowing the parties themselves to determine the (often divergent) objectives of industrial conflict, and intervening only when absolutely necessary via the cautious application of existing norms. Alternatively the judiciary can approach all disputes in the field of labour law according to specific external criteria (such as the interests of public policy or the state), evaluating individual and collective conflict in terms of predetermined, though often inexplicit, socio-political objectives. Kahn-Freund argued that, between 1927 and 1931, the Reich Labour Court consistently tended to adopt the second approach.

The second main use of ideal types in Kahn-Freund's study can be found in his definition and elaboration of a typology of four 'social ideals' which, he argued, have traditionally dominated labour law and social policy (including judicial activity) in capitalist societies. He classified these four basic ideologies as liberal, social-conservative, collectivist, and fascist, and then proceeded to examine judicial practice in the field of labour law in terms of these 'ideals'. A substantial part of his monograph is taken up with a detailed analysis of judicial intervention in four specific areas of industrial relations (collective conflict, the individual employment relationship, welfare provision for the 'disadvantaged' employee, and industrial arbitration) and the demonstration of the fact that, in all its decisions, the Reich Labour Court tended to apply a 'fascist' social ideal.[38]

In the context of this chapter it is not necessary to give a detailed appreciation of Kahn-Freund's analysis of specific decisions relating to Weimar labour law. However, one aspect of his study that is worthy of special mention here is his technical examination of the Court's decisions on the relation between the individual employer and the individual employee, and his sociological analysis of the social and political ideals underlying these decisions. For Wolfgang Däubler, who in 1975 published an examination of the social ideal of the West German Federal Labour Court, this analysis of individual labour law was one of the most important features of Kahn-Freund's study.[39] As Kahn-Freund himself later pointed out, the sociological approach to industrial relations tends generally

to ignore the individual employment relationship (the traditional focus of legal analysis), concentrating almost exclusively
on collective relationships at work:

'Industrial relations', as commonly understood, are collective relations, i.e.
relations between an employer or employers and bodies of employees, either
organized in trade unions or forming a distinctive group as a result of their
employment by a given employer. The relationship between the employer and
the individual employee is normally irrelevant to the social scientist, at any
rate in so far as he is interested in the social and economic factors which
contribute to the development of wages and other conditions of employment.
For the lawyer, however, this individual relationship between employer and
employee is the corner-stone of the edifice.[40]

In *The Social Ideal of the Reich Labour Court*, though, Kahn-Freund
examined both individual and collective industrial relations
and successfully integrated the legal and the sociological
approach into what can be called legitimately a sociology of
labour law. He showed the complex yet systematic nature of the
social ideal pursued by the Weimar judiciary in all areas of case
law concerned with the employment relationship. He also combined a detailed study of the technical reasoning of the judiciary
(and the legal norms contained in statute law) with an examination of the social interests and objectives that lay behind them.
For Kahn-Freund the law was 'a method of fulfilling social
objectives',[41] a 'technique for the regulation of social power'.[42]
However the social and political objectives of the actors in the
field of labour law (particularly those of the judiciary) are often
masked by seemingly objective legal concepts and methods of
argumentation. In this sense the critical sociologist of law per-
forms the function of the 'well-informed expert and vigilant
observer',[43] understanding rules and technical reasoning in
their own terms, but also able to advance beyond a purely
positivistic analysis to an appreciation of the social values and
political ideals underlying state-established and state-enforced
law. Here again the task of the sociologist of law is identical to
that of the comparative lawyer as outlined by Kahn-Freund in
1965: 'An academic lawyer who wishes to understand the legal
process as a process of policy making as well as deductive
reasoning must seek to penetrate the social objectives pursued
by legislatures, judges and administrators, and he must seek to
do so whether or not they have been made explicit by those who
made the decisions.'[44]

In *The Social Ideal of the Reich Labour Court* Kahn-Freund
brought together the legal-positivistic, sociological, and comparative methods and was able thereby to expose the dangers
inherent in the judicial transformation of Weimar labour law in
the direction of a fascist social ideology. The events of the years
following the publication of his monograph only served to confirm the validity of his analysis:[45]

> ... the key to the approach of the *Reich* Labour Court can be found in the
> tendency of all civil service bureaucracies to de-politicize and de-revolutionize
> the collective social forces. To see conflict as something abnormal, as a
> disturbance of the regulated flow of social events, is ... characteristic of the
> civil service bureaucracy.... If it is a fact that the practice of the *Reich* Labour
> Court in Germany is, consciously or unconsciously, captive to the same or
> similar tendencies as the dictatorial regime in Italy, then I am simply pointing
> to a danger inherent in the inner transformation of labour law by judicial
> decisions. It is evident that things which have been brought about by political
> dictatorship in one country can be achieved in another country by indepen-
> dent judge-made law still operating within a democracy. The aim of my
> monograph is to show this.[46]

The Relation between Legal Norms and Social Reality: Labour Law, the Economy, and the State

At the beginning of his article 'The Changing Function of
Labour Law', written in 1932 a few months before Hitler's
assumption of power and published in Germany's leading
sociological journal,[47] Kahn-Freund formulated in general
terms the object of the sociology of law:

> The task of the sociology of law may be described as the portrayal of the
> relation between legal norms and social reality. On the one hand it must
> examine the effect of the law on society, the 'social function' of legal institu-
> tions. On the other hand it must investigate how the external social world,
> how economic, social and political events influence the sum total of legal
> norms.[48]

He acknowledged that such a sociological approach to the law
owed a substantial methodological debt to Karl Renner's *Institutions of Private Law and their Social Functions*,[49] but claimed
justifiably that its elaboration in the article represented a
development rather than a wholesale take-over of Renner's
ideas.

This can be seen, for example, in Kahn-Freund's use of the
term legal norm, which he defined, like Eugen Ehrlich but

unlike Karl Renner,[50] as comprising written and unwritten law, statutes and judicial decisions, but also 'crystallized custom'.[51] Following from this extensive definition Kahn-Freund argued for a historical, sociological understanding of the relation between legal norms and social reality, stressing that the law (the sum total of legal norms) could change over time while the content of its statutes (the sum total of its written regulations) remained unaltered:

The appearance and disappearance of legal norms is a continuous process which takes place through and outside the corpus of written law. Society is working ceaselessly on the sum total of legal norms. It creates new norms, for example through contractual practice. It causes existing norms to disappear by refusing to apply them. It alters the content of existing legal rules through changes in 'interpretation'. The statement that the law is a product of the social relations of power must not only be understood in political terms. Social forces not only shape the law through political institutions, but also by their influence on judicial, administrative, and contractual practice, and by their involvement in conflict and the resolution of conflict.[52]

Having set out his general theoretical and methodological assumptions, Kahn-Freund proceeded to outline the specific focus and objective of his article. His aim was to show how the sum total of norms of German labour law had changed between 1918 and 1931, to analyse their changing function, and to uncover the basic social and political trend underlying this development.

In some respects the article had a similar objective to his monograph on the Reich Labour Court: it was a study of the social and political ideology underlying the legal norms applying to the employment relationship. However the focus was now more comprehensive, with a more detailed examination of the changing objectives of statute law, and a much more explicit attempt to draw ideological and historical connections between specific legal developments and traditions, and the development of socio-economic and political relations in Germany between 1869 and 1932. Again this approach represented in a certain sense a departure from Renner, who drew a fundamental distinction between legal (i.e. positivistic) and sociological-functional (i.e. social, historical, economic, and political) analysis. Renner argued that the lawyer should be concerned only with the normative purity of legal institutions, and should leave the study of the social objectives of the law, and the social and economic forces which create and change it, to the social scientist.[53] Kahn-Freund was able to show, however, that an integrated 'sociology of law' approach provided not only a historical understanding of the development of legal norms and differing technical interpretations of legal institutions, but also an insight into the policy alternatives open to the development of labour law in the future.

The first example of this integrated approach to the sociology of labour law was concerned with the changing social function of the contract of employment between 1868 and 1914, and the changing nature of the legal norms arising from it in the same period. Kahn-Freund was able to demonstrate how particular technical interpretations of the individual employment contract were linked to wider legal traditions, but also ultimately derived from, and supportive of, the socio-political objectives of specific social strata and classes. Thus the conceptualization of the contract of employment as an exchange relation embodied in mutual obligations, itself rooted in the Roman law tradition of jurisprudence, was a legal expression of the socio-political ideology of the industrial bourgeoisie, which was based on the principle of the formal equality and freedom of all persons under the law. On this analysis the idea of the 'free' contract of employment, a fundamental tenet of the technical-positivistic approach, is in fact a highly partisan interpretation derivative of liberal-capitalist ideology.[54]

However there was another, competing interpretation of the contract of employment, this time rooted in the German law school of jurisprudence (associated with the name of Otto von Gierke), which saw it as a legally regulated bond of fidelity between individuals, a personal relation of obedience and protection. According to Kahn-Freund this approach was derived from a social-conservative system of ideas, a legal expression of the semi-absolutist ideology of the German landowning classes. In fact German employment legislation before 1914 was an amalgam of different regulations, codes, and statutes, a complicated mixture of liberal-individualist and social-conservative legal ideas. For Kahn-Freund this could only be explained in social and political terms 'by the unique character of power relations in Germany'.[55] The political alliance between the German landowners and the Prussian state (army, civil service, Church, and Kaiser) effectively excluded the German bourgeoisie from direct participation in the exercise of legislative power, and meant that much of pre-1914 industrial legislation 'did not correspond to the wishes and supposed interests of the large industrial capitalists. . . . The much deplored "fragmentation of labour law" is to a large extent an expression of the uneven distribution of political power between different sectors of the economy.'[56]

But Kahn-Freund's analysis of the contract of employment had one further and decisive sociological component. Both the Roman and the German law interpretations, which were both embodied in legislation, were nevertheless 'in complete contradiction to social reality'.[57] Both regarded the employee as an isolated individual, either as an isolated subject freely and equally entering a contract involving mutual obligations (the Roman school), or as an isolated object subordinate to the employer and thus requiring the protection of the employer and the state (the German school). In reality, though, Kahn-Freund argued, employees were combining together in collective organizations and creating, together with the employers, a corpus of extra-statutory legal norms in the form of collective agreements. These socially created and enforced norms often overrode in practice the legal norms deriving from the contract of employment and other legal institutions established under statute law. Once again Kahn-Freund's historical-sociological method, clearly influenced by Sinzheimer,[58] was indispensable for a full understanding of these developments:

A rising class regularly uses social, extra-political methods to create for itself a series of legal norms which supplement and often override state legislation. In this way large sections of the German working class . . . were successful in creating a corpus of norms in the form of collective agreements. Admittedly they were without statutory force, but the trade unions were generally able to guarantee their observance through the social methods of external organizational pressure. These extra-statutory norms were often more important than legislation in establishing the rights and obligations arising out of the employment relationship. The state played virtually no role in securing their acceptance.[59]

However the state did intervene in other ways in the employment relationship before 1914, and Kahn-Freund's analysis of the introduction in 1911 of a special insurance scheme for salaried employees again illustrated the importance of a sociological approach to the development of labour law and social policy. German employment legislation had traditionally distinguished between different categories of employee (manual workers, salaried employees, and career civil servants), but between 1890 and 1914 the growth of large-scale industry and the rise of the trade union and labour movement had combined to foster a growing awareness amongst salaried employees of their common interests with manual workers. At this point the government introduced a special insurance scheme which gave them substantial material advantages over manual workers and reinforced traditional occupational differences. Kahn-Freund commented: 'Perhaps there is no other example which demonstrates so conclusively the social function of legal institutions, their tendency consciously to create and change ideologies.'[60] This piece of social legislation was clearly intended to influence the thought and behaviour of salaried employees 'in order to prevent the active collective intervention of the workers as a class'.[61]

The main focus of Kahn-Freund's article, however, was on the changing function of labour law in Germany from 1918 until 1932, to which the developments described above provide the necessary historical background. Here again the sociological method was of fundamental importance, particularly in the elaboration of the origins, theory, and development of what he called the 'collectivist system'[62] of labour law in Weimar Germany. As a system of labour law and industrial relations, collectivism arose out of the unique economic and political situation in Germany in 1918 and 1919, which, on Kahn-Freund's analysis, had 'led to a temporary state of equilibrium in the balance of power between the bourgeoisie and the working class'.[63] The decisive change in the ideology and legislative practice relating to labour law was the recognition by the state of the organizations of employers and employees as law-creating institutions. Responsibility for the development of legal norms was formally transferred by the state from the political to the social sphere, the recognition of a development which had already taken place in social reality. In this sense formal law was essentially being made consistent with legal reality. Collectivism therefore assumed the primacy of the collective social regulation of industrial relations over unilateral employer or statutory regulation. The rules governing employment were to be derived, agreed, and administered autonomously by the collective social forces. The role of the state (here mainly the legislature, the judiciary, and the administrative authorities) was to recognize and encourage 'the idea of social self-determination in the law'.[64] Labour law was to be formed as 'an accommodation arising out of the conflict between the collective forces in society'.[65]

But what would happen to the primacy of collectivist rule-making if the balance of power between capital and labour changed fundamentally, if the degree of equilibrium between them was disturbed? This is what Kahn-Freund set out to examine in his article, analysing in detail a number of institutions and legal provisions of Weimar labour law (the arbitration system, the judiciary, the 'extension' of collective agreements, collective bargaining, and the role of the works councils) and observing whether changes in economic and political reality had brought with them a change in legal norms even though the content of written law had remained unaltered.[66] In many respects this detailed analysis was an extension, a refinement, and above all a sharpening of the ideas first developed in the monograph on the Reich Labour Court. Through numerous examples he was able to show that external intervention by the state (above all by the legislature and judiciary) had perverted the collectivist ideal, restricting the relatively free expression of class conflict and making the development of labour law subject to the 'imposition of the will of a dictatorial civil service'.[67] The period from 1923 to 1932 saw 'the retreat of the autonomous forces and the advance of the state in the field of social policy'.[68]

What general lessons did Kahn-Freund draw from this analysis of Weimar labour law?

Firstly, he argued that deep economic crisis had undermined the extra-legal basis of collectivism and thereby fundamentally changed the nature of labour law. In times of high demand for labour (full employment), employees can use their collective strength and organization as a counterbalance to the superior social power of the employers which arises from their ownership of the means of production and their control of jobs. In this way a certain degree of equilibrium is created in the balance of power between employers and employees, which finds expression in the processes of collective bargaining, industrial conflict, and collective agreements. In times of over-supply of labour, however, the collective social power of employees is weakened and the social basis of labour law rights (employment protection, freedom to strike, etc.) is undermined. Neither Sinzheimer nor Kahn-Freund had any illusions that labour law loses all meaning in times of large-scale unemployment, 'if it is at best just a law for an elite of workers, if, alongside the living reality of labour law, an economic graveyard of "structural unemployment" opens up'.[69] The economic crisis served only to expose even more clearly the structural contradiction between the social, emancipatory purpose of Weimar labour law and the individualistic, anti-social character of the capitalist economic order.

Secondly, Kahn-Freund was critical of the ever-increasing state intervention in industrial relations in Weimar Germany, for according to the theory of collectivism the state should play a secondary, subsidiary role. A particularly ironic aspect of this increased state intervention was that Hugo Sinzheimer, the champion of collective autonomy in the field of labour law, himself advocated compulsory arbitration between 1929 and 1932 as a means of determining wages. His hope was that compulsory arbitration would provide some kind of political support for the trade unions whose social power was almost completely undermined by unemployment. In fact Kahn-Freund never fully accepted this view, arguing that compulsory arbitration actually undermined independent trade unionism and weakened the democratic defences against the rise of Fascism. Indeed he had already argued in *The Social Ideal of the Reich Labour Court* that involvement in arbitration committees, labour tribunals, and social insurance bodies had furthered psychologically a peaceful, non-combative, depoliticized tendency within the trade unions and encouraged their integration into the state.[70]

Thirdly, Kahn-Freund argued that collectivism could function successfully only if the judiciary was prepared to adapt to the spirit of the new labour laws. In fact, of course, the Weimar judiciary maintained its static conception of society and its adherence to the social ideal of 'peace, order and *consensus omnium*',[71] which were in complete contradiction to the collectivist system of ideas.

For Kahn-Freund collectivism was an innately unstable and fragile system, conditional on a particular balance of power between capital and labour. When this balance of power, the extra-legal basis of collectivism, changed fundamentally in favour of the employers, so did the function of labour law. In his essay one senses at many points Kahn-Freund's growing doubts about the long-term adequacy and viability of any statutory system of employment rights in capitalist society:

The road which labour law has taken since the revolution [of 1918–19] proves that collectivism has come up against difficulties which have their origins in the fundamental nature of the capitalist system and in the sociological composition of the proletariat. . . . Perhaps it was a mistake to believe that it was possible to realise a collectivist system in a capitalist economy without recognising that the economic conditions of capitalism allow this system to function only under quite specific circumstances. It was inevitable that the function of collectivism would change fundamentally when confronted by the crisis.[72]

In his conclusion Kahn-Freund felt unable to pronounce on the future development of collectivist labour law and the role of the state in industrial relations. These were, he argued, dependent on two main factors, the economic situation and the organizational strength of the working class.

Is it possible to legalise the class struggle in a class-divided society and to make it a component of the legal system? Can the state recognise the idea of class and yet remain 'neutral'? Must not the conflict eventually break up the legal system or the legal system suppress the conflict? It is impossible to answer these questions from the perspective of the present crisis. Only a renewed strengthening of the organisational power of the working class when the economy starts to grow again can teach us whether the collectivist system can achieve new life in a different economic situation.[73]

Conclusion

So far in this chapter the main concern has been to analyse the major German writings of Otto Kahn-Freund with a special emphasis on their theoretical and methodological implications for the study of labour law. It is now possible, building on this analysis, to advance some more general statements about the main elements of a sociology of labour law.

The foundation of such an approach is the sociological analysis of employment relations in capitalist society and the understanding of the relationship of the individual employee to the individual employer as one of social subordination.

However, this relationship (and the legal apparatus which regulates it, the contract of employment)[74] has been modified historically by a series of norms which regulate both individual and collective employment relations. These norms can be socially as well as legally created and enforced, and are expressed in processes and institutions such as employment protection legislation, collective agreements, conciliation and arbitration, industrial conflict, industrial tribunals, and workplace organization. A sociology of labour law requires therefore a legal and a sociological understanding of legal and extra-legal norms governing both individual and collective employment relations.

A sociological approach to labour law differs significantly from a traditional 'positivistic' approach in terms of both theory and method. Before these differences are pursued further, however, it is perhaps necessary to note the often conflicting uses of the term 'positivism' and to clarify its meaning in this specific context. The term is *not* used here as a philosophical or epistemological concept expressing a particular assumption about the scientific status or objectivity of knowledge;[75] *nor* is it used in the sense of 'positive law' in contrast to 'natural' law.[76] Positivism in this context refers to 'positivism within jurisprudence' as opposed to 'functional' or 'sociological' analysis of law. It will be argued here that there is a fundamental distinction between these two approaches to the analysis of law, and that a sociology of law (and thus a sociology of labour law) requires the integration of both approaches. David Schiff's recent article on Timasheff's sociology of law provides a useful starting-point:

The tests of a sociological theory of law and that of a jurisprudential theory are . . . distinguishable. The former depends on whether the theory adequately presents legal reality as part of social reality (without misconstruing either element), the latter is a presentation of a differentiated or distinguishable reality per se (. . .).[77]

The significance of this definition of the sociology of law lies in its emphasis on legal reality as part of social reality 'without misconstruing either element'. This is entirely consistent with what Sinzheimer called the 'critical' sociology of law, whose task is to compare legal norms with the real rules governing human behaviour; this requires both a jurisprudential and a descriptive sociological analysis. Unlike both Timasheff (the sociologist) and Kelsen (the lawyer), who as Schiff has shown elevated jurisprudence to a position of primacy over sociology, the critical sociology of law unites both approaches 'without misconstruing either element'. Despite this it would be wrong to assume that the use of the sociological method has no impact on the technical analysis of positive law. As we have seen in our examination of Sinzheimer's theory of the contract of employment, the sociological understanding of the nature of work in capitalist society has a significant bearing on the legal-positivistic analysis of the employment relationship.[78] As Kahn-Freund wrote of his teacher Sinzheimer:

Like all good lawyers he worked his way through the black-letter analysis of the law, in other words, he neither went round it nor got stuck in it. He demanded the same of his students. He would have had nothing in common with those members of the younger generation who are afraid of positivistic training, of 'learning how to think', for fear of weakening their own convictions, nor with those who make a cult out of their own social blindness. . . . For him the practical problems of the application of the law were combined with general insights into the economic and social structure of the employment relationship and into the general problems of the law.[79]

The theoretical distinction between jurisprudential analysis and the sociology of law thus has profound methodological implications for the study of labour law, a proposition illustrated by Sinzheimer's analysis of the origin and function of collective agreements and by Kahn-Freund's examination of judicial decisions in Weimar Germany.[80]

The sociology of law is also distinguishable from jurisprudential analysis by its 'methods' in the narrower sense, i.e. its methods and sources of collection of data and evidence. This can be demonstrated by reference to two of the central methods of sociological analysis: observation and interview. If the sociologist of labour law is concerned, as Kahn-Freund wrote in 1954, 'with the law as it is and not with the technical processes through which it precariously maintains the fiction of its self-sufficiency and immutability',[81] then it is necessary to examine the law in reality, or, to use Ehrlich's phrase, 'living law'. One of the fundamental questions raised by the increase in labour legislation in Britain since the early 1960s is whether and how this growth in legal regulation influences the actual behaviour and thinking of employers and employees, management and unions, in the day-to-day conduct of industrial relations. The social (as opposed to the legal) significance of this new legislation is a prime subject for the sociology of labour law, and can be adequately assessed only by interviewing the actors in industrial relations (to find out their perceptions of and attitudes towards the law in industrial relations) and observing their actual behaviour (to gain an independent view, for example, of the extent to which day-to-day industrial relations have become 'juridified'). This question of the social effect(-iveness) of legal norms in the field of labour law is a fertile field for study, particularly when linked to a study of their changing social function (as in Kahn-Freund's article of 1932) and the social purpose underlying them (as in his monograph of 1931).

All these questions relate to problems and issues arising from the continually changing status and function of law in social and political relations, and they point to possibly the most distinctive feature of a sociology of labour law—its practical implications for the development of legal policy. In this respect it is no coincidence that the final work of perhaps the foremost twentieth-century exponent of a sociology of labour law, Hugo Sinzheimer, was called *A Theory of Legislation* and culminated in a theory of 'legislative jurisprudence'.[82] The practical problems of legal policy in fact bring together the three main substantive concerns of a sociology of labour law: the relation between law and social domination (the function of the law in social relations of domination and subordination); the relation between law and the political structure (the law, political power, and the role of the state); and the relation between law and the economy (the role of the law in processes of industrial and economic control).

Finally it should not be forgotten that a sociology of labour law building on the pioneering work of Kahn-Freund and Sinzheimer has one further ingredient without which it would not be complete. It is what Kahn-Freund called 'legal anthropology',[83] a conviction that the true function of the law is to assist in the achievement of a wider social and political purpose, namely the advance of human freedom and the dignity of man. Such a conviction cannot of course be derived from theoretical conceptions of the sociology of labour law, but it is impossible nevertheless to understand the pioneering contribution of Kahn-Freund and Sinzheimer in this area without recognizing the indivisible unity in their life and work between a sociological understanding of the law on the one hand, and political commitment and a concern for human emancipation on the other.

Human freedom and the dignity of man were, for Sinzheimer the socialist, as for every true socialist, the alpha and omega of intellectual and political life. . . . His whole work is a call to the emancipation of man. One can only do justice to his sociological writings if they are seen in this light.[84]

1. See, for example, H. L. A. Hart, 'Positivism and the Separation of Law and Morals' (1958) 71 *Harvard Law Review* 593; J. Stone, *Social Dimensions of Law and Justice*, London, 1966; V. Aubert (ed.), *Sociology of Law*, Harmondsworth, 1969; A. Hunt, *The Sociological Movement in Law*, London, 1978; D. Schiff, 'N. S. Timasheff's Sociology of Law' (1981) 44 *Modern Law Review* 400; A. Podgorecki and C. Whelan (eds.), *Sociological Approaches to Law*, London, 1981.
2. The three main German writings are available in English translation with an editorial introduction by Roy Lewis and Jon Clark. See O. Kahn-Freund, *Labour Law and Politics in the Weimar Republic*, Oxford, 1981.
3. At the beginning of Kahn-Freund's celebrated article of 1954 on the legal framework of British industrial relations, there are some fascinating comments on the differences between the 'legal' and the 'sociological' approach to industrial relations, but these are not taken up in the rest of the analysis. See O. Kahn-Freund, 'Legal Framework', in A. Flanders and H. A. Clegg (eds.), *The System of Industrial Relations in Great Britain*, Oxford, 1954, esp. pp. 42–5. Probably the best example of a sociological approach to labour law in Kahn-Freund's English writings is the first chapter of *Labour and the Law*. His reflections on law and power are heavily indebted to Max Weber, among others, but there is no reference to specific sources in either text or notes. See O. Kahn-Freund, *Labour and the Law*, London, 2nd ed. 1977, pp. 1–17.
4. O. Kahn-Freund, 'Hugo Sinzheimer 1875–1945', in *Labour Law and Politics*, p. 96.
5. See ibid., pp. 73–9; also R. Lewis and J. Clark, 'Introduction' to *Labour Law and Politics*, pp. 37–41.
6. *Labour Law and Politics*, pp. 73–107.
7. These basic elements of Sinzheimer's conception of labour law are discussed more fully in H. Sinzheimer, *Grundzüge des Arbeitsrechts*, Jena, 1927, pp. 3–42.
8. 'Hugo Sinzheimer 1875–1945', p. 77.
9. Both Sinzheimer and Kahn-Freund used to illustrate this point by quoting from Marx's study, *Wage-Labour and Capital* (1847–9): 'Labour has no other container but human flesh and blood.'
10. See Kahn-Freund's comment of 1962 on this point: 'The semblance of co-ordination of expressed intentions which is the essence of contract making may be a veil for an act of subordination to private rule-making power. . . . This is a sociological commonplace.' 'English Law and American Law—Some Comparative Reflections', reprinted in O. Kahn-Freund, *Selected Writings*, London, 1978, pp. 336–7. Or the more famous formulation in his 'Introduction' to Karl Renner's *Institutions of Private Law and their Social Functions* (London, 1949, p. 28): 'The contract (of employment) itself is, like all legal institutions, a blank without intrinsic social significance, and adaptable to an infinite number of social objectives. In industrial capitalism, however, it is also "blank" in a more poignant sense. Whatever the law may say, from a sociological point of view this is a "contract" without contractual content. It is a command under the guise of an agreement.'
11. Sinzheimer, *Grundzüge des Arbeitsrechts*, p. 4.

12. 'Hugo Sinzheimer 1875–1945', pp. 92–3.
13. W. Däubler, *Das Arbeitsrecht*, Reinbek bei Hamburg, 1976, p. 40.
14. H. Sinzheimer, *Der korporative Arbeitsnormenvertrag*, Leipzig, 1907–8.
15. See on this point Wedderburn above, p. 31: 'In 1947, there were only two British Universities offering a course to students in "Labour Law" in a modern form (relating the subject to collective bargaining)'.
16. Interestingly, neither Sinzheimer nor Kahn-Freund used one of the most important sociological research methods, i.e. observation, in their sociological studies of labour law. Eugen Ehrlich went as far as to describe sociology as a 'science of observation', arguing that 'the sociological method . . . demands absolutely that the results which are obtained from the judicial decisions be supplemented by direct observation of life'. E. Ehrlich, *Fundamental Principles of the Sociology of Law*, New York, reprint ed. 1975, pp. 473, 495.
17. H. Sinzheimer, *Ein Arbeitstarifgesetz*, Münich and Leipzig, 1916, p. 13.
18. For a more detailed discussion of these concepts see Kahn-Freund, 'Hugo Sinzheimer 1875–1945', pp. 82–6, 96–100.
19. Ehrlich, *Fundamental Principles*, pp. 160, 162, 390, 493. Cf. Kelsen's criticism of Ehrlich's concept of 'living law' as discussed in Schiff, 'Timasheff's Sociology of Law', p. 405.
20. See *Labour Law and Politics*, pp. 35, 48–9, 86–91, 103, 113–7.
21. For an elaboration of this point see M. Rheinstein, 'Introduction' to Rheinstein (ed.) *Max Weber on Law in Economy and Society*, Cambridge, Massachusetts, 1954, pp. xxv–xxvii.
22. See ibid., pp. xxv–xlvii.
23. H. Sinzheimer, *De taak der rechtssociologie*, Haarlem, 1935. For a concise summary of certain parts of this work see Kahn-Freund, 'Hugo Sinzheimer 1875–1945', pp. 96–100.
24. See esp. pp. 251–300.
25. Published in English translation in *Labour Law and Politics*, pp. 162–92. Hereafter cited as 'Changing Function'.
26. Published in ibid., pp. 108–61. Hereafter cited as *Social Ideal*.
27. Ibid., p. 109.
28. O. Kahn-Freund, 'Comparative Law as an Academic Subject', reprinted in *Selected Writings*, p. 278. Hereafter cited as 'Comparative Law'.
29. H. Sinzheimer, 'Über soziologische und dogmatische Methode in der Arbeitsrechtswissenschaft' (1922), reprinted in H. Sinzheimer, *Arbeitsrecht und Rechtssoziologie*, eds. O. Kahn-Freund and T. Ramm, Vol. 2, Frankfurt and Cologne, 1976, pp. 38–9. A full bibliography of Sinzheimer's writings is given in Appendix 1 of *Labour Law and Politics*, pp. 208–13.
30. See n. 26.
31. See n. 25.
32. *Social Ideal*, p. 155, n. 2.
33. Ibid., p. 108. For an examination of the role of the judiciary in British labour law see Clark and Wedderburn below, text to n. 187 *et seq.*
34. For further details on the organization and procedure of labour tribunals in Weimar Germany see *Labour Law and Politics*, pp. 34–5, 93–4.
35. See Wolfgang Däubler's interesting comment on Kahn-Freund's approach: 'The fact that the question is rarely if ever raised as to whether individual judgments and decisions are based on unified conceptions of those making the decisions, whether a "system" lies behind them, has the major disadvantage that the further question of the social causes of certain prevailing evaluations is also not raised.' W. Däubler, *Das soziale Ideal des Bundesarbeitsgerichts*, Frankfurt and Cologne, 1975, p. 11. Hereafter cited as *Das soziale Ideal*.
36. 'Comparative Law', p. 277. For a more detailed examination of Kahn-Freund's use of the comparative method see Lewis below, text to n. 2 *et seq.*

37. For a discussion of Weber's use of the 'ideal type' see M. Rheinstein, 'Introduction', pp. xxxvii–xliii.
38. See *Social Ideal*, pp. 113–50. For a more detailed analysis of these points, particularly of Kahn-Freund's typology of 'social ideals', see Lewis and Clark, 'Introduction' to *Labour Law and Politics*, pp. 42–5.
39. Däubler wrote of Kahn-Freund's study: 'His analysis, unrivalled to this day, stands out . . . because of the completeness of the case material cited, which also includes the generally much less considered field of individual labour law.' *Das soziale Ideal*, p. 13.
40. Kahn-Freund, *System* (1954), p. 45.
41. 'Comparative Law', p. 279.
42. *Labour* (1977), p. 3.
43. *Social Ideal*, p. 151.
44. 'Comparative Law', p. 278.
45. For a discussion of Nazi labour law, including references to certain continuities with judicial decisions in the Weimar Republic, see T. Ramm, 'Nationalsozialismus und Arbeitsrecht', and Hientzsch, *Arbeitsrechtslehren im Dritten Reich und ihre historische Vorbereitung*, both cited in Däubler, *Das soziale Ideal*, p. 14, n. 18.
46. *Social Ideal*, p. 152. O. Kahn-Freund, Letter to Clemens Nörpel of 21 February 1931, published in English translation in *Labour Law and Politics*, p. 230.
47. This was the *Archiv für Sozialwissenschaft und Sozialpolitik*.
48. 'Changing Function', p. 162.
49. See n. 10.
50. See on this point Kahn-Freund's own comment in his 'Notes' to *Renner* (1949), p. 60: 'A reader who is familiar with Ehrlich's *Fundamental Principles of the Sociology of Law* . . . will perceive that Renner's conception of law is the antithesis of Ehrlich's. All that Ehrlich calls "the living law" (see in particular chp. xxi of his work), is from Renner's point of view no law at all. It is the extra-legal functioning of the legal norm.'
51. The term 'crystallized custom' is used by Kahn-Freund in his essay on the 'Legal Framework' of British industrial relations (*System* (1954), pp. 58–9), but the formulation appears in virtually equivalent form ('zu Zwangsgeboten erstarrte Sitten') in the first page of his 1932 article on 'The Changing Function of Labour Law' (p. 162).
52. 'Changing Function', pp. 162–3.
53. See Kahn-Freund's assessment of this point in his 'Introduction' to *Renner* (1949), p. 1: 'It is one of the tasks of the sociology of law to explore the social forces which bring about the creation of legal norms and institutions and changes in positive law. Renner's work does not deal with this aspect of the inter-relation between law and society.'
54. See Kahn-Freund's comment: 'The capitalist environment of the law favours the positivist approach.' Ibid., p. 16.
55. 'Changing Function', p. 164.
56. Ibid.
57. Ibid., pp. 164–5. It is interesting to compare this analysis with Freedland's comment on the British law of the contract of employment: 'Writers on the law and sociology of employment have demonstrated extensively [its] social irrelevance . . . and its failure to express the realities of the contemporary employment relationship.' M. Freedland, *The Contract of Employment*, Oxford, 1976, p. 1.
58. See above, text to n. 12 *et seq.*
59. 'Changing Function', pp. 165–6.
60. Ibid., p. 166.
61. Ibid., p. 165.
62. See ibid., pp. 167 *et seq.*; also Lewis and Clark, 'Introduction' to *Labour Law and Politics*, pp. 46–51.

63. Ibid., p. 167.
64. This was the subtitle of Sinzheimer's work of 1916, *A Statute on Collective Agreements*, Münich and Leipzig.
65. *Social Ideal*, p. 155.
66. See 'Changing Function', pp. 167–89.
67. *Social Ideal*, p. 155.
68. 'Changing Function', p. 173.
69. H. Sinzheimer, 'Die Krisis des Arbeitsrechts', reprinted in *Arbeitsrecht und Rechtssoziologie*, Vol. 1, p. 141.
70. *Social Ideal*, pp. 153–4.
71. 'Changing Function', p. 178.
72. Ibid., pp. 189, 176.
73. Ibid., pp. 190–1.
74. For a more detailed analysis of the contract of employment see Clark and Wedderburn below, text to n. 73 *et seq.*
75. For a discussion of this concept of positivism and the debate surrounding it see Schiff, 'Timasheff's Sociology of Law', pp. 410 *et seq*. Schiff also provides a detailed reference to sources relating to the critique of 'positivism' within sociology, ibid., p. 412, n. 78.
76. See on this point Karl Olivecrona, *Law as Fact*, London, 1971. Chapter 1 is entitled 'Legal Positivism and Natural Law Theory', ibid., pp. 7–64.
77. Schiff, 'Timasheff's Sociology of Law', p. 402. See also Georges Gurvitch's contrast between 'legal positivism' (which 'projects law into a sphere quite removed from living social reality') and the 'functional attitude' (which 'requires that judges, jurists and lawyers keep perpetually in mind the relation between law and living social reality'). G. Gurvitch, *Sociology of Law*, London, 1947, p. 4, p. 2.
78. See above, text to n. 7 *et seq.*
79. 'Hugo Sinzheimer 1875–1945', p. 77.
80. See above, text to n. 12 *et seq.*; text to n. 30 *et seq.*
81. *System* (1954), p. 118.
82. H. Sinzheimer, *Theorie der Gesetzgebung*, Haarlem, 1949. For a discussion of this book see Kahn-Freund, 'Hugo Sinzheimer 1875–1945', pp. 100–1.
83. Kahn-Freund, ibid., p. 102.
84. Ibid., pp. 74, 103.

Chapter 5

Method and Ideology in the Labour Law Writings of Otto Kahn-Freund*

Roy Lewis

Until quite recently legal method tended to revolve around the technical analysis of legal rights and obligations with the emphasis on case law. Lawyers were of course concerned with public policy but their framework of ideology was usually implicit. Kahn-Freund's approach to the study of labour law was of strikingly different order: a unique combination of technical legal analysis, the perspectives of the social sciences, and international comparisons.[1] Since other chapters in this volume deal with the importance of the social sciences in his writings, this chapter will attempt to analyse Kahn-Freund's use of comparisons.[2] His method also involved raising fundamental issues of a political character: the relationship between the 'autonomous' social forces of capital and labour, the objectives of public policy, and the role of the state in industrial relations. His views on such issues were naturally underpinned by ideological assumptions, which were of immense significance for both his writings and his involvement in public policy.[3] His political beliefs were already manifest in his German publications in the early 1930s,[4] when he achieved notoriety by his condemnation of his fellow judges' crypto-fascist tendencies, and were no less strong (though his viewpoint was modified) in 1965–8 when he was a member of the Donovan Royal Commission,[5] and in 1978 when, as a Fellow of the British Academy, he offered his final prescription for industrial conflict in Britain.[6] Indeed the intellectual and political milieu of the Weimar Republic continued to exert a powerful influence on his endeavours after 1933. As a preliminary to a discussion of his method and ideology, therefore, the initial task of this chapter is to sketch

* I would like to thank Jon Clark, Paul Edwards, Ben Roberts, and Bill Wedderburn for their helpful comments on an earlier draft of this chapter.

some of the connections between Kahn-Freund's Weimar
experience and his later work.

The Legacy of Weimar

What was the cultural inheritance which Kahn-Freund
brought with him from Germany to Britain in 1933? That
Kahn-Freund had trained as a lawyer under Hugo Sinzheimer
was of supreme importance. As has been explained in a previous chapter, it meant that Kahn-Freund was immersed in a
tradition not merely of 'black letter' legal analysis but also of
sociological jurisprudence and ultimately of the entire range of
German social science, which was dominated by the giants
Marx and Weber. Moreover Kahn-Freund lived and worked
within a specific political and social environment. In Weimar
Germany he was first and foremost a committed social democrat—not a Communist or an adherent of the centre—but a
democratic socialist. For him the hallmark of both political
democracy and socialism was a free trade union movement
autonomous from the state.[7] Such conviction underpinned his
critique of the German labour movement's over-reliance on the
state and on labour law and also no doubt encouraged him, as a
judge in the Berlin Labour Tribunal, to make the fateful
decision in March 1933 to uphold the appeal by the union
militants who had been dismissed from the state radio station
shortly after Hitler's assumption of power.[8] This courageous
act compelled his flight from Germany. But sooner or later
Kahn-Freund would have had to leave or suffer persecution or
worse because he was a Jew. As he remarked, to be born a Jew
in Germany at the turn of the century fostered a critical view of
society.[9] Jewish intellectuals were prominent in the German
labour movement, and many of the left-wing labour lawyers
were Jews: Phillip Lotmar, the pioneer of the subject before
Sinzheimer, Sinzheimer himself, and the brilliant circle of
Sinzheimer's pupils including Ernst Fraenkel, Franz
Neumann, and Otto Kahn-Freund himself.

Kahn-Freund remained subject to these influences for the
rest of his life.[10] On reading his famous monograph of 1931, *The
Social Ideal of the Reich Labour Court*, and his article of 1932, 'The
Changing Function of Labour Law', one sees that the origin of

his later work in Britain is located in the critical and theoretical labour law of Weimar Germany. Here is to be found a sophisticated discussion of ideas such as the primacy of collective bargaining over legislation and of law as a secondary force in society twenty-five years in advance of his elaboration of the theory of legal 'abstention' and of 'collective *laissez-faire*'. Indeed Kahn-Freund's initial attempts to theorize about British labour law in the 1940s were largely an adaption of Sinzheimer to a British context. Thus he characterized the individual contract of employment as a 'command under the guise of an agreement'.[11] Its main function was to support and legitimate the employer's prerogative, his domination, and the employee's subordination. The true purpose of labour legislation was (as Sinzheimer had argued) to regulate and mitigate the dependency of the employee. This dependency, this inherent inequality of the individual employment relation, was also the justification of trade union organization and collective bargaining. According to Sinzheimer collective bargaining had creative law-making functions which in 1943 Kahn-Freund introduced into the analysis of British labour law.[12] He expounded on the British versions of the 'normative' function—the codification of terms and conditions of employment, mainly through the incorporation of collectively agreed provisions into the individual contract of employment, and the 'contractual' function—the laying down of the mutual obligations of the collective parties through agreed recognition and disputes procedures.

At first Kahn-Freund assumed that the contractual function implied the enforceability of collective agreements as contracts, which had been the case in Germany. By the late 1940s however he had perceived that British collective agreements were not contracts in the legal sense because the collective parties lacked the intention to create legal relations.[13] This insight was later adopted by the Donovan Commission, the High Court, and Parliament.[14] Kahn-Freund's analysis was of course original, even revolutionary, but it was in part a product of the German legacy. Kahn-Freund (like Sinzheimer before him but quite unlike British lawyers at that time) had made his own empirical study of the raw materials—collective agreements. At a more theoretical level, Ehrlich's theory of 'living law' assisted him in raising the fundamental question of whether autonomous collective regulation could be enforced entirely through social sanctions.

Method

Kahn-Freund'a theory of the non-contractual status of collective agreements is a perfect illustration of his 'legal method'. The doctrine in the law of contract of intention to create legal relations is interwoven with a profound and unrivalled awareness of the historical, political, and industrial relations contexts of the law and of the contrasts between Britain and continental Europe. His explanation of British labour law as a whole was based on this indivisible combination of sociological and comparative jurisprudence. In 1943, when he still thought that British collective agreements were legally enforceable contracts, he was nevertheless able to write:

> British collective labour law is in one respect unique among the legal systems of the larger industrial countries. Trade union recognition was achieved in this country by purely industrial as distinct from political and legislative action. No Wagner Act, no Weimar Constitution, no Front Populaire legislation has imposed upon British employers the duty to enter into negotiations with trade union representatives. The proud edifice of collective labour regulation was built up without the assistance of the law.[15]

The Social Ideal of the Reich Labour Court was Kahn-Freund's first attempt at comparative labour law. Its central thesis was based on a comparison of the social ideal of the Reich Labour Court with the collective labour laws of Fascist Italy. The comparison was possible for Kahn-Freund because he had mastered the Italian language; subsequently his outstanding linguistic ability, in Wedderburn's words, 'lay at the heart of his commanding position internationally in comparative legal studies'.[16] Kahn-Freund, Hepple tells us, 'was fond of saying that it was his enforced transition from the Continental civil law systems to the English common law (extended by his visits to the United States to American Law) which made him a comparatist not by choice, but by fate. . . . He was universally acclaimed as the world's leading scholar of comparative labour law.'[17]

It is surprising therefore that Kahn-Freund's first sustained essay in English on the specific theme of comparative labour law appears to be little known in Britain or on the Continent, though it may have had a wider circulation in the USA. In 1960 a book was published—*American Enterprise in the European Common Market: A Legal Profile*[18]—with a lengthy chapter (145 pages) by Kahn-Freund. After surveying the impact of the Treaty of Rome on the labour and social security laws of the then six member states of the EEC, it provided a fairly detailed analysis (Kahn-Freund modestly called it a 'sketch map') of the labour laws of the Six. The comparison focused on five key issues: (a) the role of legislation and constitutions in shaping collective labour relations; (b) the methods and legal effect of collective bargaining, including the structures and ideologies of employer and trade union organizations; (c) industrial democracy and participation (apart from collective bargaining); (d) grievance settlement methods, including labour courts; and (e) the law of industrial conflict. This chapter must stand as one of the great testaments of Kahn-Freund's comprehensive legal and sociological erudition. It is moreover the unified vision of one man, indeed perhaps the only man capable of such work on his own without a team of international colleagues. On the other hand, he was first in the field of 'co-operative' comparative labour law. He wrote the editorial introduction to *Labour Relations and the Law: A Comparative Study*, which was based on an international colloquium held in 1962.[19] Some of the participants went on to form the Comparative Labour Law Group, whose distinguished research and publications were inspired by Kahn-Freund's approach.[20]

In 1964 Kahn-Freund left the London School of Economics on his appointment as Professor of Comparative Law at the University of Oxford (his eventual 'retirement' six years later was purely nominal). From then on the comparative element in his work was, if possible, even more pronounced. He wrote a series of papers in which international comparison was the main theme; including his important article on 'The Impact of Constitutions on Labour Law'.[21] His two final books on labour law—*Labour and the Law* and *Labour Relations: Heritage and Adjustment*—are peppered with comparative insights and analysis. One example must suffice. In *Heritage* he explained how the British (and North American) traditions of trade union 'direct democracy' and 'job control' give rise to a particular kind of legal intervention, namely, the rights of individuals not to be excluded or expelled from trade unions. In contrast this area of law (and of public policy debate) does not exist in countries where unions have not attempted to limit numbers or impose closed shops. In Italy and France, for example, there is the quite different set of legal problems arising from a multiplicity of unions with different political affiliations. This insight, according to Kahn-Freund, shows 'how dependent the comparative lawyer is on the help he must derive from the empirical social sciences'.[22]

If Kahn-Freund used the social sciences to facilitate comparison he turned comparison into a method of the social sciences and, in particular, of sociological jurisprudence. To Kahn-Freund's way of thinking, compartive law was not a separate topic or subject but rather a method, a tool of analysis. Ultimately it led to a better understanding of one's own law. It had moreover to embrace a comparison not merely of formal legal rules but also of the different social and economic contexts. This facilitated a functionalist approach, that is, the study of the purposes of laws and other kinds of rules. Legal rules might satisfy social needs in one country, whereas forms of 'living law' (to borrow Ehrlich's indispensable phrase) might have the same function in another country. 'One of the virtues of legal comparison (which it shares with legal history) is that it allows a scholar to place himself outside the labyrinth of the minutiae in which legal thinking so easily loses its way and to see the great contours of the law and its dominant characteristics.'[23]

This was Kahn-Freund's explicit theory of comparative method which he elaborated in his inaugural lecture at Oxford. But it underpins all his writings, including the quotation from 1943 about the 'proud edifice' of autonomous 'collective labour regulation' in Britain as compared with France, Germany, and the USA. Of Kahn-Freund and comparative labour law one may say (as he said of Sinzheimer and sociological jurisprudence) that he first applied a method and theorized about it afterwards.[24]

Given Kahn-Freund's preoccupation with public policy, he inevitably viewed comparative labour law not as a mere academic exercise but as a practical aid to law reform. When he wrote the chapters in the Donovan Report which advocated a law on unfair dismissals and a transformation of the role of the industrial tribunals, he was influenced by the example of the

French system of labour courts, the *conseils de prud'hommes*.[25] He believed that individual labour law, in the form of minimum standards, could be transplanted between countries at a similar state of economic development. But collective labour law was a different kettle of fish. An important part of his opposition to the Industrial Relations Act 1971 was based on its reckless use of North American labour law concepts without regard to the vastly different political and constitutional contexts in Britain. This was an 'abuse' rather than a legitimate 'use' of comparative method.[26] In contrast his positive attitude towards the development of individual labour law reflected his faith in the minimum standards stipulated by international law, in which he was himself involved as a technical expert.[27] It also reflected his strong belief in the harmonization of law stemming from the European Commission. The Commission was a beneficial neutral force—a 'Socratic Midwife'—to the member states.[28] But by the late fifties he saw the state itself as a theoretically neutral instrument, and we must now turn to the 'ideology' (in the sense of a set of moral assumptions) that lay behind his analysis of law and society.

Ideology

Kahn-Freund's classic analysis of industrial relations law was elaborated in the 1950s.[29] This was a period of rising prosperity, industrial peace, and a degree of consensus over such issues as public ownership of the basic industries, the 'Welfare State', the maintenance of full employment, and the legitimacy of the trade union movement. Against this background Kahn-Freund worked out an explanation of the historical development and dominant characteristics of British labour law, a task in which he was assisted by the work of others—Allan Flanders, Hugh Clegg, and Henry Phelps Brown—who were developing the literature of British industrial relations. The non-contractual status of collective agreements was an integral part of a broader analysis of legal non-intervention or of the law's 'abstention' from industrial relations. Statutory protections for individual employees (outside the area of industrial safety) were largely conspicuous by their absence. There was no law to compel employers to recognize and bargain with trade unions, no positive legal right to associate in unions, and, unlike many other West European countries, there was no positive statutory, let alone constitutional, right to strike. The legal freedom to take strike action rested rather on a structure of negatively expressed statutory immunities from judge-made liabilities. The fact that Parliament had enacted statutes (the principal one was the 1906 Trade Disputes Act) to legislate the judges out of industrial conflict was the supreme expression of a public policy of legal abstention, of the paradox of non-interventionist legal intervention. 'There is, perhaps, no major country in the world', wrote Kahn-Freund in 1954, 'in which the law has played a less significant role in the shaping [of industrial relations].'[30] In Britain the historic emphasis was not on legal regulation but on voluntary self-regulation by autonomous employers' and workers' organizations. Kahn-Freund extolled this characteristic: 'there exists something like an inverse correlation between the practical significance of legal sanctions and the degree to which industrial relations have reached a state of maturity'.[31] He encapsulated this desirable state of affairs in his notion of 'collective *laissez-faire*'[32]—the belief shared by unions, employers, civil servants, and for a time even by the judges (and by Kahn-Freund himself) in the virtues of industrial self-rule backed up by purely social sanctions.

Collective *laissez-faire* was a thoroughly pluralist concept. Pluralism may have many meanings, but it usually signifies a limitation on the sovereignty of the state, and specifically that 'groups' in society (such as religious organizations and trade unions) should be independent from the state.[33] The existence of the independent or autonomous groups disperses power and so, it is argued, safeguards freedoms against an all-powerful state. In this sense the right to strike exercised by a trade union movement which is not the creature of the state may be regarded as a guarantee of political freedom. Within the sphere of industrial relations there is further scope for a pluralist frame of reference.[34] Union organization and also labour legislation disperse the employer's power and safeguard the freedom of the individual employee. Employers and unions moreover may develop a joint system of industrial self-government through collective bargaining. A mature system of collective bargaining mitigates the inequality of the individual employee, and regu-lates and contains the inherent conflicts between management and unions. If conflict is sometimes the immediate result of collective bargaining, its strategic aims are order, peace, and social justice.

Under collective *laissez-faire*, Kahn-Freund's version of industrial relations pluralism, it was axiomatic that collective bargaining had priority over the state's legal enactments. Legal abstention was therefore more than a mere instrument of legal technique: it was an integral part of the moral ethos of British industrial relations. The state nevertheless retained a critical if residual role. It intervened where there was a serious disequilibrium between the autonomous forces of management and unions. Thus the immunities for industrial action, Kahn-Freund tells us, were enacted 'to restore social equilibrium in industrial relations.'[35] The dominant public policy however was one of 'abstention and neutrality'[36] and, even in the exercise of its residual role, the state was in theory above the conflicts of the sectional interest groups.

In the unsettled economic and industrial relations climate of the last decade and a half, the pluralist analysis of British industrial relations became more explicitly prescriptive and ideological. The reform programme of the Donovan Commission was advanced in the name of pluralism.[37] The pluralist definition of the problem was how to preserve and protect the voluntary institutions of industrial relations and yet to restore order, peace, and efficiency. The solution was a voluntary reform of the institutions whereby management and trade union officials would regain control over workplace activity through factory-wide and comprehensive collective agreements. But new labour laws and incomes policies as well as the reform of collective bargaining featured in the Donovan diagnosis and in the policies of British governments from the mid-1960s until 1979. In fact the labour legislation of the 1960s and 1970s is a permanent legacy of the movement for the reform of British industrial relations.

Many new jurisdictions were added to the work load of the industrial tribunals: minimum notice periods, written 'particulars' of employment, redundancy pay, unfair dismissal, appeals against the imposition of health and safety orders, race and sex discrimination, maternity rights, guarantee pay, insolvency obligations, protective awards where employers fail to consult on redundancy, and individual rights in respect of union membership—not to be unfairly dismissed, not to be subject to employer action short of dismissal, and to paid and unpaid time off for union activities. Although a few of these measures were the result of union political pressure during the Social Contract phase, the principal provisions (redundancy pay, unfair dismissal, maternity rights, equal pay and sex discrimination, redundancy consultation) were conceived within the Department of Employment as steps towards both the reform and modernization of British industry and the harmonization of British law in conformity with international and EEC standards, which, as Kahn-Freund remarked, 'powerfully contributed to the growth of regulatory legislation in this country'.[38] Union aspirations were more clearly reflected in the development of collective labour law: the repeal of the Conservatives' Industrial Relations Act 1971, the re-enactment and enlargement of the statutory immunities to protect against new developments in the common law liabilities, and the creation of ACAS, an institution which epitomized the spirit of tripartite voluntarism. There were also new rights and procedures for the benefit of trade unions as such: a union recognition procedure, a duty on employers to disclose information in collective bargaining, compulsory arbitration for the 'general level' as well as the more traditional 'recognized' terms and conditions of employment, and compulsory consultation with recognized unions on redundancy, industrial safety, and occupational pensions. These provisions were designed to extend collective bargaining but they were also intended to assist in its reform.

In principle the new laws were to be consistent with the continuation of a modified version of the tradition of legal non-intervention. True, as Kahn-Freund acknowledged, this tradition had not been maintained in the field of individual labour law; but in collective labour law it would be maintained for otherwise the sphere of autonomous regulation would be so narrowed, and that of state intervention so enlarged, that the pluralist system would be transformed into something else. The repeal of the 1971 Act, the affirmation of the non-contractual nature of the collective agreement, the strengthening of the traditional statutory immunities, the creation of ACAS, and the largely indirect nature of the sanctions attaching to the new trade union bargaining and consultation rights would all ensure that the legal profession would be kept out of the central arena of collective bargaining and industrial conflict.[39] The policy of the law, Kahn-Freund concluded in 1977, was once again to 'allow the two sides by agreement and practice to develop their own norms and their own sanctions, and it abstains from legal compulsion in their collective relationship'.[40]

Was Kahn-Freund's conclusion correct? A few years ago the present writer concluded a survey of the historical development of labour law thus: 'In 1975 it would seem that the one indubitably fundamental and irreversible trend is the ever increasing extent of the legal regulation of the British system of industrial relations.'[41] Kahn-Freund specifically disagreed with this statement in respect of collective labour law,[42] and Wedderburn has also questioned it.[43] This is not the place for a full discussion of the extent of the legal regulation of British industrial relations, which would involve a fairly detailed analysis of the statutory provisions, the case law, and the relevant empirical industrial relations research. The point of raising the issue in this context is to pose the question: what degree of legal abstention, if any, is a necessary characteristic of a 'pluralist' system of industrial relations? In the British context, it would seem that the answer in the 1950s might have been rather different from that in the 1970s.

From Pluralism to Corporatism?

Industrial relations pluralism has been subjected to a radical critique.[44] The critique contrasted the postulate that union organization and collective bargaining produce a rough equlibrium between capital and labour with the persistence of major inequalities of wealth and power. It criticized the supposed degree of consensus in industrial relations and the wider society as a denial of fundamental social and economic conflict, which has intensified throughout the Western world since 1968.[45] It insisted that ultimately the state in practice was not a neutral arbiter. Not surprisingly Kahn-Freund rejected the radical critique. He maintained that pluralism should be regarded merely 'as a method of explaining what happens in a non-totalitarian society, not as an ideology', citing as a 'largely convincing counter-critique'[46] Professor Clegg's reply to the radicals.[47] In fact Clegg had acknowledged that pluralism, though not a complete philosophy, is a moral doctrine as well as a description.[48] To the extent that we accept the radical critique, pluralist assumptions would appear to be unrealistic as a description of society and to constitute a conservative basis for ideology. It is certainly arguable that Kahn-Freund's brand of pluralism gradually became more conservative in its implications. For example, Kahn-Freund strongly supported the Donovan Report's scheme for the selective legal enforceability of collectively-agreed disputes procedures, where (after their reform) 'strike proneness is due to irresponsibility to to agitation by eccentrics or by subversives'.[49] The great theorist of collective *laissez-faire* was now adamant that the issue of legal enforceability was devoid of 'moral ethos' and that the Donovan proposal was a 'clear expression of an insight that this is a question of expediency and nothing more'.[50] In order to restore equilibrium at a time of full employment, moreover, the law had to regulate the power of unions as well as management; specifically, it had a role to play in the suppression of what he regarded as the 'pathological'[51] manifestations of industrial conflict, such as the militant picketing in the coal and construction strikes of 1972.[52]

There was perhaps a slightly pessimistic note discernible in some of the later writings. As far as the Social Contract was concerned,[53] it was essentially a form of voluntary incomes policy and ought to be made permanent: 'a transformation of the present political negotiations between Government, TUC and CBI into something more regular and more regulated'.[54] At no time did Kahn-Freund indicate that he saw it as a step towards a socialist transformation of society; nor did he see the Bullock Report on industrial democracy in that light.[55] In fact he was opposed to Bullock for a variety of reasons, including the possibility that union representation in the boardroom might prejudice the very clear divide in the pluralist analysis between the function of management to manage effectively and efficiently, and the function of the union to oppose independently and permanently.[56] The trade union movement was not to be the engine of great social change, but nor was a political party. Perhaps Kahn-Freund was moving towards the centre. On the one hand, he was (despite the proposal on selective legal enforceability of agreements) opposed to the overall legal coercion of trade unions on grounds of justice as well as expediency. On the other hand, he was not advocating any major redistribution of wealth and power whether through labour legislation or any other means. What he wanted was a continuation of the present society but with a greater degree of economic efficiency and social stability.

There is of course a great contrast between the views of Kahn-Freund in the last decade of his life and of the younger Kahn-Freund. In the Weimar Republic he had described the policy of the new labour legislation as 'collectivist'. He was not unsympathetic towards collectivism in so far as it could be regarded as a transition to socialism, but he criticized it on the grounds that at a time of mass unemployment it assumed a degree of social equilibrium which did not take sufficient account of capitalist ownership and control, and because of its tendency, in practice, to encourage the corporatist integration of unions into the state apparatus. Half a century later, in a vastly different world, his pluralism still bore some resemblance to the earlier collectivism but it was largely static and no longer a transition to a new social order. Ownership had now apparently ceased to be a critical element in industrial conflict, and class conflict between capital and labour was replaced by a distributional conflict between management (the investor) and labour (the consumer).[57] This approach however did not overlook the rise of multinational conglomerates.[58] 'The power of multinational enterprise is in no way balanced by a corresponding power of labour, no more than there is any international or supranational authority to which multinational enterprise is accountable.'[59] But if multinationals posed a difficult 'challenge to our democratic and social institutions',[60] they transferred capital and wealth and, in the final analysis, were in the interests of some employees at least.

Perhaps the most striking contrast with the Weimar period arose from Kahn-Freund's advocacy of a reform policy which sought to involve trade union leaders, together with the employer and the state, in the maintenance of order, that is, in the more disciplined subordination of the employee. This is the thrust of the Donovan analysis, and also of Kahn-Freund's own final policy prescriptions in *Heritage* (the formalization of shop stewards in positions of authority over their members and a permanent incomes policy). Some contemporary sociologists

such as Leo Panitch and Colin Crouch have characterized
Donovan reformism and the attempts at incomes policy as a
'corporatist' strategy. Corporatism has been variously defined
but essentially it conveys the attempt to integrate trade union
leaders in order to control and restrain activities at local level.
In the writings of Crouch and Panitch it is not a full-blown
system or theory of the state, but rather a description of a
strategy of control within the contemporary capitalist state in
Britain.[61] Kahn-Freund would of course have rejected the
corporatist label not least because he regarded corporatism as a
comprehensive state system which was indelibly associated in
his mind with the rise of Mussolini and Hitler.[62] Such an
association was fairly common in the 1930s, which for this
purpose must be taken as Kahn-Freund's formative period, not
only in Germany but also in Britain.[63]

Corporatist ideas however are not necessarily to be equated
with Fascism. In the 1930s they had a powerful attraction for a
number of writers who were obviously not Fascists including,
for example, W. Milne-Bailey (the head of the TUC's Research
Department) whose *Trade Unions and the State* (1934) envisaged
an independent trade union movement enjoying a close
relationship with the employers and with a sympathetic and
interventionist state. Hyman has suggested that 'Milne-
Bailey's analysis would seem to have exerted an important
influence on the development of Flanders' conception of
pluralism.'[64] Kahn-Freund however always regarded corporatist tendencies, with or without specific fascist conno-
tations, as undesirable, as the very opposite of pluralism. Thus,
during the Second World War when his memories of the
Weimar tragedy were still vivid, he saw a corporatist danger in
Order 1305, the wartime measure which provided for compulsory arbitration and the prohibition of direct industrial
action, but not for a state-directed incomes policy. Under the
Order, according to Kahn-Freund, 'the collective agreement
appears as part of a plan laid down by the political organs of the
state. Employers' organizations and trade unions tend to
become instruments for the realisation of the social and economic policy of the government—their contracts no longer
reflect their own fighting strength, but the standards of
adequacy laid down by the state. . . . This war-time phenomenon was foreshadowed by an unmistakable development

which occurred between the world wars, and the theoretical expression of which can be found in Milne-Bailey's book. . . .'[65] But in the decades after the war Kahn-Freund's thoughts developed on lines which gradually put more and more emphasis on the role of the state in relation to capital and labour. Even in the heyday of collective *laissez-faire*, the state's abstention from legal regulation was implicitly a choice of the state. Later the state made another choice—it intervened to encourage the reform of collective bargaining, to initiate incomes policies, and to strengthen the legal framework. At some point Donovan reformism, an explicitly pluralist doctrine which nevertheless places a strong if subtle emphasis on the state and on the liaison of the autonomous forces with the state, converges with those forms of corporatism which envisage that organizations should enjoy a degree of autonomy from the state.

Heritage shows the ultimate extent of Kahn-Freund's revision of pluralism—it is not clear whether pluralism survives at all. The earlier criticism of militant picketing is developed to the point where direct industrial action in general is characterized as an internecine civil war between the worker as producer and the worker as consumer. Furthermore, 'the employer is in such a situation no more than the agent of the consumer, the instrument of the public (in the sense of the amorphous mass of the consumers) for maintaining or regaining the supplies and the services on which they depend'.[66] The employer is thus the agent of the consumer and workers are also consumers. Only one element is missing: the state. In principle the state, Kahn-Freund declares in his 'Postscript' to the translated German writings, represents the consumer: 'I am coming increasingly to the conclusion, outrageous from the Marxist point of view, that what the state represents is the consumer: in intention, not in actuality.'[67] The strike therefore threatens the consumer's interest, the employer's interest, and the national interest, all of which are conflated. Does this philosophy of the state, for that is what it is, permit of any exercise of the right to strike? How can it be reconciled with Kahn-Freund's own assertion that 'there can be no true democracy without a freedom to strike'?[68]

It is of course relevant that *Heritage* was written during the 'Winter of Discontent' (1978–9), a period of intense industrial conflict which saw the final demise of the Social Contract. How would Kahn-Freund have reacted to the legislation of 1980–2 and to the phenomenon of mass unemployment at a time of persistent inflation? No doubt he would have found these developments disturbing and perplexing. Full employment was the economic pre-condition of his ideological position. It was an essential component in the 1950s consolidation of the social and economic reforms achieved during and after the Second World War. Kahn-Freund himself explained how the experience of the post-war Labour government led him to modify and eventually to reject his earlier critique with its 'quasi-marxist' emphasis on class conflict and economic ownership.[69] Moreover the social disorders accompanying mass unemployment would have reinforced his apprehension (rooted in his memories of Weimar) that a fundamental breakdown in society might occur. Such fears were perhaps already implicit in his final analysis in *Heritage*.

As labour lawyers attempt to make sense of this new and depressing era, their task without Kahn-Freund is infinitely more difficult. Few would doubt that a critical evaluation of his work is an 'essential starting point for future research'.[70] Kahn-Freund was the master of a very demanding method of analysis which raised not only technical but also ideological questions. He successfully combined rigorous legal technique with an explicit consideration of the social and political objectives and interests underpinning legal developments, and of the interaction between law and behaviour. His monumental contribution will remain the most important stimulus in the analysis of past, present, and future labour law.

1. For a list of Kahn-Freund's major writings on labour law, see Wedderburn above, n. 1.

2. Kahn-Freund's major writings on comparative labour law include: 'Labour Law and Social Security', in E. Stein and T. L. Nicholson (eds.), *American Enterprise in the European Common Market*, Michigan, 1960; *Labour Relations and the Law: A Comparative Study*, London, 1965; 'Comparative Law as an Academic Subject' (1966) 82 *Law Quarterly Review* 40 (*Selected Writings*, London, 1978, Ch. 11); 'Collective Bargaining and English Law: Some Comparative Reflections', in *En Hommage à Paul Horion*, Liege, 1972; (with B. A. Hepple) *Laws Against Strikes*, London, 1972; 'On Uses and Misuses of Comparative Law' (1974) 37 *Modern Law Review* 1 (*Selected Writings*, Ch. 12); *The Right to Strike*, Strasbourg, 1974 (Report to Council of Europe); 'The Impact of Constitutions on Labour Law' (1976) *Cambridge Law Journal* 240. *Labour and the Law*, London, 1972 (2nd ed. 1977), has a strong comparative element.

3. The discussion of Kahn-Freund's ideology in this chapter develops some of the

arguments in R. Lewis, 'Kahn-Freund and Labour Law: An Outline Critique' (1979) 8 *Industrial Law Journal* 202.

4. See O. Kahn-Freund, *Labour Law and Politics in the Weimar Republic*, edited and introduced by R. Lewis and J. Clark, Oxford, 1981.

5. *Royal Commission on Trade Unions and Employers' Associations 1965–68, Report*, London, Cmnd. 3623, 1968.

6. *Labour Relations: Heritage and Adjustment*, Oxford, 1979.

7. This is particularly apparent from Kahn-Freund's own criticisms of Sinzheimer's role in the development of compulsory arbitration in Weimar Germany; see Lewis and Clark in *Labour Law and Politics* (1981), pp. 40–1.

8. Ibid., p. 5.

9. Ibid., Kahn-Freund's 'Postscript', pp. 196–7.

10. Ibid., pp. 51–8 for a more detailed account of the Weimar legacy.

11. O. Kahn-Freund, 'Introduction' to K. Renner, *The Institutions of Private Law and their Social Functions*, London, 1949, reprinted 1976, p. 28. See further Clark and Wedderburn below, text to n. 73 *et seq*.

12. 'Collective Agreements under War Legislation' (1943) 6 *Modern Law Review* 112.

13. See R. Lewis, 'Collective Agreements: The Kahn-Freund Legacy' (1979) 42 *Modern Law Review* 613.

14. Donovan Report, Ch. VIII; *Ford Motor Company* v. *A.U.E.F.* [1969] 2 Q.B.303; Industrial Relations Act 1971, ss. 34–6; Trade Union and Labour Relations Act 1974, s. 18.

15. (1943) 6 *Modern Law Review* 112, 143.

16. 'Professor Sir Otto Kahn-Freund' (1979) 42 *Modern Law Review* 609, 611; see too K. W. Wedderburn, 'British Labour Law and Otto Kahn-Freund: 1971', *Industrial Law Society Bulletin*, No. 11, September 1971.

17. 'Sir Otto Kahn-Freund, Q.C., F.B.A. 1900–1979' (1979) 8 *Industrial Law Journal* 193, 194, 196. Kahn-Freund also made excellent use of his 'enforced transition' in his writings on other subjects, notably private international law, on which see his treatise *General Problems of Private International Law*, Leyden, 1976.

18. See above, n. 2.

19. Ibid.

20. The members of the group were T. Ramm (Germany), G. Giugni (Italy), F. Schmidt (Sweden), B. Aaron (USA), X. Blanc-Jouvan (France), and K. W. Wedderburn (Britain). See B. Aaron (ed.), *Dispute Settlement Procedures in Five Western European Countries*, Los Angeles, 1969; K. W. Wedderburn and P. L. Davies, *Employment Grievances and Disputes Procedures in Britain*, Berkeley and Los Angeles, 1969; B. Aaron (ed.), *Labour Courts and Grievance Settlement in Western Europe*, Berkeley and Los Angeles, 1971; B. Aaron and K. W. Wedderburn (eds.), *Industrial Conflict: A Comparative Legal Survey*, London, 1972; F. Schmidt (ed.), *Discrimination in Employment*, Stockholm, 1978. See further Wedderburn above, n. 31.

21. See above, n. 2.

22. *Heritage* (1979), p. 56.

23. O. Kahn-Freund, 'Comparative Law as an Academic Subject' (1966) 82 *Law Quarterly Review* 40.

24. *Labour Law and Politics* (1981), p. 101.

25. Donovan Report, Ch. IX and X. The leading study in English of the French system is W. H. McPherson and F. Meyers, *The French Labour Courts: Judgment by Peers*, Illinois, 1966 (reviewed by Kahn-Freund in (1967) 81 *Harvard Law Review* 263). See further Clark and Wedderburn below, text to n. 230 *et seq*.

26. 'On Uses and Misuses of Comparative Law' (1974) 37 *Modern Law Review* 1.

27. Kahn-Freund was a member of the committee of experts under the European Social Charter and he acted as an expert for the International Labour Organiz-

ation. These experiences gave great authority to his writings on international labour law; see, for example, 'The European Social Charter', in F. J. Jacobs (ed.), *European Law and the Individual*, Amsterdam, 1976.

28. O. Kahn-Freund, 'European Community Law and the English Legal System' (1972) *University of Tasmania Law Review* 1, 14.

29. In particular in *System* (1954), *Ginsberg* (1959), and 'Intergroup Conflicts' (1954).

30. *System* (1954), p. 44.

31. Ibid., p. 43.

32. *Ginsberg* (1959), passim.

33. In Germany a variant of pluralism was advanced in O. Gierke's monumental *Das deutsche Genossenschaftsrecht* (1868) (three further volumes were published in 1873, 1881, and 1913); parts of Gierke's work are translated in W. F. Maitland, *Political Theories of the Middle Age*, Cambridge, 1900, and E. Barker, *Natural Law and the Theory of Society*, Cambridge, 1950 edn. Gierke's ideas influenced Sinzheimer, though Kahn-Freund's description of the latter as a 'pluralist' (in 'The Study of Labour Law—Some Recollections' (1979) 8 *Industrial Law Journal* 197) is arguably misleading: Lewis and Clark in *Labour Law and Politics* (1981), p. 40 and n. 115. Pluralist ideas have pervaded much Anglo-American philosophy and social science, including the work of some writers who wished to distinguish their own brand of socialism from the accumulation of centralized state power; see, for example, G. D. H. Cole, *The World of Labour*, London, 1913, and *Self Government in Industry*, London, 1917. For a discussion of pluralist (and corporatist) ideas with reference to the relationship between the state, capital, and labour in Britain: W. Milne-Bailey, *Trade Unions and the State*, London, 1934.

34. Industrial relations pluralism was expounded by an influential group of American academics in the 1950s, see particularly C. Kerr, *Industrial Relations and the Liberal Pluralist*, Berkeley, 1955 (discussed by R. Hyman in 'Pluralism, Procedural Consensus and Collective Bargaining' (1978) 16 *British Journal of Industrial Relations* 16, 19–20).

35. *System* (1954), p. 105.

36. Ibid., p. 123. See Wedderburn above, text to n. 59 *et seq.*

37. A. Fox, *Industrial Sociology and Industrial Relations*, Donovan Research Paper, No. 3, 1966, and 'Managerial Ideology and Labour Relations' (1966) 3 *British Journal of Industrial Relations* 366. See Allan Flanders, *Management and Unions*, London, 1970, and 'The Tradition of Voluntarism' (1974) 12 *British Journal of Industrial Relations* 352.

38. *Labour* (1977), p. 42. See B. A. Hepple and P. O'Higgins, *Employment Law*, London, 4th ed. 1981, Ch. 20; and further Clark and Wedderburn below, text to n. 232 *et seq.*

39. See, in particular, Kahn-Freund's 'Notes' to *Ginsberg* (1959) in *Selected Writings*, 1978, pp. 39–40.

40. *Labour* (1977), p. 276.

41. 'The Historical Development of Labour Law' 14 *British Journal of Industrial Relations* 1, 15. The argument was developed somewhat in (1979) 8 *Industrial Law Journal* 202, 218–21.

42. *Labour* (1977), p. 46, n. 55.

43. 'Industrial Relations and the Courts' (1980) 9 *Industrial Law Journal* 65, 82–6. See too Wedderburn, 'The Employment Protection Act 1975—Collective Aspects' (1976) 39 *Modern Law Review* 169; 'The New Structure of Labour Law in Britain' (1978) 13 *Israel Law Review* 435; and Clark and Wedderburn below, text to n. 293 *et seq.*

44. A. Fox, 'Industrial Relations: A Social Critique of Pluralist Ideology', in J. Child (ed.), *Man and Organization*, London, 1973, and *Beyond Contract: Work, Power and Trust Relations*, London, 1974, Ch. 6; J. Goldthorpe, 'Industrial Relations in Great

Britain: A Critique of Reformism', reprinted in T. Clark and L. Clements (eds.), *Trade Unions under Capitalism*, Glasgow, 1977; R. Hyman and I. Brough, *Social Values and Industrial Relations*, Oxford, 1975, Ch. 6; R. Hyman, *British Journal of Industrial Relations*, loc., cit.
45. C. Crouch and A. Pizzorno, *The Resurgence of Class Conflict in Western Europe Since 1968*, 2 Vols., London, 1978.
46. *Labour* (1977), p. 15, n. 30.
47. H. A. Clegg, 'Pluralism in Industrial Relations' (1975) 13 *British Journal of Industrial Relations* 309.
48. Ibid., pp. 310–11.
49. Donovan Report, para. 508. Cf. Clegg above, text to nn. 8–9.
50. *Labour* (1977), pp. 128 and 130. But for a review of some of the 'moral' arguments: R. Lewis, 'The Legal Enforceability of Collective Agreements' (1970) *British Journal of Industrial Relations* 313. The conservative implications of the Donovan proposal are explored by Fox, 'Industrial Relations: A Social Critique of Pluralist Ideology', pp. 221–2.
51. *Laws Against Strikes*, p. 53.
52. O. Kahn-Freund, 'The Industrial Relations Act 1971—Some Retrospective Reflections' (1974) 3 *Industrial Law Journal* 186, 200; *Labour* (1977), pp. 261–5.
53. See J. Clark, H. Hartman, C. Lau, and D. Winchester, *Trade Unions, National Politics and Economic Management*, London, 1980; and Clark and Wedderburn below, text to n. 289 *et seq.*
54. *Heritage* (1979), p. 87. Cf. Kahn-Freund above, pp. 12–13.
55. *Report of Committee of Inquiry on Industrial Democracy*, London, Cmnd. 6706, 1977. O. Kahn-Freund, 'Industrial Democracy' (1977) 6 *Industrial Law Journal* 65; cf. P. Davies and Lord Wedderburn, 'The Land of Industrial Democracy' (1977) 6 *Industrial Law Journal* 197.
56. For an analysis of union function in terms of legitimate but permanent opposition under collective bargaining: H. A. Clegg, *A New Approach to Industrial Democracy*, Oxford, 1960.
57. *Labour* (1972), pp. 18–19; (1977), pp. 15–16; see too Kahn-Freund's 'Postscript' to *Labour Law and Politics* (1981).
58. O. Kahn-Freund, 'A Lawyer's Reflections on Multinational Corporations' (1972) *Journal of Industrial Relations* 351 (Australia); *Labour* (1977), pp. 250–1.
59. *Journal of Industrial Relations* (1972), p. 359.
60. Ibid., p. 360.
61. L. Panitch, *Social Democracy and Industrial Militancy*, Cambridge, 1976; C. Crouch, *Class Conflict and the Industrial Relations Crisis*, London, 1977; P. C. Schmitter and E. Lehmbruch, *Trends Towards Corporatist Intermediation*, London, 1979. Panitch clearly distinguishes his own version of corporatism as a tendency in the relations between the state and the collective parties under capitalism from the analysis which sees recent developments in Britain as a transition to a total corporatist system, an alternative to capitalism and socialism: 'Recent Theorisations of Corporatism: Reflections on a Growth Industry' (1980) 31 *British Journal of Sociology* 159. Contrast J. T. Winkler, 'Law, State and Economy: The Industry Act 1975 in Context' (1975) 2 *British Journal of Law and Society* 103, and 'The Corporate Economy: Theory and Administration', in R. Scase (ed.), *Industrial Society: Class, Cleavage and Control*, London, 1977.
62. Cf. *Labour Law and Politics* (1981), p. 198.
63. B. Pimlott, *Labour and the Left in the 1930s*, Cambridge, 1977, pp. 63–7.
64. R. Hyman, *British Journal of Industrial Relations* (1978), p. 37, n. 35. The theorization of the Social Contract as 'bargained' corporatism (Crouch, op. cit.) is a more recent example of the compatibility of corporatist ideas with pluralism.
65. (1943) 6 *Modern Law Review* 112, 142.

66. *Heritage* (1979), p. 76.
67. *Labour Law and Politics* (1981), p. 202. See further Wedderburn above, text to n. 189 *et seq.*
68. *Heritage* (1979), p. 77. See further Clegg above, pp. 26–7, Wedderburn above, text to n. 175 *et seq.*; and R. Lewis (1981) 44 *Modern Law Review* 239.
69. *Labour Law and Politics* (1981), pp. 199–200.
70. B. A. Hepple and W. Brown, 'Tasks for Labour Law Research' (1981) 1 *Legal Studies* 56, 58.

Chapter 6

Modern Labour Law: Problems, Functions, and Policies*

Jon Clark and Lord Wedderburn

State Intervention and the 'Voluntary' System Since the 1960s

As Kahn-Freund depicted it public policy in modern Britain has encouraged the regulation of industrial relations—and especially of collective bargaining and industrial conflict—not by the law, but, in the main, by autonomous or 'voluntary' social forces. That has not been the direction of developments in labour law during the years immediately following his death in 1979. Indeed since the mid-sixties that traditional policy has been increasingly challenged by successive waves of state intervention. In this period the state—not only Parliament and Cabinet, but civil service and judges too—has apparently pursued two rather distinct and fluctuating strategies, which may be described in the broadest possible terms as policies of 'reform' and 'restriction'.[1] As we shall see, these strategies have rarely been followed in a 'pure' form, but they are clearly distinguishable from one another by their fundamentally different approach to the role of labour law, trade unions, and voluntary collective bargaining in industrial relations.

The policy of reform grew out of 'non-intervention' but used the law where it thought fit exceptionally to do so, for example in the extension of recognized terms and conditions of employment and (in its more radical form after 1975) in the expansion of individual employment protection and even on collective issues such as trade union recognition. But these were seen as exceptions: the aim, successful or not, was to maintain the primacy of voluntary collective bargaining and to maintain or even extend—as in the proposals for industrial democracy—the

* We would like to express our thanks to our co-editor, Roy Lewis, for his assistance in the preparation of this chapter.

influence of trade unions in joint regulation. The aim of the strategy of restriction was the reduction of trade union power in collective bargaining and in the day-to-day conduct of industrial relations. It sometimes offered carrots of reform and of integration into a new system to 'responsible' unions—as in the offer of registration rejected by the trade union movement in 1971; but its stick was always aimed at trade union rights and their independent organization and activity; and it sometimes destroyed—as in 1980—even the exceptional legal 'props' permitted by the system of non-intervention to push black-sheep employers into collective bargaining. If at times reform also offered trade unions a more integrated role in the economy and in a more orderly system of industrial relations, its intent was always to extend the collective influence of workers. To say this by way of explanation of the categories does not of course answer the question of whether, or how far, the measures of reform helped to create a climate which was favourable to measures of restriction or even deflected trade union resistance to them.

The policy of restriction, which has received little attention in the book so far, is examined in some detail in the next section of this chapter. The particular focus here is on the development of Conservative government strategies towards the role of the law in industrial relations since the early seventies. Kahn-Freund's hostile attitude to the Industrial Relations Act of 1971 was briefly described in Chapter 3; but he did not live to see the Employment Act of 1980, or the further legislation that followed. After its victory in the general election of May 1979, the Conservative Party adopted an almost single-minded policy clearly intended to restrict the effectiveness of independent trade unionism. Certainly the immediate tactics of this strategy tended to obscure the differences between those in government who wished to limit trade union 'power' but to retain unions as enfeebled parties to 'reformed' or 'realistic' collective bargaining, and those who saw trade unions by definition as instruments of monopoly and therefore unwelcome distortions of the market. In contrast to the early seventies, the legislation of the early eighties adopted the language and the concepts of the traditional system of labour law. Many of the threads of the reform strategy were woven into a texture which was nevertheless dominated by a pattern of restriction.

Of course it would be wrong to see the policies of 'reform' and 'restriction', and other developments in labour law over the last two decades, as having mainly a legal origin. Throughout the 1950s and 1960s the British economy went through a period of continuous absolute growth but relative international decline, suffering from a low level of internal capital investment and a distinct lack of industrial and managerial innovation. At the same time the sustained period of full employment strengthened the economic position of organized labour and facilitated the growth in workplace trade unionism and decentralized collective bargaining. From the 1960s onwards, however, successive governments have shown increasing concern with these autonomous developments in the economy and industrial relations, and have been drawn into attempting to manage what has generally been perceived as a deep-rooted social and political crisis. In other words, the combination of low or even negative growth rates, the erosion of Britain's manufacturing base, and the steady increase in unemployment, has led governments to intervene in areas which they have traditionally (outside wartime) left largely to self-regulation. The increasing politicization of industrial relations may be seen as an almost direct consequence of these social and economic changes.

In this context it is not surprising that much of labour law has also changed. For one thing there has been a vast quantitative increase; and it is arguable that there has even been in some areas a qualitative transformation. The problematical role of two central concepts of labour law—contract of employment and trade dispute—in this changing environment is discussed in the third section of this chapter.

Earlier chapters have described the reform strategy with which Kahn-Freund himself was personally identified. Much has been written about the respective, sometimes conflicting, roles of the legislature and the courts in this strategy, the pendulum which has swung between judicial erosion and statutory reconstruction of the immunities.[2] In the fourth section of this chapter, under the heading of unresolved problems of reform, we examine the role of the judiciary in labour law and the contribution of the civil service to the changes over the last twenty years (in particular its role in initiating the system of tripartite industrial tribunals). In that section we also discuss the labour legislation of the 'Social Contract' era, which was seen by Kahn-Freund and others as part of the reform strategy of the Donovan Royal Commission,[3] with the added ingredient of a 'voluntary' incomes policy. But that legislation has sometimes also been interpreted as part of an attempt to reach beyond a more efficient and orderly legal framework for industrial relations towards a more radical social transformation, a view which raises fundamental issues concerning the limitations of labour law itself. In our final section we look to the future, reviewing some implications of the policy of restriction and concluding with a discussion of the place of labour law in a wider programme of social and political reform in the 1980s.

In short, this chapter will discuss recent policies in labour law, certain legal and social problems within them, and the place of labour law in the rest of this decade.

In all such discussions it is well to remember the lesson on which Kahn-Freund insisted so often—the secondary place of law in industrial relations. The question of the 'success' of a new law in this part of the social fabric is a matter of great delicacy. The power of other social forces is usually more important here than any impact of the law. Indeed, in reacting to its impact, workers or employers or both may—as in 1971 to 1974—confirm the secondary status of law itself. And when the Conservative government claimed in June 1981 that 'secondary' action had declined in trade disputes and that 'one of the reasons why it happens very little is the passage of the Employment Act [1980]',[4] ministerial tongues must have been lodged firmly in cheeks. Unemployment had by then reached well over 2.5 million and there were few who did not regard the state of the labour market and of the economy as the decisive causes of the decline in workers' industrial action. On the other hand, the new laws of the early eighties must be seen as reserve counter-strike weapons, to be used if and when the labour movement recovers its economic strength sufficiently to mount an effective challenge on an industrial as well as a political front. To that extent the first half of the eighties is potentially a period of trial for the instrumental efficacy of restrictive labour law.

The Policy of 'Restriction'

The essence of this policy for labour law is to restrict the social power of trade unions through the use (or threatened use) of legal sanctions. It takes its place as part of a wider strategy to increase the power of employers and strengthen managerial control in industrial relations as a means of promoting greater efficiency and productivity in the economy. Unlike the policy of 'reform' the policy of 'restriction' sees the law as an important, or even as a main, instrument of achieving the reconstruction of industrial relations, but it typically oscillates between two different approaches towards the function of trade unions and their role in collective bargaining (particularly in the regulation of workplace behaviour).

The dual nature of the policy of 'restriction' was clearly exemplified by the Industrial Relations Act of 1971.[5] On the one hand it purported to encourage unions to behave more 'responsibly', and indeed 'responsible' trade unionism was one of the Act's general principles set out in its first section. On the other hand it was also manifestly an attempt to break the independent strength—and thus the effectiveness—of trade unions.

The core of the Act's conception of 'responsibility' was that unions should control their shop stewards and members and be liable to injunctions and in damages for acts committed in breach of collective agreements and for other 'unfair industrial practices'. In reality the only practical consequence of making the union legally liable for breach of a collective agreement is to permit the employer to sue for acts committed in breach of the 'no-strike' or 'procedure' clauses in the agreement. At a time of relatively full employment, the unofficial strike in breach of a collectively-agreed procedure was seen as the great mischief which the law had to confront. If only collective agreements were made legally binding as 'contracts', it was believed that 'management could normally depend on support from trade union leaders in any just action they took against unofficial strike leaders'.[6]

The aim of making unions responsible for their shop stewards on pain of legal sanctions was thus also the underlying rationale of the Act's restoration of the principle of *Taff Vale* (whereby trade unions as distinct from individuals could be held legally liable) and of the numerous 'unfair industrial practices' to which they were made subject. This policy message was sympathetically received by the Law Lords. The clear implication of their decision in *Heatons Transport Ltd.* v. *TGWU*[7] was that unregistered organizations of workers were to be liable in respect of industrial action generally, even for the apparently unofficial acts of their stewards.[8] Although the extent of legal liability could be reduced for those organizations which registered as statutory 'trade unions', the task of policing their membership was still unavoidable. Registered unions were required to have rules on a wide range of issues, including 'any body by which, and any official by whom, instructions may be given to members of the organization on its behalf for any kind of industrial action, and the circumstances in which any such instructions may be so given'.[9] The Act's presumption that the negotiators of written collective agreements intend to create legal relations was also designed to encourage 'responsible' trade unionism. Parties to a legally enforceable agreement were required 'to take all such steps as are reasonably practicable' to prevent members and persons acting or purporting to act on their behalf from breaking the agreement.[10] The question of the legal enforceability of collective agreements is inextricably bound up with the question of the liability of unions for the acts of their shop stewards. This integral connection was acknowledged a decade after the 1971 Act in the Green Paper *Trade Union Immunities*, which viewed the introduction of the legally enforceable collective agreement approvingly as a possible means of inducing unions to 'exert much greater authority and discipline over their officials and members' (thereby even recognizing that this could lead trade unions not only to reform their internal organization and rule books but also to 'turn themselves into more authoritarian organizations' in the process of exercising 'greater control over their members').[11]

This particular aspect of Conservative strategy rests on the assumption that there is, or ought to be, some sort of 'chain of command' in trade unions, a notion often fed by lawyers' conceptions that trade unions and companies are two parallel types of 'combination'.[12] This assumption is highly suspect, for as the Donovan Report pointed out: 'Trade union leaders do exercise discipline from time to time, but they cannot be industry's policemen. They are democratic leaders in organizations in which the seat of power has almost always been close to the members.'[13] That does not of course necessarily imply that more orderly industrial relations cannot be achieved. Indeed, within the Donovan Report's prescription, that perspective was consistent with proposals to bring the spontaneity of informal shop-floor industrial relations somewhat more under the supervision of the official institutions of management and labour. What Donovan had seen as the primary objective was 'a change in the nature of British collective bargaining and a more orderly method for workers and their representatives to exercise their influence in the factory; and for this to be accomplished, if possible, without destroying the British tradition of keeping industrial relations out of the courts'.[14] To some degree, therefore, the policy of reform underlying the Report posed the question (though it was not always seen very clearly) whether 'new problems' should be dealt with by 'voluntary collective bargaining or by compulsory statute law? Or, if by both, what should be the relationship between the two methods?'[15]

In direct contrast, the architects of the Industrial Relations Act boldly proclaimed that the law was to be 'the Government's main instrument' in achieving its objectives.[16] Moreover the legal restriction of unions was accorded a key role in encouraging 'good' industrial relations as envisaged by the Industrial Relations Code of Practice issued in 1972 under the Act. The Code, like the Donovan Report, extolled the virtues of an industrial relations system in which the central institution would be the precise and detailed collective agreement, which it was hoped would be more likely to produce peace, order, and efficiency. Conflict, in so far as it persisted, would follow a more predictable and less costly pattern. The 1971 Act contained a variety of measures designed to promote such reform: the registration of trade unions, the registration of procedure agreements, a duty on employers to disclose information, a procedure for the determination of 'bargaining units' and 'sole bargaining agents', and of course the presumption that collective agreements in writing would be intended to create binding legal relations unless there was a clause to the contrary. On the union side the statutory rights arising from these measures were to be enjoyed only by registered unions; but the authors of the Act believed (wrongly as it turned out) that most unions could be persuaded or induced to place themselves on the new state register.

However, the reforming aspects of legal regulation under the 1971 Act were vitiated by its overall restrictive intent. Employers and others were in effect invited to use the law as a tactic in industrial disputes with the object of securing restraining orders and financial compensation in actions before the National Industrial Relations Court (NIRC). The Act's so-called 'unfair industrial practices' were the basis of civil liabilities analogous to statutory torts and gave rise to legal remedies equivalent to the traditional 'labour injunction' and damages. Liability for industrial action even in the case of a registered union was extensive, but in the case of an unregistered 'organization of workers' it was so wide that in practice it obliterated the right to strike.[17] Various types of 'irregular' industrial action, in which workers had broken their contracts of employment, were singled out for special prohibition. Similarly, under the 'national emergency' cooling-off and ballot procedures, the government itself could apply to the NIRC for temporary restraining orders. This restrictive rationale was inevitably underlined by the application of quasi-criminal sanctions for contempt of court to individuals[18] and to organizations[19] who refused to obey the orders of the NIRC. It was not long, though, before lawyers discovered that the imposition of legal sanctions against unofficial leaders who are strongly supported by their fellow workers is as difficult as their imposition against groups of workers themselves.[20]

The Conservative government strategy was reinforced by certain of the Act's provisions which sought to promote the liberties of individuals. These included the right to be a non-unionist—'to be a member of no trade union or other organization of workers' (i.e. of a union whether registered or not)[21] —and the right of individuals to challenge the continued existence of collective bargaining as well as union security arrangements. The 'pre-entry' closed shop agreement was declared 'void'; and a range of statutory provisions made the operation of closed shop arrangements of any kind legally hazardous (a fruitless venture because in the face of that 'stable and sturdy institution . . . even the law had to bend to the inevitable').[22] Such measures indicated an objective which went beyond encouraging 'responsible' trade union behaviour and were evidence of another more severe policy, that is a positive preference for a non-unionized as against a unionized work-force. Under the 1971 Act, therefore, the path from reform to restriction led ultimately to outright opposition to effective independent trade unionism. Reform and outright opposition are clearly irreconcilable. In fact the conflicting aims of the Act almost suggested that it might be the work of two 'phantom' draftsmen: 'The first may be thought of as a civil servant or "organization man" concerned mainly to bring "order" and a tidy structure into collective British industrial relations. The second is quite different, a Conservative lawyer imbued above all else with doctrines of individual rights, often without regard to the shop-floor problems of collective bargaining.'[23] Thus, while the Act contained in some parts a 'collectivist' flavour, recognizing the legitimacy of unions and collective bargaining, it also contained a strong 'individualist' strand indicative of a fundamental hostility towards both trade unions and the autonomous collective regulation of industrial relations.

It might be thought that opposition to the basic objectives and activities of trade unions is nowadays anachronistic. But such opposition seems to be a prevalent attitude amongst leading exponents of 'individualist' philosophy and the 'monetarist' school of economics who have provided much of the intellectual inspiration for Conservative Party policy since the late 1970s. According to this view trade unions are a distortion of the market relation between employer and employee, and trade union aspirations to regulate jobs and labour markets, even by way of joint regulation, are incompatible with individual liberty. Thus Professor Hayek has proclaimed the moral and practical superiority of individual market relations and denounced the 'legal privileges' of trade unions as the 'chief cause' of inefficiency, poverty, and unemployment.[24] Politicians of the same school tend to berate many trade union activities as being 'immoral, unethical and unacceptable to very large numbers of people';[25] and some of their supporters claim that 'the unions have, from the beginning of the industrial age, operated as a regressive and impoverishing influence'.[26] Indeed, so serious do they find modern interferences with 'the market' that they regard them as 'a critical test of democracy about the outcome of which we must feel apprehensive'.[27]

Given the support of leading ministers for such views it was not surprising that the first casualty of Conservative labour law policy after their return to government in 1979 was the long-established principle of state support for collective bargaining. From the start it was clear that this administration was influenced far more than the government of 1971 by those who rejected trade unions as an impediment to market forces. In advance of the Employment Act 1980, one of the 'July Orders' of 1979 reduced the statutory period within which employers must consult with recognized unions over redundancy.[28] The Act followed this up by cutting away many of the statutory props for joint negotiation, 'auxiliary' laws as Kahn-Freund called them. It repealed the union recognition procedure embodied in the Employment Protection Act 1975[29] (whereby an employer was under a duty to recognize and bargain with a union properly recommended by ACAS), the unilateral arbitration provisions in Schedule 11 of the same Act (which enabled a union to compel an employer to observe at least the minimum conditions of employment agreed collectively for the trade or industry or, in the absence of such agreement, the 'general level' of such conditions) and, for good measure, the 'fair wages' machinery in the Road Haulage Wages Act 1938.[30] It is in this context that those provisions of the 1980 Act must be judged which erode individual employment protection and try to restore management's unilateral prerogative to discipline and dismiss employees.

Conservative labour law policy since 1979 has also limited the right to take industrial action, a right which is, as Kahn-Freund always insisted, essential to independent trade union-ism.[31] Although the then Secretary of State for Employment, James Prior, promoted the 1980 Act as a moderate and reason-able first measure in a 'step-by-step' approach to labour law reform, its potential impact on the freedom to take industrial action was highly restrictive. In judging the nature of its pro-visions, regard must be had to the character of the usual remedy in labour litigation, the interlocutory 'labour injunction'. This 'discretionary' remedy is in theory an 'interim' measure main-taining the status quo until trial. But an employer or other plaintiff (and there are many such likely plaintiffs, e.g. a cus-tomer, a supplier, an individual, or another company) has rarely wanted to pursue any remedy other than this order to stop the union from continuing with its industrial action.[32] Moreover, even where trade unionist defendants in such proceedings prove that there is a strong likelihood that their acts are lawful because of defences based upon the 'trade dispute' immunities, the judges have nevertheless insisted on retaining a residual discretion to grant injunctions against them, for example in cases which could cause 'disastrous' damage to an employer, the 'public', or the 'nation'.[33] Restriction of trade unions' industrial rights by way of reducing the immunities inevitably invites the 'labour injunction' to flood back into industrial relations at the choice of employers and other plaintiffs in whose favour the judges will normally dispense their discretion.

With the advent of the 1980 Act, the scope of the substantive 'trade dispute' defences has been much more severely curtailed. Its provisions cut wide swathes in the 'immunities' which protect those engaged in various kinds of industrial action in contemplation or furtherance of a trade dispute, outlawing 'secondary' action,[34] picketing away from workers' 'own' place of work, and industrial action to compel union membership.[35] Union officials, organizers, and workers involved in industrial action are thereby placed in serious legal jeopardy, at least to the extent that employers or other plaintiffs wish to sue. To these sections of the Act must be added the Secretary of State's Codes of Practice on the Closed Shop and on Picketing, the latter arguably affecting even the application of the criminal law to pickets.[36] Some of the most tortuous provisions of the Act have even been understood by the Court of Appeal to mean that 'an act of a trade union official which *induces* a workman to break a contract of employment or *threatens* to induce it is to be regarded as "unlawful means" and although it is not actionable by the employer [because of the remaining immunities] it can be used by a third person for the purpose of establishing liability in tort', i.e. for an injunction and damages.[37] This interpretation was not shared by the House of Lords;[38] but even without such a severe interpretation, the bans in the 1980 Act upon 'secondary action' (which includes—with minor exceptions— all industrial action where the employer of the workers concerned is not in law a 'party' to the trade dispute)[39] and upon picketing otherwise than at the place of work, greatly reduce the capability of trade unions lawfully to undertake ordinary industrial action.

The surrounding provisions of the Act and the Codes have combined to strengthen this restrictive structure. The Secretary of State's Code on the Closed Shop, for example, provides that a trade union should not take disciplinary action against a member on the ground that he has refused to take part in industrial action called for by the union (in accordance with its rules) if the strike would constitute a 'serious risk to public safety, health or property'[40] or where the strike action 'had not been affirmed in a secret ballot'.[41] A tribunal or appellate court would, for example, be obliged to take account of that provision in deciding whether the expulsion of such a member from the union was 'unreasonable' and therefore unlawful under the new jurisdiction created by the Act where the relevant employment is the subject of a closed shop agreement.[42] The Act also provides for public funds to be available for secret ballots in an attempt to encourage them; but this provision is such an integral part of the overall restrictions in the Act that the TUC's policy is that no affiliated organization should apply for this state subsidy. The Codes, moreover, contain many paragraphs which could operate to the disadvantage of a trade union (or its officials) if 'joined' in proceedings before the tribunal by an employer sued by an employee who alleges unfair dismissal by reason of his not being a union member. This new procedure introduced by the 1980 Act is of great potential importance;[43] and it does not, as is commonly thought, apply only in a closed shop. It means that in any unfair dismissal on the ground of non-unionism where there is evidence of 'pressure' by way of actual or threatened industrial action, the union (or official) may be ordered to pay a 'just and equitable' contribution to the employer who thereby can claw back part or all of the money he has been ordered to pay to the dismissed worker.

The legal freedom to withdraw labour has been further undermined by the Conservative government's measures of 1982. These go to the heart of the 'immunities' by narrowing the definition of 'trade dispute' in four ways: (i) requiring a dispute to be 'wholly or mainly' in connection with industrial matters (this is said to be needed to exclude 'political' disputes); (ii) excluding disputes between workers and workers (thereby adding to the difficulty of establishing the relevant immunity where the employer can find some reason, however technical, whereby he is not a 'party' to the dispute); (iii) restricting disputes relating to matters abroad to those likely to affect the strikers in the United Kingdom; and (iv) excluding all disputes not strictly between an employer and his own employees.[44] Also the statutory right of a union (or employers' association) to be a 'party' to a trade dispute on behalf of workers (or employers) is repealed, notwithstanding the fact that it has been allowed that right even under the common law.[45] The definition of 'worker' is significantly restricted as well. Only workers of the employer in dispute can be parties and the content of the dispute must be *their* employment conditions (not those of other workers, as the traditional formula permitted). The unemployed worker cannot any longer have a trade dispute with his ex-employer unless his employment was terminated in connection with the dispute, or was one of the circumstances giving rise to it.[46]

In addition, the principle of liability in tort established by the *Taff Vale* judgment in 1901 is reintroduced, making trade union funds widely available in claims for damages and the union itself subject to the orders of the ordinary courts in that area of civil liability on the basis, as we shall see later, of a very extended doctrine of 'vicarious liability' for its officials.[47] In 1982 the government was clearly determined not to leave 'vicarious liability' to the courts, as the 1971 Act had for the most part done. It therefore made the union liable for a list of statutory agents (including the national executive, the President and General Secretary, and other officials) unless their acts are 'repudiated' in the fashion required. In fact these developments in 'vicarious liability' display, we shall suggest, the philosophy of the policy of restriction in its most revealing form.

Because closed shops are anathema to it, the Conservative government also decided to render 'void' all contractual provisions requiring a 'union only' work-force. All commercial conduct (tenders, contracts, refusing to contract, and the like) which evinces such a purpose is unlawful, affording a civil action to 'any person adversely affected'.[48] The basic 'immunities' are removed from industrial action taken to support any call for 'union labour'. Indeed, under these provisions industrial action is unlawful and open to the same remedies of damages and injunctions if any supply of goods and services can 'reasonably be expected' to be interrupted (even where there is no contract), and if one of the reasons for the interference is that the work is to be done by employees of another employer who are either members of trade unions or of a particular union, or are not members of unions or of a particular union.[49] By all the yardsticks of the policy of 'reform' (even at its most conservative) these new legal provisions, should they succeed, look set to achieve the impairment of effective trade unionism by the creation of disorder in the labour market—disorder which would no doubt be defended as an increase in 'competitiveness'.[50]

Indeed it is difficult to see how the restriction policy can rest here. If workers refuse to work alongside others because they are 'undercutting' union rates, does that fall within the illegality? Is it one of their reasons, in reality, that those others are non-unionists? The same is true for injunctions. Even under the 1980 Act, problems were encountered in enforcing injunctions, which normally apply only to those named. Early in 1982 two union officials fulfilled their obligation to the High Court to withdraw their recommendation to members to 'black' newspapers, but the union members voted to continue the boycott and the plaintiffs faced the prospect of taking proceedings against each of the 300 workers individually.[51] The answer for the future is, as we have seen, to allow an injunction against the union. The statutory immunity which has since 1906 protected unions against orders in the High Court in tort actions—'the British solution of the problem of the "labour injunction" which has been so much discussed in the United States'[52]—is jettisoned.[53] To make that work, though, the union must be put under an obligation to police a return to normal working. Under the new policy, demands for 'union only' labour are to be unlawful. If there is a union, then its primary job is to regulate the work-force.

Moreover the procedure of 'joinder', whereby the union or its officials or members can be made liable to pay for an unfair dismissal, is now placed in the hands of the dismissed employee, an innovation (as we shall see) of great significance.[54] And the employer is to have greater legal power to dismiss striking employees[55]—a new weapon which can be used to erode the solidarity of strikers. The machinery of employment protection law is in both respects pressed into service to weaken trade union action.

It is very significant that these measures do not (as in 1971) attempt to replace the traditional structure of 'trade dispute' immunities from common law liabilities. They nevertheless effect through statutory enactment the policy so often espoused by the judges in the past, namely, the narrowing of the immunities. This method of proceeding reverses the historic function of statute law in this field. Instead of shielding trade unionists from restrictive judicial doctrines, the laws of 1980 to 1982 seek to minimize the statutory protection and thereby allow the courts to impose the doctrines of the common law, with all the uncertainties that judicial interpretation of those doctrines implies. The only certainty about the common law in this field is its implacable hostility to the legality of trade unions and their activities. The retention of the form of the traditional structure of negative statutory immunities is a strategy which renders the Conservative government's claim to moderation superficially the more plausible in contrast to the radical restructuring attempted in the 1971 Act with its new institutions and statutory 'unfair industrial practices'.

It also gives credence to the argument that all the government is doing is to make trade unions subject to the same laws as everyone else and to cut back their anomalous legal 'privileges'. This strategy of intervention via an apparently non-interventionist structure is proclaimed, for example, as 'restoring to employers and others, who are harmfully affected by the consequences of people acting as pickets inducing breaches of contract, their common law rights that statute has taken away'.[56] This line of reasoning fails to take into account the fact that in the face of common law liabilities trade unions have no rights to function or even to exist, a fact that was acknowledged not once but several times in the government's own Green Paper.[57] The immunities do not make trade unions privileged persons above the law; they are the British legal form of democratic liberties, the equivalent of what in other countries often takes the form of a positive right to organize, to bargain, or to strike, guaranteed by legislation or by the Constitution.[58] In Britain 'every economic common law right "restored" is an industrial trade union right destroyed'.[59]

The relentless logic of the policy of restriction leads on from a desire to encourage 'responsible' trade unionism to a preference for no trade unionism at all. That was the direction of those parts of the Industrial Relations Act which sought to promote individual liberty at the expense of trade union organizational strength and the stability of collective bargaining arrangements. An analogous pattern emerges even more clearly from the recent legislation. For example, the system of joint regulation is potentially weakened at the expense of 'individual rights' by the section in the Employment Act 1980 giving individuals the right not to be subjected to action by their employer short of dismissal in order to 'compel' union membership. In that section, by a stroke of the draftsman's pen, what was previously an 'individual' right for trade unionists not to be compelled to join unions which are not independent is turned into a right for non-unionists not to be 'compelled' to join a trade union.[60]

In similar vein, TULRA's indirect support for the closed shop was transformed by the 1980 Act, which gives redress to an individual dismissed for non-membership if he comes within one of three broad categories: if he genuinely objects to union membership on grounds of 'conscience or other deeply-held personal conviction'; if he is a non-member at the time when the closed shop is introduced; or if he has remained a non-member in an unapproved new closed shop after the commencement of the Act. New closed shops must be approved by at least 80 per cent of those eligible to vote in a secret ballot if the employer is to avoid liability for unfair dismissal; and even if the required majority is obtained, a non-member who has been employed since the date of the ballot is protected.[61]

But this was not enough for the policy of restriction, and it was soon found necessary, while retaining the provisions for closed shops after 1980, to add to the conditions which permit a 'fair dismissal' of a non-unionist. Under the 1982 Employment Act closed shops are now forced to undergo a regular ballot for approval because any such dismissal is unfair if it takes effect more than five years after such a ballot. In the case of closed shops dating from before the 1980 Act, it is sufficient to obtain a majority of either 80 per cent of the electorate or 85 per cent of the employees who vote; and no subsequent ballot on any closed shop is sufficient unless it results in approval by 80 per cent of those entitled to vote or 85 per cent of those voting.[62] Also the 1975 protection of workers against dismissal by reason of their refusing to join a union which is not independent is changed into protection against dismissal for workers who refuse to join a union or a particular union.[63] This is a formulation which (when taken with sections 4 and 5 of the Act of 1980) could fragment the TUC and other inter-union arrangements for stable patterns of worker representation in multi-union plants.

In a remarkable clause not hinted at in their *Proposals* three months earlier,[64] the government introduced in the 1982 Act a scheme for compensating non-unionists dismissed between 1974 and 1980 if their dismissal would have been unfair under the provisions of the 1980 Act (except the ballot provisions). That compensation is to be paid by the Secretary of State out of public funds to those applying within twelve months.[65] These retroactive prizes from public expenditure to dismissed non-unionists would apply, it has been estimated, to about 400 workers over the six years in question (a figure which has not gone unchallenged).

But this was not enough to purge the system of the malady diagnosed by this policy. Compensation was increased in the 1982 Act for those dismissed by reason of refusing to join a union. In addition to the basic and 'compensatory' awards, when they seek re-employment a 'special award' is added, ranging from a minimum of £12,000 to a maximum of £22,000.[66] These figures are almost the same as the government's proposals of three months before, notwithstanding the CBI's representation that such compensation could 'bankrupt small firms'.[67] Moreover, the new 'special award' applies, perhaps logically, to a non-unionist dismissed by reason of his refusal to join a union whether or not there is a closed shop.[68]

This whole approach represents a fundamental reversal of public policy. What in the legislation of 1974 to 1978 had been a preference for trade unionism, with protection of non-unionists only as far as it was thought necessary to maintain pluralist values, now turns into a preference for non-unionism. Many of the threads of this scheme were apparent in the earlier Code of Practice on the closed shop issued by the Secretary of State in 1980. In effect that provided guidance for the progressive elimination of union security arrangements.[69] The 1982 legislation is consistent with those provisions of the 1980 Act under which a worker was given (in addition to his common law rights) a right against the union in closed shop situations not to be 'unreasonably' excluded or expelled from membership, whatever the rules of the union say.[70] All these jurisdictions are given to the tribunals, whose role we discuss below.[71] And in cases of unfair dismissal by reason of non-membership of a union, the compensation is recoverable (as we have noted) from a trade union, which may be 'joined' by the dismissed employee as well as by the employer. 'Union only' practices of all kinds are attacked and associated industrial pressure is made unlawful. The 1982 measures, when combined with the provisions of the 1980 Act, represent a frank rejection of the basic trade union objective of achieving common standards in the trade.

Whether these provisions will even offer individuals or minority groups any real protection is highly debatable. The precise effect of such legislation is not easy to predict; it may not always be that which is intended by its sponsors, as in the case of some of the employment protection legislation of 1975 to which we return later. Account must be taken not only of the surrounding social and legal environment but also of the condition of the very legal concepts employed in the statutes, some of which are discussed below. But, without doubt, the statutes of 1980 to 1982 could have extremely damaging consequences for collective organization. They could weaken the ability of trade unions to maintain collective discipline (i.e. solidarity through the union) in industrial disputes. They could easily be employed to undermine the TUC's voluntary arrangements (the Disputes Principles and Procedures which have emerged from the 'Bridlington Agreement') for containing inter-union competition. They could severely damage the stability of collective bargaining arrangements. And they even appear to ignore the interest which many employers have in the maintenance of the closed shop.[72] The many technical difficulties in the new legislation—such as the meaning of 'deeply-held personal conviction' or the labyrinthine provisions outlawing 'trade union only' requirements—are likely to provide lawyers with a profitable field-day. But on one central point there can be no doubt: the opposition to effective independent trade unionism underlying this legislative offensive. To this theme we shall return in the last section of this chapter.

A Crisis in Fundamental Concepts

If inquiry into the labour law of the early 1980s discloses a political strategy to restrict the autonomy and effectiveness of independent trade unionism, recent developments in labour law also seem to point to a deeply rooted crisis in its legal concepts and beyond them in the wider society. All modern

systems of industrial relations in fact require certain fundamental legal concepts: one of these must express the relationship of the individual worker to his or her employer; another
must relate the collective action of workers (normally through
their independent trade unions) to their obligation to work. In
the British system these are largely supplied by the term 'contract of employment' and by principles which rest in great
measure upon the term 'trade dispute'. Both these concepts
pose problems for contemporary policies in labour law.

The Contract of Employment

In labour law the contract of employment is, as Kahn-Freund
observed, the 'cornerstone of the edifice'.[73] Its importance lies
in the provision of an indispensable legal apparatus for regulating the individual employment relationship and related areas of
law, for example, redundancy payments, industrial safety, and
unfair dismissal.[74] As such it is a 'necessary element' in our
labour law.[75] The 'employee' or (to use the older term) 'servant'
is fundamentally distinct in English law from the 'independent
contractor', i.e. the worker who is self-employed or works under
a contract not 'of service' but 'for services'. Most workers are
employees. If therefore there is today, as we suggest, a crisis
which threatens that very legal concept, it is of the most profound moment for the whole of our labour law.

Before investigating the difficulties which beset labour law
today in this area, three qualifications must be made to Kahn-
Freund's statement that the contract of employment is the
'principal actor in the drama'.[76] First, when the law deals with
collective labour relations, such as the regulation of 'combinations' or strikes, it has often used for obvious reasons a
wider category so as to include all 'workers', 'workmen',
'journeymen', or other persons which it intends to cover,
whether for repressive or for liberal purposes.[77] Secondly, the
employment protection legislation of this and the previous
century has attached rights to employment only rarely by way
of inserting them into the contract of employment as such.[78]
More often it has created a code aimed at protecting the worker
from injury or damage (as in laws about safety or dismissal) and
provided remedies resting not upon 'contractual' rights but
upon 'statutory' rights. Because of 'a gap in the conceptual
equipment of English law',[79] these rights are still separate in

character from the contract of employment. The 'severance of statutory and contractual rights'[80] has been perpetuated, and today statutory rights are even enforced through a separate judicial process (i.e. the industrial tribunals)[81] quite distinct from the procedures and courts in which 'ordinary' contractual employment rights are enforced.

The third qualification is of a different nature. Few students of labour law are today unaware that the employment relationship is fundamentally 'a command under the guise of an agreement', a 'submission' by and 'subordination' of the worker, concealed by that 'indispensable figment of the legal mind known as the contract of employment'.[82] No doubt the law defends the inalienable right to choose whether or not to serve a particular employer—for that is 'the main difference between a servant and a serf'.[83] But it also permits economic forces as well as the utmost indirect legal pressures (such as removal of social security benefits if he refuses to take a job) to determine the worker's choice.[84] It is perhaps curious that Kahn-Freund, who so often stressed this reality about the 'contract', showed less interest in the social content of the other part of the concept— the 'employment' or 'service'.

The 'individual contract of employment' has long contained a myth and a reality. The myth, that it is a consensual 'agreement', must be sustained by existing society, despite its manifest character as a figment concealing subordination. But the very concept of employment itself contains a reality, and one which must be upheld if the system is to survive. Even in the heyday of *laissez-faire*, the substantive content of the relationship reflected the extensive obligations of the pre-industrial servant and the command power of the master. As Fox has argued: 'contract, as the pure doctrine defined it, could not be seen by the property-owning classes as an adequate foundation for governing the employment relation. Their needs were met by infusing the employment contract with the traditional law of master and servant, thereby granting them a legal basis for the prerogative they demanded.'[85] The language may have been contractual but the employer's control embodied in, for example, the common law's implied obligations harked back to an earlier era of master–servant relations. Even in 1972 the judicial mind could describe an industrial work-to-rule which held up the employer's commercial operation but did not depart 'from the literal letter of the agreement' (because the workers had zealously observed the working rules of the employer) as 'a breach of an implied term of the contract to perform the contract in such a way as not to frustrate that commercial object', and as involving a breach of 'the implied term to serve the employer faithfully within the requirements of the contract'.[86]

Victorian judges were content to reaffirm the master's right to command or to control the servant, i.e. the reality of subordination inherent in employment (or, as it was still known, 'service'), viewing the 'independent contractor' in contrast as someone who had derogated little from his own personal autonomy. 'As they viewed both subordinated service and autonomous independent contracting as necessary and stable features of the social structure, they found it reasonably straightforward in practice and in accordance with their social and political principles to apply this two-fold distinction rigidly.'[87] By the late ninteenth century that distinction was summed up in the so-called 'control' test, which defined a servant as 'a person subject to the command of his master as to the manner in which he shall do his work'.[88] The servant, as against the independent contractor for services, is told not only the what but also the how.

But the judges did not sit down and invent such a concept to fit their social predilections. There was no need for that. The common law as it came down to them fashioned the content of the test and in part the manner in which they applied it. To a considerable extent the refinement of the definition of a 'servant' took place in litigation concerning the doctrine of 'vicarious liability', whereby the 'master' is liable in civil law for certain acts of his 'servant'.[89] The origins of this doctrine lay not in any abstract definition, but in the structures and certainties of medieval Britain. The 'labourer' was obliged not only to perform his allotted work but also to accept work; and when the Black Death decimated the supply of labour in 1348, statute quickly moved in to correct the imbalance in the labour market.[90] Elizabethan legislation such as the Statute of Artificers 1563 developed and extended that scheme, imposing wage-fixing by justices for 'all classes of workmen'.[91]

Although as early as the fourteenth century there is evidence that some types of employment were not within 'the letter' of such statutes,[92] throughout four centuries there is little evidence that lawyers experienced serious difficulty with the generic term *serviens*, which comprised in feudal society persons as far apart as a mason, a bailiff, and a household labourer.[93] Such statutes developed into what became known as the 'Master and Servant' Acts of which the last consolidation was in 1867. It must never be forgotten that the nineteenth-century judges grew up in a society where the workman's breach of his contract of service was not just a civil wrong but also with few exceptions a crime punishable by imprisonment by reason of these Acts. The Master and Servant Acts were repealed only in 1875.[94]

Moreover the law gave to the master a proprietary interest in his servant. If anyone wrongfully injured the servant, the master could—and can today in respect of an uncertain category of 'menial' or 'domestic' servants—sue the wrongdoer for injury to the master's *servitium* or property in the service. That earlier tort is distinct from the modern tort of inducing the employee to break his contract of employment (a tort of primary importance to labour law which was invented by the judges in 1853).[95] It reflects the way in which 'ideas which had come down from the days of serfdom and villeinage lingered on, so that a master was regarded as having a proprietary right in his servant'.[96]

This then was the flavour of 'employment' when the problem of vicarious liability and the legal definition of 'servant' came into greater prominence in the eighteenth century, as *laissez faire* supplanted status. Before that time the issue had been obscured behind the technical distinctions between 'trespass' (where the wrong was directly inflicted on the plaintiff) and actions 'on the case' where 'injury was merely consequential upon some otherwise neutral act'. The latter was the remedy against a master sued for the negligence of his servant.[97] If damage was done at the master's express command, a remedy might consequently lie in 'trespass'; but in 'case', the master was responsible for the wrongful act of his servant by reason (it was said) of his 'implied command', i.e. the authority given to the servant or inferred from the nature of the general course of the employment. Today that is only one of a variety of explanations given for the doctrine of vicarious liability which has, as we shall see, returned to primary importance in labour law.[98] It is not difficult to see how, from the law which imputed such an 'implied command', judges constructed the test for deciding who was and who was not a servant, namely whether the employer could control the manner in which the servant is to do his work.

This formula was at once important and difficult. The importance lay partly in the contemporaneous expansion of civil liability at a time when the modern torts (especially the tort of negligence) emerged from the older 'forms of action'. The difficulty arose partly from the fact that the common law—as is its habit, perhaps its function—had not kept abreast of changing social conditions. Kahn-Freund pointed out that the renowned jurist Blackstone, writing in 1765, discussed only four categories of servants: domestic servants, apprentices, labourers 'only hired by the day or the week', and 'superior' servants such as bailiffs.[99] This picture was 'a portrait of a society which had long ceased to exist'.[100] No reference was made to the areas of shipbuilding, mining, potteries, iron foundries, or even textiles, in all of which labour was starting to be employed in capitalist production, soon to be enhanced by the introduction of steam power. So authoritative was Blackstone that no jurist overtook his categories until the industrial revolution was in full swing. But, as contract supplanted status, eighteenth-century judges tended in their general statements to refer to a 'servant' as 'a person who contracts with another to do certain work for him'.[101]

When, therefore, the nineteenth-century judges turned to define the 'servant' or 'employee', they were still educated in the concepts of an almost pre-industrial society; still strongly affected by the belief that a master had property in his servant; conscious before 1875 of the crime committed by a servant if he broke his contract of service; and still sensitive in the time of the Poor Laws to the old obligation of working people to accept work.[102] They now needed a general definition of 'service'—what more natural than to keep the concept of 'command' and to find the mark of the servant in the master's control over the manner in which the work is done? Other factors of course entered into the juridical debate, but that became the ultimate test.[103]

Scorn has frequently been poured on this test in modern times. Kahn-Freund himself called it 'unrealistic and almost grotesque' to call the ship's captain, aeroplane pilot, train

driver, or crane driver the 'servant' of the employer because the
latter 'controls the performance of his work'—and the point is
even more obvious if the servant is a surgeon.[104] The employer
may well not know how to 'perform the work', let alone control
its execution. A more refined test appeared in judgments of this
century, namely whether the employer is entitled to give orders
as to how the work should be done. If a crane driver gave to his
master a 'sturdy answer', which meant that he was 'a skilled
man and knew his own job and would carry it out in his own
way', ultimately he would still do so at his peril because of the
employer's power of dismissal.[105] But there were crane drivers
and train drivers in the nineteenth century; and the crisis in the
'control' test did not occur, as has been suggested, because it
became a 'legal fiction' instead of the reality it had reflected in 'a
simple industrial society, such as England was until this
century', when employers had 'the same or even greater skill
than their workmen'.[106] It is true that technological and social
developments have made any realistic application of the
'control' test more difficult. But very early cases were concerned
with workers likely to be more skilled than the employer; and
one of the earliest cases which carried the seeds of modern
vicarious liability involved a servant who was the master of a
vessel.[107] Few judges expressed serious disquiet even in the
early twentieth century about this test which rested on 'the
nature and degree of control over the person alleged to be a
servant'.[108]

The deep crisis in the modern law is recent and connected
with both legal and social factors. The legal—if secondary—
factors include the determination of the judges to uphold the
ancient and (as they see it) the essential character, in Davies
and Freedland's phrase, of 'subordinated service'. In 1850, for
example, they invented a principle complementary to their
vision of vicarious liability which was one of the more splendid
articulations of their class solidarity with the masters. This was
the doctrine of 'common employment'. A master was held not
to be vicariously liable in damages to his servant injured by a
fellow servant because the former had 'accepted' the defaults of
the latter by entering into the master's service (a preposterous
doctrine not repealed until 1948).[109] A century later, in 1957,
the Law Lords relied upon equally antique principles in holding that, where an employee's negligence in the course of his

employment as a lorry driver had injured a third party, the employer's insurance company (which paid the damages and had acquired the right under the policy to sue in his name) could sue the same employee to recoup the money because he had broken the implied obligation in his contract of employment to use proper 'skill and care' in his employment.[110] Their refusal to allow the realities of modern insurance to overtake the ancient right of an employer to claim damages and an indemnity from his careless employee has still not been totally excluded from the law.[111]

In discussing the social factors influencing the crisis in the 'control' test, it is not sufficient just to refer to such obvious explanations as the increasing division of labour and technological change. After all the society in which the test emerged in its recognizable form cannot simply be described (as even Kahn-Freund once appeared to suggest) as one in which 'the ownership of the means of production coincided with the possession of technical knowledge and skill . . . handed down from one generation to the next by oral tradition'.[112] That generalization was no longer accurate by the time the 'control' test was fully elaborated, and though there were difficulties, it lasted for another hundred years without serious judicial demand for its replacement. The 'control' test naturally demands greater judicial ingenuity as the number of 'servants' increases who possess skills superior to or different from those of the 'master', especially after 1855 when more and more 'masters' became companies. But the legal crisis of the contract of employment is essentially a phenomenon of the last forty years. It is only since the Second World War, in a period when wider social and economic developments seem set to herald social change as great as that which saw the introduction of the factory system, that the courts have sometimes despaired of the 'control' test and turned to different tests, only to flounder helplessly.

Cases in the courts are not of course necessarily typical of any society. Millions of workers will work as employees whether or not the lawyers can define their status. Nevertheless a pathological eruption in the law may be a signal that serves notice of a more general social distress. By the 1950s, when the application of the 'control' test had been perceived to be an adequate instrument to distinguish the ship's master, chauffeur, and newspaper reporter (employees) from the ship's pilot, taxi-man, and newspaper contributor (self-employed), it was judicially suggested that a new 'organization' test could be used to distinguish employment—work done as 'an integral part of the business'—from services—work done for the business but not 'integrated into it'.[113] Such a test has more recently been joined by others, such as: 'Did the worker work as his own boss?'[114] Other definitions have met with even less success; and judges have fallen back despairingly on the ultimate test of inquiring whether a worker would appear to be an employee 'to the ordinary person'.[115]

Since the 1970s there has been a further challenge to the traditional foundations of the concept. Previously the arrange-ments made by the parties themselves, especially their descrip-tion of the relationship, were a very important factor. After all employment is supposed to be a consensual relation. If the parties agreed that the contract was one of 'services' not 'service', what right had the court to deny them that choice? Today, however, judges feel that this cannot always be per-mitted. The employer and the worker may collude in order to give the 'employment' relationship the colour of self-employ-ment, so that one or both of them may derive tax, national insurance, or other advantages denied to them if they adopt the ordinary contract of service. The advent of the Welfare State has introduced the complication that for certain purposes it might suit both of them to transmute employment into self-employment. Indeed sometimes the modern 'master' appears to be willing to give up the appearance of control of the job in order to retain his ultimate right to command without the obligations society has begun to demand of him as an employer. Even the company director, to whom the old learning forbade the status of an 'employee', seeks that haven for the purpose, for example, of alleging unfair dismissal.[116]

The courts are now to be found, therefore, insisting that in certain cases there is an ordinary contract of employment even where the parties said there was not. For example, where a sheet metal worker had on engagement chosen the option of working as 'self-employed' (i.e. paying his own tax, etc.) but had otherwise worked on the normal employment conditions, the court held him to be an employee. To permit the parties in this situation to determine the legal nature of the relationship, said the court, would in effect permit them 'to contract out of the Act' (on unfair dismissal).[117] When things reach this state, the juridical concepts approach anarchy. Thus the courts have decided that an oboist working for an orchestra was self-employed; an avowedly 'self-employed' television reporter was an employee under a contract of service; a sub-postmaster was self-employed, 'in reality carrying on business on his own account'; a sales representative clearly offering 'services' was an employee; the change of status of a driving instructor from employee to self-employed, effected merely by a written document, was binding and good; a labourer engaged expressly 'on the lump' (the construction industry's mode of self-employment) was an employee; while a 'self-employed' manager of an insurance company was indeed self-employed.[118] Even when legislation permits the Minister to determine whether a worker is an 'employee', the court may decide that the worker is in 'reality' self-employed, as in the case of an architect held not to be an 'employee' because he had undertaken no 'obligation to present himself for service' or 'even to provide a specific number of hours' for the association for which he worked some twenty-eight hours a week during two years, shoulder to shoulder with its other architects who clearly were employees.[119] Once again the judge preferred not to deal with 'the relevance of the intention of the parties to the contract'.[120]

The social problems arising from artificial 'self-employment' have been widely publicized, particularly since an official inquiry which was set up to investigate and report on the construction industry.[121] Although for that industry legislation now makes some attempt to deal with evasions of income tax and social security payments,[122] Parliament has generally found it difficult to intervene on this issue. There is indeed no easy solution by way of a statutory ban on self-employment which is adjudged not to be economically beneficial or 'genuine' (such as the small partnership or workers' co-operative). For 'the very idea of a distinction between artificial independent contractors and genuine independent contractors presupposes that the distinction between contracts of service and contracts for services exists as a clear concept of social organization'.[123] It may no longer sufficiently do so.

One significant legislative intervention, however, has been

the regulation of the supply of temporary workers by employment agencies.[124] These must now be licensed,[125] though
the parties are still allowed to determine whether the ultimate
contract is for 'service' or 'services' and, perhaps just as important, how far it is of a temporary nature. But—and here the
modern law advances a cautious step towards regulation—the
supplier of a temporary worker is obliged to act today as if he
were the employer in certain respects, namely, by giving the
worker a written statement of the terms of the employment and
securing that certain national insurance contributions are
paid.[126] Such statutory intervention is exceptional both in
respect of self-employment and also the various other practices
often associated with it. Thus Parliament has not thought fit to
regulate the so-called 'task' contract. This—though technically
in most cases a contract of 'employment'—terminates automatically on the performance of the task, so there can be no
dismissal and no claim for unfair dismissal or redundancy.[127]
Many short-term or casual workers are in practice deprived of
statutory employment protection.[128] Outworkers or home-
workers who often labour for a pittance are a further example of
their legally vulnerable position, especially in times of high
unemployment. The failure of much protective 'legislation to
"deem" outworkers to be employees of the employer supplying
them with work is an important gap'.[129] Such practices are of
course initiated in one way or another by employers. But
increasingly the state is financing employment schemes which
may cause analogous difficulties. The application of protective
legislation to a growing number of young and other workers on
temporary-training or job-creation schemes is a matter of great
difficulty and concern.[130]

Some forms of 'self-employment' will no doubt receive state
encouragement as a commendable form of economic activity;
but the trend towards artificial 'self-employment' and its
associated practices, devised only in the interests of parties who
wish to avoid laws about taxation, social security, welfare,
safety at work, prohibition of discrimination, and employment
protection, may now disclose such a confusion in the labour
market that more vigorous state intervention is demanded. No
doubt Kahn-Freund was right in 1951 to say that the inade-
quacies of the common law were compelling the courts to move
on from the 'control' test by reason of 'the irresistible power of

economic necessities';[131] but the concepts available to the courts now seem less than adequate to mirror, let alone shape, the changed relationships.[132]

If the Conservative government's strategy on employment continues unchanged, no major legislative interference with the workers' 'freedom' to choose to contract either as employee or as self-employed (for so it will be presented) can be expected. Indeed the Employment Act 1980 offered further incentives for the spread of artificial self-employment by giving small employers a new defence against unfair dismissal complaints by employees with less than two years' service providing the workforce does not exceed twenty 'employees'.[133]

Self-employment not only means the avoidance of legal imposts but also has another consequence which conveniently conforms with the overall strategy of 'restriction', namely great and often insuperable difficulties for the maintenance of trade union membership.[134] Paradoxically the nominal conversion of the relationship of subordinated employment into apparently autonomous 'self-employment' weakens the link between worker and worker. The employment patterns in the construction industry have consistently shown how 'the lump', administered by small firms, can obstruct the establishment or maintenance of trade union organization. And employers generally do not lack expert consultants whose advice on how to avoid a strong union regularly includes the promotion of self-employment.[135] Moreover the 1980 and 1982 Acts include provisions which can be used to put at risk industrial action intended to eradicate self-employment practices.[136] The courts meanwhile meander from case to case, upholding self-employment here, discovering a contract of employment there. To the mystification of 'contract' is now added the confusion of 'employment'. Some will perhaps say that this trend represents the great pragmatic British tradition. But for most workers it will mean only a general weakening of employment protection and of trade union organization. And it is open to question how far the forces available to autonomous trade unions can provide an answer to these fundamental problems without the aid of the state by way of legislation.

Trade Disputes

Kahn-Freund was always aware of the fragile character of the term 'trade dispute', long before disillusionment with aspects of British trade unionism developed in his last years. In 1954 he declared that the concept of trade dispute in the Trade Disputes Act 1906 rested 'on a theory of society and of politics which, even in 1906, was open to grave doubt and which today is plainly untenable. It rests on the assumption that one can separate economic from political motives and economic action from political action.'[137] Millions of workers were employed by public corporations; the level of wages depended 'in all sorts of ways' on government policies; and government was 'somehow involved' in all major industrial disputes. Perhaps in the nineteenth century it was possible to divide the sphere of the 'State' and the sphere of 'Society'; but now (in the fifties) such an attempt was 'doomed to failure'; and we ought to be aware that the foundations of the law were therefore 'shaky'.

The subsequent efforts to distinguish 'political' from 'industrial' action have hardly solved the problem. Indeed some judicial decisions suggest that the solution may often lie merely in the semantic manner in which workers put their claim. For example, where workers took industrial action by refusing to transmit television programmes to South Africa in support of an anti-apartheid campaign, the dispute was held to be a 'political dispute';[138] but it 'could readily have been turned into [a trade dispute] . . . by a demand by the union that the contracts of employment . . . should be amended to incorporate a term that they should not be obliged to take any part in the transmission' to South Africa.[139] In that event it would have contained the requirements of the definition of trade dispute: a dispute between workers and employers or workers and workers connected with 'industrial' matters as set out in the Trade Union and Labour Relations Act of 1974[140] (which were substantially the same as under the Trade Disputes Act of 1906). In a sense, therefore, all 'political' disputes have been excluded since 1906 from the 'golden formula', within which a person 'in contemplation or furtherance of a trade dispute' has immunity from specific areas of liability (certainly not all liabilities), mainly immunity from the so-called economic torts.[141]

It has been suggested that the problems inherent in protections based upon the concept of 'trade dispute' could and should be solved by transforming the legal 'immunities' bequeathed to British labour law between 1871 and 1906 into 'positive' legal rights (to associate, to bargain, to strike and lock-out, etc.). The Conservative government's inquiry into this matter in 1980 concluded that this would be a 'formidable task', not least because such rights would need 'detailed definition and limitation in legislation', especially in 'insulating a right to strike from the common law'.[142] Indeed the creation of a 'positive right to strike' is, whenever it is proposed, naturally made subject to 'reasonable limitations being created'.[143] Those limitations invoke precisely the same questions as the definition of trade dispute which draws the boundaries around the current protective immunities. Would the positive right to strike include go-slows, stoppages against government policies, or sympathetic strikes which even by 1926 had 'been the practice for over fifty years'?[144] What are to be the limits on the right to lock-out?

A change in its semantic presentation does not alter the fundamental problem. For those who insist that the conflict between workers who sell labour and those who purchase it as employers is no longer a central reality of life in the late twentieth century, the concept of trade dispute (or its equivalent 'limitation'—for there will be one—in a system of positive rights) must be even more narrowly confined. For them the law cannot for much longer provide shelter to those who are seen as irresponsible organizers of industrial stoppages in pursuit of old-fashioned, class-ridden objectives which no longer represent present-day reality. There was on occasion common ground here between the strategies of 'restriction' and of 'reform', for the latter often contained a warning note to the unions that if they did not co-operate and exercise self-restraint, more restrictive measures might have to be taken.

In 1954 Kahn-Freund believed that it would be possible to carry on with the 'shaky' legal foundations of British labour law 'for many years to come'. But by the time of his death, whilst affirming 'the need for the freedom to strike', he was upbraiding as 'senseless' what he saw as industrial action in which one group of workers damaged others in 'internecine civil war' and where the employer was perceived as the agent of the consumer or the 'instrument of the public'.[145] The tension thus created between the inability of the law to intervene effectively and the need to adjust 'collective *laissez-faire*' would have forced him, had he lived, to confront the shaky definition of 'trade dispute' anew.

Such a redefinition is an ideological as well as a pragmatic exercise.[146] Foreign systems of law which express trade union rights in positive terms clearly illustrate the point. They also show that the social, industrial, and political history of their country is reflected in their answers. Thus the Italian Constitution of 1948 guarantees 'the right to strike within the limits of laws passed to regulate it' (Art. 40). No general regulatory laws have been passed; and it is not possible to understand this constitutional law without understanding its emergence both from the years before Fascism and from the uprising of Italians—especially workers—against Fascism from 1943 onwards.[147] When the Italian Constitutional Court was faced in 1974 with the question of the legality of a 'political' strike organized against 'fascist revanchism' and in defence of 'the values of the Resistance', it looked to the Code of 1889 (which, 'inspired by principles of freedom', did not penalize political strikes), to the general practice of 'democratic social systems', to the fascist law prohibiting strikes, and to the Constitution as a whole, in deciding that strikes for political purposes (i.e. not connected with conditions of employment) could not constitutionally be penalized unless they amounted to 'subversion of the constitutional order' or obstruction of the machinery of 'popular sovereignty'.[148] By contrast, although the right to strike is recognized in the preamble to the French Constitution, juridical developments in France have left illegal the strike for 'predominantly political objects' (which is even a good reason for dismissal), even though a stoppage for a day of 'protest' is legitimate.[149] What limit would a British Constitution or 'Bill of Rights' set in the eighties?

A system of labour law needs fundamental and fixed points of reference—a defined 'right to strike' or, in the British case, an acceptable concept of 'trade dispute'. If the logical validity of such a concept is dubious, nevertheless, like God, it was and is necessary to invent it. In 1875 and 1906 the trade unions were only too willing to accept it as the basis of their immunities for the purpose of legitimacy inside the criminal and civil law. After defeat in the General Strike they could not, and had no wish to, challenge it in the 1930s. By the 1960s it was an almost hallowed touchstone for the labour movement in the face of political and judicial attack, sanctified and blessed by half a century of history. In 1971 Conservative legislation imposed severe liabilities (to be administered by a new court) in 'industrial disputes'. What was more natural for the legislation of 1974 and 1976 than to restore the traditional trade dispute as the basis of immunities (in a modern form, of course, adapted to meet the innovations of the judges' expansion of liabilities for economic torts), taking the law 'back to what Parliament had intended when it enacted the Act of 1906—but stronger and clearer than it was then'?[150] Only thereafter did the next government make inroads into the traditional immunities. In 1980 it restricted the effectiveness of the 'trade dispute' protection and challenged the legality of 'secondary' action;[151] and in 1982 it mounted a direct assault upon trade disputes and upon trade unions, whose funds it wished to lay open to injunctions and damages for the first time since 1906.[152]

The Conservative programme for the eighties is indeed more restrictive than is generally understood. In 1958 the Conservative barristers' society (then a prestigious group) produced a report on trade unions which was widely thought at the time and long afterwards to be a particularly retrogressive document. It declared: 'The power to strike sympathetically is politically, socially and economically justified *if, without it, employees will have insufficient bargaining power*; but not otherwise.' On that test, concluded the authors, sympathetic strikes should not be (as they normally were) lawful because 'in conditions of full employment and a delicately balanced economy' they were 'almost certainly unnecessary'.[153] Twenty-four years later their successors in the Conservative government were commended by the media as 'moderates' when they had done their best to outlaw sympathetic action at the very time that mounting unemployment was striking at the jugular vein of workers' bargaining power.

The historical wheel has turned even though the formal structure of the 'immunities' continues. The 'reform' policy has been abandoned. The contrived concept which emerged from the battles in the thirty years after 1871 as an acceptable if intellectually 'shaky' foundation for a system of labour law is now a natural target for redefinition in a society where consensus is notably less manifest. In fact that area of consensus which emerged from social struggle rested upon the 'British solution of the common problem of illegality of trade unions'.[154] It was imposed in the 1920s and 1930s; it was in part imposed but in part desired on both sides during the world wars; and it was grudgingly accepted by the middle class in the 1950s until their patience ran out at the upstart strength of organized workpeople a decade later.[155] By the early 1980s the attack on the concept of 'trade dispute' was in full swing.

The debate in 1981 about the redefinition of the concept of 'trade dispute' was presented by the government and the media as though its object was to prevent improper 'political' disputes, when even on the most conventional definition such disputes have been rare in Britain compared with many continental countries. In its *Proposals for Industrial Relations Legislation* of November 1981, the government not only proposed that disputes must relate 'wholly or mainly' to 'industrial' matters, must exclude disputes between workers and workers, must not relate solely to matters abroad, and must be restricted to disputes between an employer and his own employees (all part of a policy rendering effective industrial action unlawful), but also made it very clear that a primary objective was to outlaw disputes 'mainly political or personal in character'.[156] This presentation did not lack method. In a situation where government strategy towards the economy and industrial relations aimed to weaken the effectiveness of trade union action and (ostensibly) to promote more competition in the market, trade union and worker opposition to restrictive state intervention could be undermined by the apparent reaffirmation of a basic principle of the old labour law, the distinction between lawful 'industrial' and unlawful 'political' action.

In such an environment, cases of potentially unlawful political action by trade unions become ever more numerous. In response, for example, to the Conservative government's (later postponed) plan in 1981 to privatize the showrooms of British Gas, union leaders in the gas and also the electricity and water industries threatened strike action, and local government workers planned action in support. At the TUC Congress in September 1981 a motion pledging support for such action was passed, and a revived triple alliance of railwaymen, steel workers, and miners took the occasion to declare that they would take joint industrial action to stop 'privatisation' in their sectors.[157] 'The only power now left to defend these public assets', declared John Edmonds of the GMWU, 'is the organised power of the trade unions.'[158] The point would no doubt occupy hours of lawyers' argument, but it would not be surprising if the courts pronounced some such strikes to be 'political' (concerned with government policy)[159] rather than 'trade disputes'.

The threat of 'political' action by trade unions was also a subject of concern in the closing weeks of 1981. One law professor devoted his Christmas Eve to a letter to *The Times* protesting that he had that very day read in its columns not of one but of two threats of political strike action aimed 'against the operation of the law in our society'.[160] They were the TUC's 'consideration' of industrial action against the government proposals on labour law, and reports of transport union plans to strike in protest at the House of Lords decision outlawing the GLC's cheap fares policy.[161]

The response to industrial action in the public sector too was rapidly becoming harsher and with similar overtones. A special study group in the Lord Chancellor's department initiated the prosecution of an official of the inland revenue union in the civil service pay dispute for the crime of 'persistently following' a tax collector who was carrying 'blacked' cheques, thereby activating a somnolent provision of an Act of 1875 which applies whether there is a trade dispute or not.[162] The civil service attitude to another central area of state concern was evidenced the very next day when the Ministry of Defence called for 'no-strike clauses' to be inserted in their civil servants' conditions of service so that 'key defence areas are effectively protected from industrial action'. This policy had been recommended in the 1981 Green Paper in cases where 'the national interest' was at stake.[163]

But the new labour law policy of the early eighties was also alert to a different danger. In 1979 the House of Lords had affirmed that a 'connection' with industrial matters was all that the law required (and all that section 29 of TULRA 1974—and the 1906 Act before it—stated) for a person engaged in a trade dispute to fall within the ambit of the protective immunities. Lord Diplock rammed home the message that the connection still qualified the dispute as a trade dispute even if 'the predominant object were to bring down the fabric of the present economic system by raising wages to unrealistic levels'. These remarks were seen by some as 'thinly disguised justifications for changing the law, if not an invitation to the government to propose changes'.[164] The warning (not the only one delivered by the Law Lords in this period)[165] was not lost on the government. Having heeded the call to narrow the ambit of immunities for sympathetic action in 1980, thereby effectively destroying the right of action in disputes between 'workers and workers',[166] it was ready by 1981 to squeeze the golden formula yet further by not just requiring *a* 'connection' (or even a 'substantial' or 'real' connection) but by insisting on the 'main' connection with the 'industrial' content of the stoppage. Such a test allows wider scope to the employer (and even third parties such as his customers or suppliers) to edge the content of the dispute outside the boundaries of the immunities, and of course it gives much greater discretion to the judges in deciding whether a dispute has that 'main' connection which will be needed to qualify it as a trade dispute. This applies, for example, to disputes connected with redundancy. So far the decisions of the courts have varied on the question of how 'real' or 'objective' fears of redundancy must be before a dispute— like the gas showrooms case, for example—qualifies as a trade dispute.[167] The Conservative government's Employment Act 1982 points the way out of that difficulty.[168]

This pathway to attack the immunities has of course been travelled before, but not so hopefully since 1906. For example, judicial statements were made in the middle of the General Strike of 1926 to the effect that it was 'unlawful' because, if it was a dispute between the TUC and the government about 'political' matters, it had—so it was said—neither the right parties nor the right connection for a 'trade dispute' (this view of the facts was convincingly shown to be wrong by an academic lawyer with no pronounced radical leanings).[169] However, the then Conservative government resisted pressure upon it from employers' organizations to remove the immunities and end the 'privileged legal position' of the unions.[170]

How far the restriction policy could go in the eighties can be measured further by the provisions of the 1982 Employment Act concerning industrial action connected with the refusal of trade unionists to work with non-unionists. The new law removes, as we have seen, the immunities from the widest range of activity which might be used to uphold requirements that work must be performed by trade union members (either generally or of a particular union).[171] Such 'union-only' terms in commercial contracts become void. Failure to include an employer in a list for tenders or suppliers 'on the ground of union membership', or to end a contract (however lawfully in other respects) or to refuse to make a contract for that reason, is unlawful and permits any person 'adversely affected' to sue for damages or an injunction. In fact the 'union-only' reason need be 'only one of the grounds' on which action is taken. Industrial action which attempts to induce someone to take any such action is stripped of the immunities. So too is industrial action where interference with the supply of goods and services (whether or not under contract) is reasonably to be expected and where one of the reasons is that the work is being done by non-unionists.[172]

The restriction policy is here being applied in its most explicit form, in order to free the labour market from trade union 'obstruction'. Although the government did acknowledge that 'it has to be accepted that it is not possible to eradicate "union-only" practices simply by changes in the law',[173] the implications of these new legal provisions are clear. At a time of large-scale unemployment, falling union membership, and weakened union strength, it will become illegal to refuse to work alongside those who are willing, in their desperation for jobs, to be employed on an employer's unilateral conditions which undercut the rates negotiated by the union (or in construction, for example, 'on the lump'). The crisis in the law of trade disputes intersects here with the crisis which besets the contract of employment,[174] bringing with it echoes of the old illegality for combinations which dared to aspire to improve on 'regulated wages' fixed by employers sitting as Justices of the Peace.[175]

One other development in labour law fits the pattern of increasing restriction. Consideration had to be given to the possibility of industrial action by some of the three million unemployed. True some trade unions would find it difficult to organize them: of the forty-four unions in the largest fifty who in 1981 were permitted by rule to retain unemployed members, twenty-four were found to have rules prohibiting them from actually recruiting the unemployed.[176] In fact labour law policy in the eighties has moved clearly towards restriction of the rights of the unemployed. Adjustments in 1980 in social security law have impoverished their position when engaged on industrial action during which they are sacked; the 1982 Employment Act gives the employer increased power to sack them selectively; and under the 1980 Employment Act the right to picket by a worker 'not in employment' is permitted only at his 'former place of work' where his 'last employment was terminated in connection with a trade dispute', a formula replete with sufficient difficulties to exclude most sacked workers.[177] As we have seen, a 'trade dispute' will in future be more difficult to prove; and the 1982 legislation, by restricting trade disputes to disputes between an employer and only his own 'employees', may immediately indicate a safe escape route to the employer; so much so that the government's proposals plaintively said that it would be 'necessary' to ensure that he could not abort a legitimate trade dispute 'simply by sacking those with whom he was in dispute'—and presumably those with whom he was about to be in dispute.[178] The attempt in the legislation to deal with this point does not provide any marked protection for the worker. He is permitted a trade dispute with his ex-employer only when his employment was 'terminated in connection with the dispute' or when that termination was one of the 'circumstances giving rise to it'.[179] The well-advised employer is likely to sack the ringleaders of impending trouble long enough before the actual dispute to make it difficult to prove that 'connection' or those 'circumstances'. In this legislation the amendments on trade disputes take their natural place in a policy justly described as 'punishing the unemployed'.[180]

By restricting its ambit and, in particular, by insisting that it must not cover any type of 'political' dispute, Conservative government policy in the eighties has confirmed the continuing unreality of the concept of 'trade dispute' and simultaneously adapted the concept to its own political ends. It may be said, not without foundation, that the latter is what 'reform' policies of various kinds have been doing since 1906. By the eighties, though, the boundary between the 'industrial' and the 'political' had been made even more 'shaky' by the process of state intervention in social and economic activity (even under a government pledged to privatize.) Indeed many people argue, as did Kahn-Freund in his last lecture,[181] that the increasing interdependence between different sectors of the economy means that many industries and services are 'essential' and that in such a situation the government 'is equally involved as a target of industrial action' and 'cannot stand by seeing the

public deprived of them'.[182] It is therefore not unlikely that the
state may resort in future to direct intervention against the
liberty to withdraw labour in 'essential' services of some
category; the indications are that such measures await only a
solution to the 'very great difficulties in making strikes by key
groups of workers illegal'.[183] The obstacle is inexpediency, not
principle.

The overall logic of the policy of restriction in this area of
labour law, clearly confirmed by the legislation of 1982,[184] is to
undermine further what is left of the fragile golden formula of
'trade dispute' itself, thus challenging the very right to strike.
For those, however, who foresee successful resistance to this
onslaught, another fundamental question arises. If the policy of
restriction is defeated, what is to take its place? Should the
limitations on the right to strike and the right to lock-out be the
same (as they are not in every legal system)? What should be
the equivalent to the boundary now drawn by the concept of
'trade dispute'? For every system of labour law must have one.
Should it be co-terminous only with the legal boundary which
guarantees the primacy of 'popular sovereignty', as in Italy?[185]
That might be a less 'shaky' foundation on which to build the
freedom to take industrial action in the future. After all, much of
the 'industrial action' permitted to owners and controllers of
capital is already inhibited only by that frontier.

Some Unresolved Problems of 'Reform'

The policies of 'reform' since the sixties have raised very
directly the question of how far the state should introduce 'a
greater use of legal sanction' in the handling of industrial
disputes; and they have exposed the need to choose between 'an
uncertain experiment of that kind', and 'new initiatives . . .
within the pattern of negotiated procedures, voluntary arbitration and public inquiry, where legal sanction and lawyers make
their greatest contribution to industrial life by being self-
effacing rather than obtrusive'.[186] In this section we aim to
discuss some of the unresolved problems of labour law reform,
examining in particular the introduction of industrial tribunals
and the legislation of the Social Contract period. Like all other
areas of labour law, however, these problems have in part

reflected the special relationship between the judiciary and the trade unions, and we therefore begin with the role of judiciary in labour law.

The Judiciary and Labour Law

The story has been sufficiently told for it to be established that this relationship can be understood only in the framework of a class analysis. Not only did the judges in the nineteenth century reflect the attitudes to trade unions of the 'middle class',[187] the judgments on labour law by their counterparts of the 1960s also gave 'the impression that the repressive tendencies of the courts, which in the 19th and early 20th centuries had to be repeatedly counteracted by Parliament, are on the point of being revived'.[188] Few students of labour law were shocked, as others seemed to be, by Professor Griffith's reminder that 'judges are the product of a class and have the characteristics of that class'; they are 'not the stuff of which reformers are made, still less radicals'; they are likely to insist that 'stability above all is necessary for the health of the people and is the supreme law'.[189] Moreover English judgments are personal judgments; workers' antagonism to 'the law' can be expressed against a person—'Bramwell', 'Lindley', or 'Denning'. And after all, Griffith was only developing the theme which Lord Justice Scrutton (a powerful conservative lawyer) expressed in 1920:

The habits you are trained in, the people with whom you mix, lead to your having a certain class of ideas of such a nature that, when you have to deal with other ideas, you do not give as sound and accurate judgments as you would wish. . . . Labour says 'Where are your impartial Judges?'. . . it is very difficult sometimes to be sure that you have put yourself into a thoroughly impartial position between two disputants one of your own class and one not of your class.[190]

Although senior judges have sometimes been accepted, perhaps surprisingly readily, as investigators of industrial disputes (in Courts of Inquiry, for example),[191] the traditional hostility of the working class to the judiciary has in fact been soundly based. The repressive judgments of the nineteenth century were matched for the most part in the twentieth by 'startling innovations in trade union law' and the generally negative attitudes of the judges towards strikes, so that in 1969 'even as the print dried, whole passages in the Donovan Report itself were obsolescent in the face of them'.[192] This is indeed a problem for any reform strategy. One independent member of the Donovan Commission (Mr Wigham) confessed that 'all through the deliberations' what worried him was, even if the Commission made the 'right' recommendations and the government enacted them, 'how long would it be before the judges turned everything upside down?' The labour movement's response to the judiciary and indeed to lawyers has therefore remained basically unchanged. British trade unions and British industrial relations as a whole have traditionally recognized only rarely 'legal' methods and reasoning (such as the formal distinction between 'rights' and 'interests'). Even when in 1968 the TUC accepted the proposal for an extension of the jurisdiction of industrial tribunals, the General Council declared that it did 'not consider that there is a conclusive case for all chairmen to be legally qualified' because of the need to emphasize 'informality of procedure and the adoption of a conciliatory approach'.[193] We shall see later that this proposal to reject legal chairmen did not succeed;[194] but it illustrates the fact that hostility to judges is based not only upon the perceived oppression of trade unions by the courts, but on a rejection of the methods of thinking employed by lawyers—which in turn often causes the latter to accuse trade unions of attacking the 'rule of law'.

The reason, however, for the special place of the judges in labour law goes much deeper. British labour law did not acquire immunities as its base for the liberty of collective trade union action by choice of the judges but by reason of the special circumstances under which Parliament conceded legality to trade unions in the decades before 1906. It achieved that result not by granting rights (as in many comparable countries) but by the creation of the now famous immunities to protect trade unions from the illegalities that stemmed from the common law.[195] 'In substance, behind the form, the statute provides liberties or rights which the common law would deny to unions. The "immunity" is mere form.'[196] The protections established for trade unions in trade disputes did not therefore mean, as has been alleged, that 'the trade union and its members of today occupy a privileged position under the law', or enjoy 'special legal protection'.[197] Indeed by 1981 even the Conservative government appeared to have appreciated the truism that 'the immunities are not simply legal privileges. . . . without some legal protection—however circumscribed—it would be impossible for trade unions or individuals to organize industrial action' lawfully; and because of the common law liabilities, a lawful 'withdrawal of labour would be effectively nullified'.[198]

It remains doubtful, however—and this was and is the special difficulty for the policies of 'reform'—whether many judges have yet learned that simple historical truth about the labour law which they administer in the courts. Even in the eighties they usually seem as blind as the judges of 1900 to the character of the old dialectical interplay between legislation and judicial innovation in the common law. Time and again they display the attitude summed up with characteristic clarity by Lord Denning: 'when Parliament granted immunities to the leaders of trade unions, it did not give them any *rights*. It did not give them a *right* to break the law or to do wrong by inducing people to break contracts.'[199] The parliamentary statute is seen here as an intruder invading the domain of 'the law'—a law which is in fact the common law created by judges; which in this case (the 'wrong' of inducing breach of contract) was invented by them in 1853; which was regarded as 'bad law' by judges including Lord Chancellor Loreburn even as late as 1906; and which in some comparable countries (such as Sweden) does not exist at all. It is only if one appreciates this judicial attitude (not confined to labour law, but particularly significant in its effect on that field) that one can begin to understand how it is possible for present-day members of the judiciary to debate, as they did in 1981 and 1982, whether, when Parliament declared in 1974 that acts done in furtherance of a trade dispute should not be 'actionable in tort' under common law doctrines, Parliament also meant that those acts should remain inherently 'unlawful' in that same common law of tort.[200]

Certainly judges do not seem aware that political actions and demonstrations have been a normal and necessary part of the pressure needed to obtain democratic reforms or to defend the fundamental rights of workers (just as it was in the case of women's political rights), from Peterloo in 1819 to demonstrations against the Industrial Relations Bill in 1971.[201] But trade unionists themselves cannot have failed to recognize the significance of the judges' willingness to accord a 'right to demonstrate'[202] to other groups while undermining the right of workers to picket peacefully, defining it by reference to the rights of a hitch-hiker[203] (an approach which Kahn-Freund, in his later attitude to picketing, rather surprisingly saw as 'obvious'.)[204]

Without doubt the judges have the power—and today are clearly conscious of it—to narrow or expand common law liabilities and the 'immunities'. In the 1920s, in the shadow of the Great War, some judges like Lord Justice Scrutton stayed their hand from further developments in case law which would once again have rendered trade union activity unlawful.[205] But for a century the dominant note has been that of Lord Lindley—'You cannot make a strike effective without doing more than is lawful'[206]—and the imposition by the judiciary of new liabilities upon trade unions. Just such a manipulation of the little-known tort of conspiracy in 1901 caused one commentator to say that the judges 'first invented a new civil offence and . . . then created a new kind of defendant against whom it could be alleged'.[207]

Certainly the hostile judicial attitude was rampant in the 1960s, when self-doubt seemed to be quite forgotten in a series of judgments which once again drove the common law by way of 'judicial creativity' around the flanks of statutory immunities. The House of Lords went so far as to render part of a section of the Trade Disputes Act 1906 'nugatory' or 'pointless' when it seemed to protect trade union defendants. That part, said Lord Reid, was inserted by Parliment as *necessary* 'to achieve their object if the law' (i.e. the common law, of which he was master) 'should go one way but *unnecessary* if it should go the other away' (which was the way he took it).[208] This was but one of a number of creative judgments[209] which in the sixties revived for the trade union movement the consciousness of judicial hostility more sharply than in the decades immediately preceding them. In the 1930s, notable for extensive judicial 'creativity' in other areas of the common law (such as the law of negligence), there was no call for expansion of the common law liabilities for it was unnecessary against the weakened trade unions. And most of the exceptional judgments (favourable to unions) in the first fifty years of the century turn out on examination to illustrate the point that a narrowing of liabilities occurred only if it was in the joint interests of the employers and the established union, or in the interests of the war effort, or both.[210]

In the most recent developments following a period of characteristically repressive judgments by the Court of Appeal,[211] the Law Lords in 1979 and 1980 appeared at first sight to have played the opposite of their traditional role. In the now famous 'new trilogy' of cases they in fact reaffirmed the proper ambit of protection for the immunities and the meaning of 'furtherance' of a trade dispute, thereby re-establishing the legality of sympathetic and other industrial action.[212] But this apparent liberalization of judicial attitudes was itself expressly rejected by the very words used in most of the judgments. The same trade dispute immunities that were now reaffirmed, Lord Diplock said, 'have tended to stick in judicial gorges', and were 'intrinsically repugnant to anyone who has spent his life in the practice of the law or the administration of justice'—giving to trade unions 'a power, which has no other limits than their own self-interest, to inflict by means which are contrary to the general law, untold harm to industrial enterprises unconcerned with the particular dispute, to the employees of such enterprises, to members of the public, to the nation itself . . .'.[213] Lords Edmund-Davies, Wilberforce, and Keith took a similarly forthright view. Lord Salmon was not alone in his cry: 'If this is the law, surely the time has come for it to be altered.'[214] That was the message, whatever the decision, in these cases.

At precisely this time Parliament was at an advanced stage of its deliberations on the 1980 Employment Act and, in particular, was presented with a most important new clause which sought to outlaw solidarity or sympathetic action (now dubbed 'secondary action'). Some Law Lords may well have 'concluded that it would be wiser to leave such highly contentious political matters to the professional politicians'; but others, in the majority, 'did not hesitate to push the Conservative government in what they saw as the right direction'.[215] There can be no doubt that it was not policy which divided the majority of the Law Lords from Lord Denning MR and the Court of Appeal. They all patently agreed that trade union 'muscle' should be weakened. The only difference was about the right method of achieving it. Similarly, when the Law Lords applied the novel and rather dubious doctrine of 'economic duress' to trade unions for the first time in 1982, the majority differed only in marginal ways from the minority. None of them saw, as judges had elsewhere (for example, in Canada), that such vague doctrines of the common law should not be applied at all to collective bargaining and industrial conflict.[216]

Indeed with less than a handful of exceptions English judges—certainly the Law Lords—have not during two centuries delivered any judgments encouraging the spread of trade unionism and thereby of collective bargaining.[217] Only in one or two cases could they be said to be within reach of understanding the 'class of ideas' (to use Scrutton's phrase) which is inherent in trade unionism. It is more natural for them to see statutes which oblige employers to bargain with unions as interventions in the individual employment relationship, which deprive the individual of control of his employment contract and which therefore must be construed strictly, as in 'the case of compulsory purchase powers'.[218] They have not yet learnt that the employment contract is inherently a relationship of subordination, a thesis that Kahn-Freund understandably never renounced. Without that understanding their instinct is to apply an inadequate individualist philosophy to the collective class realities of large areas of industrial relations. Indeed their ready instinct to treat persons or companies as innocent parties 'unconcerned with the trade dispute' contrasts even with the approach of an expert committee of the Confederation of British Industry, which criticized British employers for not appreciating their common interest with other companies under attack by a trade union and for taking 'commercial advantage of the plight of others'; they should not 'poach labour' from them or, even as competitors, fill 'gaps created in a market'.[219] And even as the auxiliary laws of 1975 dragged their way into 1982, the judges displayed their consistency by interpreting the union's right to information from the employer in the narrowest possible manner.[220]

Despite his idiosyncratic language, Lord Denning was being true to the judicial tradition when he began some of his judgments in the 1970s (concerned with individuals who were members of a breakaway union confronting a recognized trade union): 'This case reminds me of the story of David and Goliath, with a difference. Goliath is winning all along the line.'[221] And yet again in 1979: 'This is another story of David and Goliath.'[222]

Such judicial attitudes will not die away, as the Donovan Commission had hoped, by providing lawyers (through the

Bar, the Law Society, and the universities) with 'at least an elementary knowledge of industrial relations'.[223] That part of the policy of reform assumed too great a power in the sector of 'education' to combat attitudes inculcated daily by their social background and everyday culture into the élite caste from which judges in England are drawn.[224] Without a massive intellectual effort the English judge is by upbringing a natural ally of those who wish to apply the law in trade disputes restrictively to the rights of organized workers. It is also doubtful, as Griffith remarks, whether an increase in the number of judges who have been to grammar or comprehensive schools and graduated at redbrick or new universities would produce a less conservative judiciary. 'The years in practice and middle aged affluence would remove any aberration in political outlook, if this were necessary. Also, if those changes did not take place, there would be no possibility of their being appointed by the Lord Chancellor, on the advice of the senior judiciary, to the bench.'[225]

Kahn-Freund himself, though, however sensitive he was to the *damnosa hereditas* of caste and craft divisions in British society in general and in the legal profession in particular, hoped that there would be 'a new generation of lawyers' entrusted with the 'supremely important role which lawyers and courts' might play 'in the vitally necessary reform of the system of industrial relations and the code of conditions of employment'; lawyers 'taught to take an interest in the living law', and not 'carefully insulated from any knowledge of the facts of industrial life'.[226] It must be admitted that this programme of lawyer reform has not been put to the test. The ranks of senior barristers are not swollen with enlightened labour lawyers; nor, as Griffith predicts, is the bench of the eighties likely to see many such appointed to it as judges. Moreover the labour lawyer, along with his colleagues in administrative law, knows how often he has to give a negative response to the question: 'Can we keep the courts out of it?' Even if there is no provision for appeal to the courts, the matter will be entertained by the High Court almost whenever desired, either by way of 'judicial review' or through the remedy of a 'declaration'—and English law is, as Kahn-Freund insisted, above all a system of remedies. Nor has it always been the apparent object, even of 'reform' legislation, to restrict the jurisdiction of the judges in trade union matters. For example, the Registrar's decisions on complaints about the political fund, one area where administrative decisions worked effectively for more than sixty years and were 'conclusive and binding on all parties . . . not removable into any court of law', were replaced in the legislation of 1975 by an appeal to the new 'tripartite' Employment Appeal Tribunal.[227]

The policy of 'reform' has never found an answer to the problem of the judiciary or of the legal profession with which it is enmeshed. There is an inherent contradiction in its wish to retain the intrinsic voluntary character of collective labour law (repeatedly damaged by decisions of uncomprehending, even hostile, judges) and its desire to create a modernized 'code of conditions of employment' and to place it in the hands of 'a new generation of lawyers'—a generation which has remained little more than an aspiration. Worse, English judges were and are able and likely to discover in the ambiguities of 'reform' those elements which, when applied by them, most resemble the policy of restriction.

On the other hand it must be asked whether an alternative approach, such as the overt recognition by the judges of class interests in industrial life, might lead not only to decisions just as hostile to trade unions but also to an increase in the 'judicial-ization' of issues which should belong to the autonomous inter-play of social forces. In other countries some judges, in pursuit of a 'civilized way of reducing conflict-proneness' in society, have advocated an increase in 'the justiciability of class or group interests', a development in the judicial process which has been described as: '[a] disquieting revolutionary platform and—*labour law possibly excepted*—a sound reformist practice'.[228] Even in that situation the exception constituted by labour law is a critical proviso. The judiciary in fact represent institutionally one of the most intransigent problems for any labour law policy based upon the promotion of strong and independent trade unionism. At best 'judges are capable of moving with the times, of adjusting to changed circumstances. But their function in our society is to do so belatedly.'[229] At worst they can frustrate any legislative programme for industrial relations. That is unlikely to change in the eighties.

Industrial Tribunals and Civil Service Policies

In 1931 Kahn-Freund thought it 'the tendency of all civil

service bureaucracies to de-politicise and de-revolutionise the collective social forces', and 'characteristic of the civil service bureaucracy' to see 'conflict as something abnormal', as a disturbance of the regulated flow of social events'.[230] In post-war Britain just such a tendency of the civil service appears to have been instrumental in the creation of 'legal' tribunals through which increasingly large areas of industrial disputes could be processed and contained. Such a policy has been undoubtedly conceived as an attempt to institutionalize areas of conflict in employment by judicializing what would (in the absence of grievance arbitration or other similar third-party intervention) otherwise lead to an extension of combat on the economic and industrial front. Such a policy has also been understood at times as a 'liberal' attempt to prevent the renewal of hostility between the ordinary High Court and the trade unions, between whom contact was 'not good for trade unions' and 'not good for the courts'.[231]

At the centre of this policy lay the creation and expansion of the system of industrial tribunals, bodies with legal chairmen appointed by the Lord Chancellor and two 'wingpersons' chosen from panels appointed by the Minister of Labour (now Secretary of State for Employment) after consultation with organizations of employers and of employees (in practice the CBI and the TUC). Today they sit in some 80 centres; in recent years they have received some 40,000 applications a year; in 1979, the year of Kahn-Freund's death, the median compensation awarded by them, in the successful 27 per cent of 11,705 employees whose complaints of unfair dismissal they determined, was £401.[232]

Yet the origin of these important new institutions is shrouded in silence, if not in mystery. They were created under the Industrial Training Act 1964 to hear appeals not by workers but by employers who wished to complain about the training levy imposed upon them; their birth was delayed until 31 May 1965 when the necessary orders were promulgated;[233] and the only public argument about their original form seems to have been between the Ministry of Labour (which wanted to appoint them *ad hoc* in each region) and the Council on Tribunals (which demanded a standing tribunal in each region)[234]—a demand gladly accepted by the Ministry which responded by setting up a national system with a President for England and

Wales and for Scotland. This system, it was thought, would offer 'flexibility' as well as accessibility of the tribunals to applicants, and also the development of 'consistent methods and decisions'.[235]

In precisely this period of the 1960s a related debate was settled—whether redundancy and other forms of dismissal should continue to be dealt with mainly by voluntary methods (the law adding little to the matter except a demand for adequate notice according to the employment contract).[236] It is notable that in 1964 a joint statement of intent by government, TUC, and employers supported government proposals for earnings-related unemployment benefit and for 'severance [i.e. redundancy] payments'; but the latter occupied a very minor place in public discussion and was rejected by many as giving 'priority to the wrong measure'.[237] In other words redundancy was widely regarded at that time as a matter not for laws but for improved negotiated schemes.[238] Yet by the end of 1965 the Redundancy Payments Act had introduced statutory redundancy payments, and the work of deciding disputes was given to the tribunals, together with disputes about the 'written particulars' which the 1963 Contracts of Employment Act required employers to provide,[239] and later in 1966 disputes about 'selective employment tax' (again complaints by employers) and about the nature of 'dock work'.

A similar, apparently *ad hoc*, pattern is to be discovered in the history of the law of 'unfair dismissal'. This is now so much taken for granted as a natural part of the 'floor of rights' in employment protection that it is often forgotten that there was little trade union pressure for such laws in the 1960s.[240] In 1967 the National Joint Advisory Council (composed of members from the TUC, the CBI, nationalized industries, and the Ministry of Labour) concluded that there were 'strong arguments against the introduction of statutory machinery' (e.g. that it would lessen the incentive to develop, and even undermine, existing voluntary procedures); and that until further review 'the immediate programme' should concentrate on 'voluntary negotiated agreements'.[241] But the 'review' came more quickly than expected. Only two years later in 1969 the Labour government declared the absence of legal safeguards against arbitrary or unfair dismissal to be an 'anomaly'; to end it they proposed legislation to give employees so dismissed a right to complain 'to the present Industrial Tribunals which will have to be extended and equipped to deal with this additional role'.[242] This jurisdiction over unfair dismissals (together with other more controversial powers relating *inter alia* to the rights to join and not to join a trade union, and to the supervision of trade union relations with members) was eventually added by the Industrial Relations Act 1971. A decade later the tribunals were hearing complaints about redundancy, unfair dismissal, itemized pay statements, guarantee payments, employer's action short of dismissal, rights to time off, maternity rights, sex and race discrimination, equal pay, health and safety notices, safety representatives' rights, questions relating to occupational pension schemes, and (after 1980) exclusion or expulsion from trade unions[243]—a wide range of statutory rights mainly across the spectrum of individual employment protection law. With the gradual extension of employment protection laws between 1971 and 1981 the tribunals came to be seen as the obvious forum in which to hear complaints mainly, though not exclusively, brought by employees.

With hindsight it is possible to see the importance of the civil service thinking in this line of development. In 1964 no political party, no employers' organization, no trade union made a central demand for new labour courts. But having established them in embryonic form in the 1964 legislation, the Ministry of Labour in its *Evidence* to the Donovan Commission wrote in 1965 of the tribunals: 'The nucleus of a system of labour courts exists potentially in these tribunals which are to deal with disputes under the Redundancy Payments Act.' If 'all disputes between an individual worker and his employer' were transferred to them, the advantages would include 'ease of access, quickness, informality and cheapness'; their composition would be 'adapted to suit the work', introducing members with industrial knowledge and 'corresponding flexibility of approach', with the incorporation of conciliation in informal procedures. Should the tribunals not deal with 'all disputes between the individual worker and his employer'? Jurisdiction could also be extended, it was added significantly, to disputes between trade unions and members if that relation 'were to be regulated more closely by law'.[244]

The Minister of Labour, Mr Gunter, in introducing the

Redundancy Payments Bill, also declared in 1965 that he 'would not rule out the possibility that as the tribunals became more established and gained experience further functions relating to industrial relations might be given them . . . [for] they will constitute a valuable experiment in our industrial relations system'.[245] He was clearly speaking not to a party, but to a departmental brief. The Donovan Commission agreed, not least through the influence of Kahn-Freund himself, devoting a whole chapter to 'Labour Tribunals'. These were desirable, it said, in order to improve the adjudication of disputes concerning employees' contractual or statutory rights against the employer; the Ministry of Labour was right, all such disputes should fall within the tribunals' jurisdiction to make available (for the resolution of such disputes) 'a procedure which is easily accessible, informal, speedy and inexpensive' and with the best possible opportunities for 'amicable settlement'. But the tribunals should not deal with collective disputes, or with disputes between unions and members, or with disputes about strikes or accidents at work.[246]

It was clear even by the end of the 1960s that the tribunals had in practice 'become maids of all work' and that, in the debates about legislation on redundancy, 'scant attention was paid to the procedural question of where disputes should go'. This was at least in part because those who criticized the High Court for its ignorance of industrial relations 'were only too ready to turn to the easy answer of a tripartite tribunal. . . . There was little hard-headed debate—at least in public outside the Ministry.'[247] It is sometimes said that the existence and nature of the tribunals reflect traditional working-class 'hostility to the ordinary courts'.[248] But while that antagonism has certainly persisted, even the proposals for new legislation that had begun to come by 1968 from the trade union side did not include any central demand for the extension of the jurisdiction of the tribunals.[249]

Few civil servants can have experienced so little opposition to a policy of such importance to the legal system. By 1969 a government White Paper asserted vigorously that the tribunals had 'proved their worth as quick and satisfactory machinery', not least because 'the presence of employer and employee members' had proved 'extremely helpful';[250] and it gladly accepted the recommendation of the Donovan Commission

that their jurisdiction should be extended (though research on
how they were operating in reality was negligible at the
time).[251] The influential position of the industrial tribunals in
'individual' employment law today[252] represents a massive
victory for civil service policy, even to the extent after the 1980
Employment Act of including within their jurisdiction (contrary to the Donovan prescription) complaints against trade
unions by those 'unreasonably' excluded or expelled—a feature
which has been said to put the 'neutrality of the tribunals . . . in
jeopardy'.[253]

So far legislation has attempted, to a great extent successfully, to draw a line between 'individual' and 'collective' labour
law for the tribunals, even if the boundary is somewhat uncertain at times. For example, the tribunals were given no
jurisdiction where all the strikers were dismissed by their
employer; for to say otherwise would put them inevitably into
the position of determining the reasonableness and merits of the
strike, a 'collective' issue not justiciable in a system of voluntary
collective bargaining. So too, for parallel reasons, they were
charged to decide on the 'reasonableness' or 'fairness' of a
dismissal without reference to the pressure put upon the
employer by way of industrial action.[254] But some of the rights
enforceable in the tribunal, such as the right to time off for
union duties for officials, or the right not to be penalized for
trade union activity, are clearly in reality of even greater
'collective' than 'individual' importance.[255] And then the 1980
Act permitted the employer, when sued by an employee dismissed by reason of non-membership of a union, to 'join' in
dismissal cases those (i.e. the union, or its officials, or members)
who pressurized him into dismissal by industrial action. In such
cases the tribunal must apportion a contribution of the compensation according to what 'is just and equitable'.[256] The 1982
legislation went further, allowing the dismissed employee to sue
the union, official, or member guilty of such pressure and to
recover compensation from them direct—a logical but, as we
shall see later, profoundly important step.[257] And even in the
original employment protection laws, the various provisions on
unfair dismissal, guarantee payments, and redundancy (which
tried to provide for the 'primacy' of voluntary collective
bargaining by allowing the parties to contract out of the
statutory provisions if the Minister by Order gave approval) are

of academic rather than practical interest, for few such agreements or Orders have been effected other than on guarantee payments; and the Minister's approval will normally require the parties to submit disputes to a third party, often to an industrial tribunal.[258]

It has been questioned whether the conceptual line or frontier between 'individual' and 'collective' labour law—like the concept of trade dispute or even of the contract of employment itself[259]—can always be maintained in the face of the trend towards legal regulation of the British system.[260] But it was the very crossing of that boundary which was historically one of the main causes of the strong opposition of British trade unions to the Industrial Relations Act 1971. That Act put into the hands of a superior new tripartite court, the National Industrial Relations Court (or NIRC) chaired by a judge, the enforcement of the new regulated system of 'collective' labour relations of which the unions would have no part. The industrial tribunals became 'the lower level of the Industrial Court' (NIRC);[261] indeed the tribunals had the power, and could be compelled, to transfer cases up to the NIRC.[262] The NIRC was both a court of appeal from the tribunals and a court of original jurisdiction in what were mainly 'collective' issues. The TUC made no extended analysis of such matters; but it had already registered some disquiet both about labour courts dealing with trade union issues and about the need to maintain an informal atmosphere conducive to conciliation (which, it thought, meant that there was no need for lawyers as chairmen—a proposal swept aside without argument in the seventies).[263]

In 1971 a new labour law system was introduced which put the legitimacy of traditional industrial action at risk. The instincts of the labour movement, so sensitive in Britain by reason of the customary attitude of judges to trade union affairs, were roused in a way that recalled 1926 or 1906. It knew a fundamental issue when it saw one. Moreover the eager style of the NIRC destroyed any lurking doubts, for it was administered by a judge who really did believe (in Lord Scarman's phrase) in being a 'backseat driver' in control of trade disputes. He subsequently revealed that, in his view, the three years' experience of the NIRC would have been different if the Act had gone the whole hog and allowed the court to judge the 'reasons' given by a union and an employer in an industrial dispute, so that it could inform the public. 'Ought they not to know who is right? . . . they would know, for the court which investigated the dispute would tell them. Those who suffered injustice would then be supported by the Courts.'[264] That singular view of the function of a labour court is strikingly similar to that of the Conservative barristers' society in 1958, which declared that strikes should be lawful only after an 'independent tribunal' had been given time 'to assess and publish the facts . . . and to clarify the issues at stake'.[265]

The action taken by the TUC in 1971 was swift and decisive. The Special Congress held on 18 March 1971 approved the recommendations of the General Council, *inter alia* advising trade unionists not to serve on the NIRC, and recommending that 'in the event of the Bill becoming an Act, trade unionists should withdraw from the employed persons' panel' from which the employee wingpersons were chosen for industrial tribunals.[266] This recommendation was made despite the correct prediction that the case load of the tribunals would rise to some 30,000 a year, of which the majority would not involve 'internal union affairs' but be concerned with unfair dismissal or redundancy 'where workpeople would stand to benefit'. Once made the recommendation was thoroughly implemented. By April 1972, 162 out of a total of 201 trade union nominees serving on the tribunals had resigned, and of the remainder only 17 had refused to resign.[267] Not until the repeal of the 1971 Act in 1974 did trade unionists resume their participation in the work of the tribunals.

But if this defiance is to be seen (as it is by some) as a gesture by the British trade union movement signalling that it would not be incorporated into a system of legal regulation in which political and civil service policies fused to put into hostile judicial channels the outcome of industrial conflict, its reaction to the subsequent history of the tribunals must also be examined. After the burial of the NIRC in 1974, the Employment Protection Act 1975 created a new appeal court to which appeals from the tribunals should be taken, the Employment Appeal Tribunal (EAT). Once again this was to be tripartite— a judge and two wingpersons (one employee, one employer from the respective TUC and CBI nominees). Some commentators (perhaps understandably, but without complete accuracy) saw this as the NIRC 'resurrected under a new title'.[268] To the trade unions it appeared to be no such judicial Lazarus. The TUC had, it is true, proposed 'a second appellate body between the tribunals and the High Court' as early as 1969 when it supported the general lines of what became subsequently the Social Contract legislation.[269] The 1975 Act contained new rights for workers and even for trade unions; together with the legislation of 1974 and 1976 the new code of labour law seemed a satisfactory basis for free trade unionism and even for voluntary collective bargaining. The EAT was thereby given the benefit of any doubts. Apart from some points about its jurisdiction (such as appeals connected with political funds) the TUC's main concern about the EAT was that trade union representatives should be able to 'act as advocates' before it.[270] By 1981 the participation of trade unionists in the tribunals and the EAT was firmly re-established. The total panel for wingpersons had risen to 2,019 compared with 600 in 1972,[271] of which it may be safely assumed some 1,000 were trade unionists.

Meanwhile, however, the Employment Act 1980 had expanded the jurisdiction of the tribunals to include complaints of unreasonable exclusion and expulsion from trade unions. Moreover here and elsewhere the government had changed the rules about unfair dismissal, allowed trade unions to be sued for civil compensation by way of 'joinder' by an employer, and generally reconstructed the law of unfair dismissal to the disadvantage of trade unionists. Even the EAT had been transformed into a court of original jurisdiction for the purpose (it seemed) of awarding large sums against a union at the suit of an expelled member or excluded applicant.[272] The Green Paper of 1981[273] heralded further government intervention; and the publication of its *Proposals* later in the same year adumbrated the Act of 1982. The Conservative government's legislative effort to weaken union membership arrangements or closed shops (by compelling the tribunals to award to most dismissed non-unionists large sums by way of compensation against either the employer or the trade union), and to prohibit the validity of any closed shop lacking a very high majority in a ballot, inevitably drew the tribunals even closer to the regulation of industrial conflict, especially when it also made industrial action against non-unionists illegal and permitted the employer to dismiss strikers if some returned to work.

The trade union reaction to this trend towards legal regulation was sharp. The Act of 1980 was condemned 'with complete and outright rejection' as removing traditional trade union rights, weakening individual workers' rights, and attacking the conditions of working women (a charge which is not difficult to sustain) and was dubbed 'a virtual re-run of that 1971 Act'.[274] The Green Paper of 1981 was seen by the TUC as 'a further phase in this Government's legal offensive against essential trade union freedoms ... injecting yet another massive dose of rigid legalism into British industrial relations'; and the government proposals of 1981 and 1982 were also condemned totally.[275]

However no withdrawal of trade unionists from the tribunals (or the EAT) took place at this time. In 1980 the General Council of the TUC stated that it would 'keep under scrutiny the operation of industrial tribunals and the Employment Appeal Tribunal which have been allotted new functions by the Employment Act'.[276] But in 1981 it continued a strong campaign to retain its exclusive right to nominate members to the employees' panel for the tribunals, a principle which the government had infringed by permitting another body which claimed to organize employees to nominate members. In fact the General Council argued that this step could 'alter the TUC's attitude towards the industrial tribunals ... [and] would undermine the standing of IT's in the eyes of many trade unionists'.[277] By the beginning of 1982, however, the TUC began to consider afresh the possibility of a general withdrawal of trade unionists from tripartite institutions.[278]

Even if the TUC continues to allow affiliated unions to nominate members to the tribunals and the EAT—indeed claims the exclusive right for them to do so—and does not demand complete withdrawal of those trade unionists sitting on them, it should not be immediately concluded that British trade unions have somehow surrendered their liberty by integration into a state apparatus which administers restrictive and repressive legislation. The issue is too delicate for such quick judgment. The tactics of 1971 may not be suitable for the eighties, especially when the muscles of the movement itself, so resilient a decade ago, are palsied by the disease of three million unemployed. Nor is it as easy to demand 1,000 resignations as 200; nor perhaps as easy to demand the resignation of lay judges accustomed to sit with a High Court judge in the Employment Appeal Tribunal (albeit he wears no wig).

Nevertheless it is difficult not to speculate whether future historians of labour law may not see some point in the early 1980s as the moment after which it became impossible for trade unions to disengage and remove their own members from a judicial system about which they had had doubts and which had come to administer justice under laws perceived to be unjust. If that is a danger for the 1980s it is not one against which Kahn-Freund ever warned. Although as early as 1967 he realized that the old tradition of legislative non-intervention would not be maintained[279] in respect of individual law, he had no apparent doubts about the work of the tribunals, welcoming them as an integral part of the reform and modernization of British industrial relations. His enthusiasm for such a new system led him, as we have seen, to advocate the 'need for a new generation of lawyers who can be entrusted with the supremely important role which lawyers and courts may be called upon to play in the vitally necessary reform of the system of industrial relations and the code of conditions of employment'.[280] Kahn-Freund was in fact disappointed that the ministerial Order was never made under the statutory section which envisaged the transfer to the tribunals of jurisdiction over contracts of employment.[281] He was aware that, in view of the widespread practice of incorporating terms from collective agreements into individual employment contracts, this would have accorded the tribunals 'a decisive role in the interpretation of the terms of collective agreements',[282] but he seemed curiously unaware that that was precisely one of the reasons why the TUC opposed the transfer.

Such issues were a far cry from the life and death conflicts of the Weimar Republic, in which Kahn-Freund saw the labour courts (and particularly the highest court, which had a majority of professional judges) acting as a 'substitute for industrial conflict' and bringing about a 'fundamental inner transform-ation of labour law' by the imposition of a 'fascist social ideal'.[283] There was of course no reason for Kahn-Freund to apply such terms to the emergent 'labour courts' of Britain; nor was there any reason for him to believe in the 1970s that the future might bring to Britain an authoritarian regime based on brutality of the kind which his sensitive ears had then begun to detect in Germany. On the contrary he found more promising in Britain an analogy with the French *conseils de prud'hommes*.[284] But perhaps he underrated the two vital facts which distinguish them from the British industrial tribunals: they operate without a legal chairman and are composed exclusively of elected lay judges (employers and employees in parity).[285] The civil service idea of industrial tribunals as a 'nucleus of a system of labour courts' never envisaged any such democratic base for Britain. The lay members were not to be—and are not—'representatives' of employers and of workers; they are individuals nominated as persons with special experience or knowledge. Much research has been concerned with such issues as procedure, remedies, informality, legalism, and costs in tribunals proceedings,[286] most of them areas in which the tribunals have fallen short of the civil service claims. However it may be of still greater importance to ask more fundamentally, as Kahn-Freund did in 1931, whether it is the tendency of 'all civil service bureaucracies to de-politicize' collective action and industrial conflicts of interest, adding one more pressure to convince workers (who believe that they do have 'representatives' sitting on the tribunals) that industrial conflict is 'something abnormal', a 'disturbance of the regulated flow of social events,'[287] and that law and litigation are the social norm. In this context it remains in the 1980s 'still an open question' as to whether the tribunals 'have won the confidence of working people'.[288] And whether they should.

The Social Contract: Collective Bargaining and Trade Union Rights

The confidence of working people was central to the 'Social Contract', the agreement between the Labour Party and the TUC which provided the corner-stone of the economic and social programme of the 1974–9 Labour government. It owed its origins to a fundamental dispute over the legality of trade union activity and the general role of the law in industrial relations. In fact it began as a 'negative' and defensive alliance against the restrictive proposals of the newly-formed Conservative government. The body which subsequently devised the Social Contract, the TUC-Labour Party Liaison Committee, was first convened in December 1970 with an immediate and short-term aim, to co-ordinate opposition to the proposed Industrial Relations Bill.[289] It was only in 1972, though, that the Liaison Committee became the forum for the development of a 'positive' economic and social strategy of the labour movement for implementation on the return of a Labour government. The reform of labour law, the rejection of the Industrial Relations Act, and the elaboration of legislation to replace it, was a central feature of this 'alternative strategy'. The compact was also the avenue through which the breach between the Labour government of 1964–70 and the trade unions, caused by industrial relations and incomes policies, could be healed.[290]

In a number of important ways the Social Contract labour legislation[291] restored the traditional non-interventionist framework of British industrial relations. Indeed mobilization of the labour movement against government interference in 'free' collective bargaining and autonomous trade union activity generated a powerful sense of unity in the 1970–4 period, which played a central role in the defeat of the Conservative Party in the 1974 elections. In 1974–6 the immunities for those acting in contemplation or furtherance of a trade dispute were restored and modernized to meet the new threats posed by judicial innovations in the common law, collective agreements in writing were presumed not to give rise to legally enforceable contracts, the voluntary arbitration and conciliation service (ACAS) was expanded. At the same time, though, the restoration of the 'voluntarism' of the sixties in collective industrial relations was tempered by a significant expansion in individual regulatory legislation.[292] Individual employees were, after 1975, to enjoy enlarged and new rights covering not only unfair dismissal and redundancy but also racial and sex discrimination, maternity leave, and rights to consultation over redundancy and health and safety issues. In this mixture of non-intervention at the 'collective' level and increased intervention at the 'individual' level the Social Contract legislation was, superficially at least, consistent with the broad reforming principles of the Donovan Report, and to some eyes was a radical version of its programme.

However, despite this obvious 'voluntarist' intention, the Social Contract may also be seen in retrospect as part of a secular trend towards greater legal regulation of industrial relations in Britain. At different times and under different governments the content of the specific legal rules may vary

substantially—for example, under the Social Contract legislation the rights of trade unions were generally strengthened,
whereas under the Employment Acts of 1980–2 they were
weakened. In both cases, though, it may be said that the law
was playing an increasing role as a mechanism of social regulation. Indeed it has been argued that the inevitable advance of
legal regulation in labour law has in practice caused the distinction between 'collective' and 'individual' to break down.[293]

When confronted in 1978 with the great increase in employment protection legislation (compared with the state of the
statute book, say, ten years earlier) it seemed obvious to say:
'This clearly represents some shift from settlement of problems
in negotiating procedure to settlement via judicial process, not
a development which British trade unions would have been
expected to welcome.'[294] But the critical question is, of course,
how great a shift? In this inquiry it may be important that the
statutory provisions were not all of one juridical type. Most of
the 'individual' laws provided protection (against unfair
dismissal, for example) with a statutory right to compensation
enforceable in the industrial tribunals. Others, like the equal
pay legislation, were given the status of a compulsory 'term' in
the contract of employment.[295] Other innovations, as in the
health and safety legislation, were not regulatory as such;
regulation (by 1974 volumes of it) had become the norm in
health and safety at work for more than a century without any
indication that it had nullified collective autonomy. The new
element in the 1974 statute was the obligation on employers to
consult with safety representatives and safety committees
composed of trade unionists—analytically an 'auxiliary' legal
provision.[296] Again, a different type of measure was the
statutory foundation for ACAS, a law which did little more than
provide machinery. Other provisions increased the area of
statutory 'props' for voluntary collective bargaining (the
obligation on employers to disclose information or to consult
about redundancies, and the extension of unilateral arbitration
to include 'general level' claims against employers who were
'black sheep' in their industry).

In this last group stood the controversial obligation on an
employer to 'recognize' a union (i.e. to bargain with it—or even
to bargain more with an already recognized union under the
obligation of 'further recognition', which was never tested) if

ACAS so recommended. The story has been told elsewhere of how the opposition of some employers (like Grunwick Ltd., who faced no penalty more daunting than an arbitration award on their employment conditions) and the obstruction of the courts (at first literally unable to understand the social problems with which they were confronted) combined to defeat these provisions of the 1975 Act.[297] But there were other reasons. Some trade unions appeared to turn to the 'obligatory recognition' procedures as a first, rather than as a last, resort (as was intended), subsequently to complain of the 'legalism' of the weapon they had chosen to use in place of the customary industrial strength. ACAS too grew to dislike the provisions, not least because they seemed to hinder what it saw as its 'real' work, voluntary conciliation (since even four-fifths of the recognition cases were settled by voluntary means). Its Chairman wrote to the Conservative government in June 1979 with in effect a request for repeal, which the government was only too happy to grant in its 1980 Act. It proved to be the case that the 'burden' of this small measure of intervention was too 'heavy' for the voluntary collective structure of industrial relations to bear.[298] There remains, therefore, a curious question in the centre of British labour law: are its idiosyncrasies so pronounced that it cannot have what comparable societies have, and other strong trade union movements operate, i.e. some legal duty on employers generally to bargain with trade unions? Or does the history of this interventionist measure teach unions that they should rely upon their own strength and mistrust like Greeks even the friendliest of governments which proffers such gifts?

The debate about the labour law impact of the Social Contract, however, has tended to concentrate upon the employment protection legislation; and at a purely juridical level it is quite clear that 'any general characterization of our labour law as either interventionist or abstentionist' must allow for enquiry about 'the extent of its regulation of the individual employment relationship' as well as about 'the processes and institutions of collective bargaining' and of conflict.[299]

What effect, then, has the 'individual' employment protection legislation had in practice? What evidence is there of what Hyman has called in another context a 'climate of legalism',[300] capable of bringing about a significant change in the conduct of British industrial relations? To what extent is the behaviour of line and personnel managers, shop stewards, and full-time officers in dealing with individual and collective employment issues determined by reference to legal (or what are believed to be legal) norms and procedures, rather than to voluntarily agreed norms and procedures or to 'custom and practice'? Certainly the Social Contract labour laws have contributed (along with other factors, but directly) to the spread of the closed shop and of procedures of greater formality across the face of industry, as well as to the increased specialization of management.[301] When, at the point of dismissal or discipline, the manager or the steward or the employee acts by reference first to norms relevant to the legal method of resolving disputes, there is a clear break with traditional practice. And the overall growth in individual employment protection rights, their legalistic influence on the actual conduct of industrial relations, and their enforcement through the tribunals must all represent some move away from voluntary negotiation. The increased 'juridification' of day-to-day industrial relations may have been an unintended consequence of the expansion of those rights under the Social Contract. Moreover there must be added the effects of the 'hybrid' legal rights (the right to take part in independent trade union activity, or the union official's rights to time off for industrial relations and trade union duties, and to facilities) which were actually intended to produce a 'collective' effect, sustaining the strength of union organization through the building blocks of individualized rights enforced by the tribunals.

On the other hand, there are indications that in practice this has not been the overall result where strong trade union organization is maintained. There, at least, the reliance on 'custom and practice' and the rejection of the distinction between 'conflicts of interests' and 'conflicts of rights' (which Allan Flanders saw as characteristic of British industrial relations and which may perhaps be one useful test of the extent of 'juridification')[302] appear to have survived. Indeed even the new, formal individual disputes procedures seem to be much less refined into 'legal' categories in British (rather than foreign-owned) establishments; and the new procedures are most prevalent where trade unionism is not at its weakest but at its strongest.[303] Legal intervention does not appear to have determined the shape of the change that has overtaken a range of institutions and behaviour (for example, the spread of job evaluation) as against other factors such as enterprise size, concentration, investment, the transnational character of enterprises, trade union development, and the move to single-employer bargaining. One of the objectives of the authors of the unfair dismissal laws ('reformers' and 'restricters' alike) was also to diminish the number of collective stoppages about dismissals by 'judicializing' such disputes individually before the tribunals; but there is little evidence as yet of that objective being attained.[304] One study in 1976 concluded that, although the intention of unfair dismissal law—and therefore of the tribunals which applied it—was undoubtedly to 'individualize' what could be collective disputes, the social effects of the law were 'less dramatic' in practice, certainly for organized workers; and that perhaps because the remedies made available to workers by the law were different in kind from those achieved by collective bargaining, collective industrial disputes over discipline and dismissal had probably not declined since the law was introduced, and would not do so after the 1975 extension.[305] Moreover the usual complaint about some of the laws of 1975–6 is that they have not been sufficiently effective (for example, the statutes which purport to outlaw racial and sex discrimination).

It would be foolish to think that this problem would not have existed without the Social Contract legislation, but equally wrong not to recognize that that legislation, whilst it did not cause, must have accentuated, the problem. In some ways it had little choice. The 1971 Act had (by adopting the 1969 proposals) enacted rights against unfair dismissal; the practical question in 1974 was whether these should be repealed along with the rest of the tottering structures of 1971. Again, the legal changes in 1974 revived the legality of the closed shop; but in so doing what should the new law say about the impact of various employment protection laws in that industrial situation?

In truth it was this feature of the management of the boundary between 'collective' and 'individual' rights (for example, between the collective right of a union and its members to agree with an employer on a closed shop, and the right of an individual employee to be compensated if dismissed as a non-unionist) that was critical for the legislation as a whole. For it is by the management of that boundary that the impact in practice of the employment protection laws upon the conduct of collective industrial relations can, in part at least, be controlled. It would perhaps be useful to examine more closely the manner in which that boundary was 'managed' (for the most part by the pull of social forces and unconsciously) in the case of safety legislation, where for a century significant regulatory legislation pervaded most of our industries at the very period of the growth and consolidation of autonomous collective bargaining; and how far in 1974 the shape of the retained law concerning unfair dismissal was moulded by an understanding of the role of that boundary.

In retrospect the Social Contract labour legislation does not evince a consistent policy towards the management of the boundaries between collective and individual rights, or between collective autonomy and state intervention. Some effects of the new laws were no doubt impossible to predict. (Who could have foreseen that so many marcescent employers' associations would be rejuvenated as advisers on the new laws?) But it is questionable how far the policy of maintaining and extending independent trade union strength was always present in the new laws. And the ambiguities of the tripartite structures spill over from the Social Contract as a whole into its labour law. Indeed, when we survey the undoubted failures of the obligatory 'recognition' provisions, we should perhaps consider them not only in the context of Grunwick Ltd. but also in the light of the tripartite character of ACAS. In the absence of any agreement between the TUC and the CBI representatives on criteria for the recognition of unions, the ACAS Council could not be rescued by its three independent 'neutral' members (or by the valiant efforts of its Chairman) from its unhappy attempt to do its best and muddle through.[306]

It cannot yet be fully assessed how far the boundaries drawn were 'failures' from the point of view of the various policies on industrial relations and how far the face of British industrial relations was finally turned towards more legalistic structures or (perhaps more importantly) more legalistic behaviour. Nor can it yet be said how successful the Social Contract was in permitting a shift away from the tradition of voluntary bargaining while at the same time maintaining a continuing commitment to its basic structure in its attempt to reconcile traditional collective autonomy with increased legislative intervention.

Yet it was not only this field of labour law which experienced the problem. It becomes even more apparent when we examine the other labour law elements of the Social Contract (industrial democracy and incomes policy) and their link with the overall economic and political strategy of the agreement. But as we approach this 'second level', Kahn-Freund as usual has a relevant reflection. After assessing various systems of compulsory and voluntary arbitration, he concluded in 1977: 'things which may have a disastrous effect in a declining labour market can be absorbed by a buoyant economy, and . . . a healthy union movement can "take" a great deal of legal intervention, whilst weak unions may be its victim'.[307]

The Social Contract proposals for the extension of industrial democracy were part of a three-stage programme of legislation to replace the Industrial Relations Act on the return of a Labour government and were first agreed by the TUC-Labour Party Liaison Committee in June 1973.[308] An initial 'Repeal Bill' (which became the Trade Union and Labour Relations Act of 1974) was to be followed by an Employment Protection Bill (which became the Act of 1975) and then a 'Companies Bill', 'which would include provisions for extending industrial democracy within companies (e.g. supervisory boards)'.[309] The significance of this latter proposal at this stage of the argument lies in the change it signalled in TUC and Labour Party policy towards voluntary collective bargaining and the role of the law in industrial relations. This change can be best illustrated by examining the arguments for trade union board representation contained in the 1974 TUC Report on *Industrial Democracy*,[310] which outlined in detail the case for reform. The Report reaffirmed the fundamental TUC commitment to strengthen trade union organization and widen the scope of collective bargaining as 'the major way to extend collective control of workpeople over their work'.[311] But it also argued that these methods had so far failed to enable trade unions to exert any real influence over strategic corporate decisions in areas such as investment, closures, take-overs, mergers, and product specialization. While in theory these issues could become subject to joint regulation, in practice they were 'not readily covered by collective bargaining'. In fact new forms of control were needed, particularly at board level, as an 'adjunct to the collective bargaining process'.[312] The main proposal arising out of this analysis was for the introduction of legislation (a 'legal' strategy) which would open the doors and allow trade unions if they so wished (a 'voluntary' strategy) to demand joint responsibility with management at board level for the determination of strategic objectives both in public corporations and in private companies with over 2,000 employees. These objectives were incorporated in the election manifesto on which the Labour Party was returned to office with an overall majority in October 1974.[313]

Like other elements of the Social Contract affecting industrial relations, the proposals on industrial democracy reflected both a continuing commitment to voluntary collective bargaining and a recognition of its inadequacy from a trade union point of view in respect of a whole number of industrial and economic issues. The remedy for this inadequacy was sought in the increasing use of legislation and legal rights to complement voluntary collective action. Even some opponents of the TUC's view on trade union board representation, such as the General and Municipal Workers' Union, advocated a legal solution to the extension of industrial democracy, arguing for the institution of a general legal obligation on employers to consult and negotiate with trade unions on issues of corporate policy—a proposal which ran into problems parallel to those affecting obligatory 'recognition'.[314]

A similar if more ambivalent questioning of the 'voluntary tradition' under the Social Contract can be observed in relation to the problem of wage determination. At the beginning and the end of the 1974–9 Labour government, autonomous collective bargaining without direct state intervention was the main method of wage determination in Britain. Between 1975 and 1977, though, voluntary wage bargaining was suspended by the introduction of national wage guide-lines. In July 1975, with inflation at around 25 per cent and rising, a major reduction in foreign investment, and severe downward pressure on the pound in the foreign exchange markets, the TUC was confronted by a government ultimatum: it had two weeks to devise an incomes policy acceptable to the government or a statutory policy would be imposed. In the event the TUC drew up a flat-rate pay policy which aimed to help the low paid. However commendable as a tactic, this could hardly be termed the product of traditional voluntary collective bargaining. Not only was it worked out by TUC leaders at national level in consultation with the government, but the eventual guide-lines were also incorporated in a government White Paper and thus given official state backing. The government also fixed cash limits for wage bills in the public sector and prepared 'reserve powers' to control private-sector wages if necessary by use of the Price Code against employers who paid above the national guidelines.

The agreement of TUC leaders, and subsequently TUC conference delegates, to central wage guide-lines between 1975 and 1977 was in itself a recognition both of the inadequacy of traditional collective bargaining and of the major influence exerted by government on traditional trade union objectives (i.e. the social and economic security and advance of working people). The initial Social Contract agreement of 1973 had not envisaged direct government intervention in wage bargaining, but had recognized that a number of proposed Labour government policies (on rents, prices, taxation, social and public services, inflation, and employment) would influence 'the whole climate of collective bargaining'.[315] Subsequently this intervention became much more direct and it was undoubtedly facilitated by the massive increase in inflation and the deep financial crisis of the summer of 1975. But trade union compliance cannot be understood simply as a response to a short-term economic crisis. It was made possible by the commitment of the TUC to the 'wider Social Contract',[316] which it defined as a 'coherent economic and social strategy . . . designed both to overcome the nation's grave economic problems, and to provide the basis for co-operation between the trade unions and the Government'.[317] At the centre of this strategy lay the fight against inflation and unemployment, the twin evils which threatened to undermine voluntary collective bargaining and independent trade unionism more successfully than the introduction of national wage guide-lines over which the TUC could exert some influence. As Jack Jones, one of the leading architects of the Social Contract, argued at the annual TUC conference in September 1975: 'Had the General Council not joined the Government in action to arrest the downward movement of the pound and the severe threat to Britain's financial stability we could have experienced an economic setback from which Britain would not have recovered for generations. . . . We have to do something to prevent this, *or unemployment will become Britain's incomes policy for a long time to come.*'[318]

Nevertheless TUC co-operation with the Labour government was conditional on the implementation of a wider range of agreed policies in favour of working people, all of which required state intervention. These included, apart from new labour legislation, subsidies on food, housing, rents, and public transport, an extension of the public ownership of key industries (docks, shipbuilding, aircraft) and of land required for house building, a large-scale redistribution of income and wealth, price controls, increased pensions and public expenditure on education and health, new regional and national employment policies, an expansion of training, and a major increase in the public control of industrial investment through the establishment of a state holding company (National Enterprise Board) and tripartite planning agreements between employers, the government, and trade unions. From the trade union point of view this conception of the Social Contract implied subjecting all areas of industrial, social, and economic policy to joint consultation and negotiation, either between the TUC and the government or between employers and individual trade unions. For employers, such a radical restriction of their right of control over the disposition of capital and their right to manage would have undermined the traditional basis of their power and authority; and therefore it could hardly be expected that they would give their positive support. For the trade unions, agreement with the Social Contract was conditional on the government fulfilling its side of the 'bargain', initially through the introduction of relevant legislation. This conception of the Social Contract was formulated clearly by David Basnett, General Secretary of the GMWU, at the 1975 TUC conference: 'One of the primary purposes of the Social Contract is to give back to the Government some economic initiative so that it can contain inflation and contain and reverse the trends of unemployment. The proposals for the development of the Social Contract are a unique and historic gesture by the British trade union Movement, but it is a gesture to which there must be a response, and that response from others must come as well from the Government itself. They must keep their part of the bargain.'[319]

It is now part of history that, after an initial period (1974 and 1975) in which the Social Contract could claim to be the vehicle for a radical change in British economic and social policy, the TUC became ever more disenchanted with the Labour government and its inability to keep its side of the bargain. A number of proposals in the original Social Contract, particularly those which would have involved radical intervention in the rights of employers, were either weakened (National Enterprise Board, planning agreements) or not implemented ('industrial democracy'). A detailed analysis of the reasons for these developments has been given elsewhere.[320] Suffice it to say that the failure of the Labour government to implement major aspects of the 'wider Social Contract' was less to do with legal problems than with the opposition of employers and senior civil servants, the lack of political commitment to the strategy within significant groups in the Labour Party, divisions within the TUC over incomes policy and industrial democracy, and (crucially) the failure of both the TUC and the Labour Party to win broad labour movement and popular support for what were and remained very much national leadership strategies.

It is clear, though, that the Social Contract labour legislation takes on a very different meaning according to whether it is viewed in isolation from, or as part of, the 'wider Social Contract'. Proposals for the extension of industrial democracy look very different if they are linked in with a legally and financially powerful state holding company and compulsory planning agreements than if they are introduced in isolation as an institutional reform of traditional industrial relations structures. Rights of individual workers to time off for trade union and industrial relations education (perhaps including courses on accounting, investment, and marketing) and rights to disclosure of information take on a very different character if they are an integral part of an overall strategy to extend the control of working people over the major decisions which affect their lives. In such a wider context the Social Contract labour legislation can be viewed as part of a radical strategy to transform the structure of power and wealth in Britain.

If, however, the same provisions are examined separately and divorced from the wider strategy, then they may not only be interpreted as just another element in the increasing legal regulation of industrial relations, but, as Tony Topham has argued, as 'a modest programme of reform, a mere belated attempt to bring British law and practice regarding employee rights and workers' participation into line with fairly standard norms in Western Europe'.[321] Alternatively the range and provisions of the Social Contract may be seen as, in practice, part of an overall trend towards the 'incorporation' of trade unions into the state apparatus and the institutionalization and channelling of the militancy of shop-floor trade unionism into collaboration with employers, a view which interprets the strategy as weakening the radical left in the late 1970s and early 1980s; or, as Ken Gill (General Secretary of AUEW-TASS and one of the most consistent critics of the Social Contract) wrote in 1979: 'The retreat of the left was due to the acceptance of the Social Contract.'[322]

What is beyond dispute, however, is that the programme of the Social Contract as a whole envisaged a shift away from *laissez-faire* voluntarism towards legislative intervention—or (a more acceptable word to some of its authors) towards 'planning'—in social and economic relations in Britain. It was, in short, 'a strategy to legislate a shift in power to labour'.[323] In industrial relations and labour law it represented—as did the employment protection legislation—an uneasy and continually shifting compromise between 'collective *laissez-faire*' and state intervention, between autonomous collective action and legal regulation. Implicit within the Social Contract was the recognition of a much more pervasive role for the state and in many areas particularly for the law. The TUC and the Labour Party were indicating the need for increased state intervention beyond its traditional role in the public ownership of basis industries and in social security, housing, education, and health policy. However, the full implications of such intervention (in the heart of industrial and economic policy) for traditional collective bargaining and the role of employers and independent trade unions were neither fully thought through nor resolved. This remains one of the unanswered questions of the Social Contract.

We have suggested that it has become increasingly difficult to isolate labour law from wider economic and political developments. Does this mean that Kahn-Freund's maxim that law is 'a secondary force in human affairs, and especially in labour relations',[324] needs to be revised?

A study of the Social Contract shows that to some degree social and political conflicts are increasingly being fought out in legal terms and in a legal framework, but that the outcome of these conflicts is not generally the result of legal 'causes'. The outcome has continued to be largely determined by the relative strength and power of employers and trade unions, management and workers, and by the social, economic, and political climate of the time. The strength and demands of British trade unions in the post-1945 era have been largely industrial and economic in character, expressed primarily in wage militancy and strong shop-floor organization. A pre-condition of this strength was the politically guaranteed economic reality of full employment. Governments in the 1950s and 1960s generally helped to promote an industrial relations climate which favoured an accommodation with this 'unpolitical' climate of voluntary, decentralized industrial relations, economic management, and trade unionism.

By the early 1980s sustained high levels of unemployment and low levels of output have weakened the traditional economic strength of British trade unions and in many respects the political climate has turned—or was made to turn—against the sectionalism, decentralization, and unplanned nature of traditional collective bargaining, looking to the state to restore social control and order. In such a situation there is a danger that the recognition of the growing politicization of industrial relations and labour law may lead on all sides (including the trade unions) to a growing reliance on the state and the law for 'solutions' to Britain's social and economic crisis. Paradoxically that danger is not decreased by the fact that the present Conservative government would vehemently—and in formal terms justly—deny that it looks to 'the state' when seeking answers to the crisis. It believes in the 'market'. We have seen, however, that a necessary part of its economic and social policy (what it would describe as reducing wages to a 'realistic level'; what Professor Lord Kaldor has called 'smashing wage resistance') is the attack upon effective trade unionism by repressive economic and, when needed, restrictive legal force (albeit that the latter is devised in the garb of muted immunities).[325] This onslaught moves not only labour law but an ever wider range of social relations generally nearer to the heart of the 'political' arena. If the disadvantaged—whether minority urban or ethnic groups, or workers whose social wage or opportunity for employment is reduced—see little hope for the future and resort to new and possibly more desperate measures, the government that rests on market forces will not be slow to call upon the resources of the state to uphold the 'rule of law'. And the law must be adequate for its purposes when the moment comes. Only in this setting can we fully appreciate the current otherwise curious concern about the illegality of 'political' strikes,[326] and the significance of the Conservative labour legislation of the eighties.

The danger of an over-reliance on the state and the law at a time of social and economic crisis, itself a constant theme of Kahn-Freund's writings to the end,[327] remains a criticial problem for labour law today. In this context the experience of the Social Contract leaves a major question unanswered: can the labour movement devise an alternative strategy which recognizes the need for increased state intervention in the economy while simultaneously guaranteeing the flexibility and self-determination afforded by decentralized control of economic power, autonomous collective bargaining, and independent trade unionism? Can it manage that boundary? And can it win support for such a strategy both within and without the ranks of the labour movement? These questions lead us to an assessment of policy alternatives for labour law today.

Labour Law in a Period of Social Transition

It has been remarked above that the policy of restriction towards independent trade unionism has so far in the eighties refrained from any major reconstruction of the existing institutions of labour law of the kind attempted in 1971. Can it continue to do so? If it attempts to adapt the institutions and concepts of the so-called 'non-interventionist' system still further, will it be compelled by its own internal logic to transform them, albeit gradually and step by step?

Trade unions are under few illusions about the nature of the legislation of 1980–2, especially the restoration of liability in tort, in respect of both injunctions and damages. Despite the disastrous experience of the Industrial Relations Act and the warnings in its own Green Paper,[328] the government has seen fit to reintroduce that liability. The range of lawful industrial action has also been drastically curtailed: the immunities have been cropped and the concept of trade dispute stripped down until the 'golden formula', that cherished child of British labour law, has assumed the appearance of a ragged-trousered waif. The legislation has made it possible to outlaw wide areas of secondary picketing and blacking, solidarity and sympathetic action, industrial pressure to maintain closed shops, union-only practices and even union consultation, a wider field of so-called 'political' strikes, and without doubt—in view of the volatile nature of common law doctrines, such as 'duress', 'unlawful means', and other new areas of tortious liability for which the fingers of some judges itch as the immunities recede—many other forms of industrial action.[329] The very right to strike—the hallmark of a pluralist society as Kahn-Freund maintained—is under threat. The state, this time, is poised to take away the right it did not give.

The legislation of 1982 makes trade unions as such liable in tort in the ordinary courts for the first time since 1966. The question immediately arises, liable for what and for whom? This problem of vicarious liability arose under the Industrial Relations Act 1971 in respect of its 'unfair industrial practices'; and it was also raised by the 1980 Act in the provisions which allowed an employer to 'join' a union guilty of industrial pressure and claim contribution towards, or an indemnity for, the compensation which he had to pay to the employee dismissed unfairly. That liability is further extended in the 1982 Act by allowing the employee the right to sue the union direct. But when is 'the union' (and its funds) liable to pay? When is it liable for the industrial action of the relevant officials or members? Few legal cases involving that question were fought in the first years of the 1980 Act; and most observers ignored the problem of vicarious liability between 1980 and 1982.[330]

The Act of 1982 and the preceding *Proposals* of 1981 forced vicarious liability into the centre of the labour law debates. It could not be otherwise, for it meant reviving the explosive *Taff Vale* judgment of 1901 imposing liability on union funds in tort, which was, wrote Lord Asquith, so novel that it was 'not surprising that public opinion was unprepared for any such decision'.[331]

It has long been a principle of English law that an employer is liable in civil law for the acts of his 'employee' done within the 'course of the employment', and a principal is liable for the acts of his 'agent' done within the scope of his 'authority'. When this doctrine approached its modern form in the eighteenth century, it rested upon the notion that the employer should be liable because the employee must have acted under his 'command'; subsequently, it was added, his 'implied command'.[332] By 1912 the master or 'principal' was made similarly liable for his 'agent' for acts done within the scope of the agency, even if the latter was not strictly an 'employee' and had not even acted for the principal's benefit.[333] Since then the area of the legal doctrine has expanded; but it is still rooted deeply in the concept of a 'command' structure—that same 'command under the guise of an agreement' which Kahn-Freund perceived behind the contract of employment.

Whatever else it is, a trade union is not based upon a 'command' structure of the kind found in an employment relationship—certainly not in respect of shop stewards; and not even in relation to its full-time officers (even if they are appointed and not elected and count in law as 'employees' of the union). Indeed the voice of reform, the Donovan Report, had warned in 1968: 'Trade union leaders do exercise discipline from time to time, but they cannot be industry's policemen. They are democratic leaders in organisations in which the seat of power has almost always been close to the members.'[334] So when the 1982 Act attempts to impose upon trade unions these 'common law doctrines',[335] this policy is bound to require legislation that goes beyond the common law and which is bound to be an assault upon the integrity and the legality of their independent activities.

That much had been learnt in 1972 under the Industrial Relations Act 1971. The intellectual gymnastics of the judges in *Heatons Transport Ltd.* v. *TGWU*,[336] who tried to decide whether the authority of shop stewards came 'up from the bottom' or 'down from the top', were essays in the absurdity of trying to apply the common law doctrine to trade unions, as they were bound by the Act to do. Indeed when Lord Wilberforce found that shop stewards 'play a dual role'—sometimes acting for 'the union', sometimes for their group of members—he thought such an idea so surprising that it would not be 'likely to occur to trade unionists'. In fact, of course, it is part of the common currency of trade union life. The House of Lords found the TGWU liable in the *Heatons* case because the shop stewards in the docks had acted with an 'implied authority' (contained in the rule book, plus the customs and practices and the policies of 'the union'). But four years later, by a majority, they held the union not liable for parallel industrial action launched by shop stewards at London Airport, in whom they could find no parallel 'authority'.[337] The 1971 Act required a wider area of vicarious liability to be effective. Indeed Kahn-Freund, who approved of the Law Lords' analysis that authority comes 'from the bottom' rather than 'the top' (how could it be otherwise in this association governed by custom and practice and direct democracy as much as by rules?), nevertheless concluded: 'it is the irony of the *Heatons* case that the same court which diagnosed the identity of unions and shop stewards imposed on "the union"' (i.e. now the permanent officials of the union) the duty to enforce the court's order 'by threatening to withdraw the shop stewards' credentials'.[338]

Had many collective agreements actually been made legally binding, the provision in the Act which made a union vicariously liable for members who 'purported' to act on its behalf, and for not preventing their activities, would have been seen to be very important.[339] Although no such development occurred in regard to collective agreements, the President of the NIRC showed just before the repeal of the Act that he was ready to extend even judge-made vicarious liability that far in respect of the 'unfair industrial practices' generally.[340] Further, in dealing with contempt of court by unions which defied the NIRC, the Law Lords demanded that the unions should order shop stewards 'in language they would understand as being an order by the union, to stop organizing' the industrial action.[341]

In framing its proposals for legislation in 1982 the government took its cue not only from the principles applied to 'common law' vicarious liability but also to those governing contempt of court. For the policy of restriction to work the union must be made to disavow industrial action wherever possible. This is the inexorable logic of the policy when it is applied to the reality of industrial life. For it is notorious that the rule books of trade unions, and even the rules plus the 'practices, customs and policies' of unions, will not always make clear whether shop stewards have the 'authority' (express, implied, or 'ostensible') which attracts the ordinary doctrine of vicarious liability.[342] So the government's 1981 *Proposals* declared that the union must be liable if the executive committee authorizes or ratifies industrial action; or if a subordinate body or official acts within its or his 'authority', or on instructions from such a body or official without a 'more senior authoritative' body repudiating action; or, in cases where the rules are not clear, if any official or body acts and a 'more senior authoritative body or official' has not repudiated the action.[343] The legal nightmare promised by such proposals (such as the problem in many unions of which body is more 'senior' or 'authoritative' than another) could not prevent a demand for legislation along these lines being made by the policy of restriction in the eighties.

In fact the 1982 Employment Act advanced a more sophisticated version of this general scheme. First, under the terms of the Act the revival of the *Taff Vale* doctrine makes the union generally liable in tort. But it is liable for torts arising from industrial conflict—the so-called 'economic torts'[344]—only in respect of acts authorized or endorsed by a list of 'responsible persons' who are by statute declared to be the agents of the union. These include the executive committee, any person empowered by the rules to authorize acts of the kind in question, and the President and the General Secretary (whatever the 'rules' have to say about their authority).[345] It is significant that under the Act's provisions the term 'rules' does not mean only the union rule book; it includes any other written provisions forming part of the 'contract' between the members of the union (though it is not at all clear which documents are thereby included).

Secondly, the union is made liable for acts authorized by two other groups of 'responsible persons', namely employed officials (who will usually be full-time officers of the union) and any committee to which any such officer 'regularly reports'. But here the liability does not arise if such persons were prevented by the 'rules' from authorizing the kind of acts in question, or if the act done has been repudiated by the executive committee or the President or the General Secretary. However, such repudiation is effective only if it occurs as soon as is reasonably practicable after the act 'has come to the knowledge' of the executive committee or either of those two top officers, and if the person purporting to authorize the act is informed of the repudiation without delay and in writing. Above all, the repudiation is not valid if the executive committee or either the President or the General Secretary 'has behaved in a manner which is inconsistent with the purported repudiation' after it has been effected.[346] How long after is not made clear. What is clear is that, if it takes the law seriously, a well-advised executive committee will have ready a stock of repudiation forms and will make them available to the President and the General Secretary just in case.

The logic of the 1982 scheme must lead therefore to the repudiation of union officers by their executive, President, or General Secretary, but perhaps at a more gentle pace than under the *Proposals* of 1981. On the one hand the union is responsible for acts of all persons authorized by the written documents which count as the 'rules' (though it is far from clear what they are) and cannot repudiate them. So too the acts authorized by the executive committee and its two top officers create liability, whatever the 'rules' may say. But those officers and that body can relieve the union of liability for acts of other full-time officials and committees to whom they answer (even if the 'rules' do not prevent them from having authority) by taking the necessary steps to effect a repudiation within the carefully defined limits of that term. It is at once obvious that the pressure upon (say) a General Secretary to repudiate industrial action apparently authorized by (say) a regional officer which has been brought to his knowledge by (say) a television announcement or a newspaper reporter will be intense, especially if the claim is already being made that damage is being done to the employer or to the public which is 'disastrous'.[347] The element of 'policing' in the 1982 version of vicarious liability is smaller on paper than in the 1981 *Proposals*; but in practice it could be as great, if not greater.

In this respect what will no doubt be claimed as a virtue of the Act, as against the 1981 *Proposals*, is on closer inspection a significant part of the policy. The union is to be liable for the industrial torts only for acts authorized by the 'responsible persons', and that does not include shop stewards unless they are persons 'empowered by the rules' to authorize the kind of acts in question.[348] It may be said that the courts will not therefore have thrust upon them the difficulties inherent in interpreting the express or implied authority of stewards, as in the *Heatons* case. But there is little in the new measures to prevent a court from discovering an implied authority in the 'rules' which empowers the stewards to authorize the acts in question. Indeed the 'rules' are defined to include written provisions other than the rule book, a formulation which might include the cards of accreditation usually issued to stewards by their trade union. In that event a rerun of *Heatons* is a virtual certainty. The difference would seem to be that the court could not rely upon unwritten custom and practice this time to establish (or, more important, to exclude) implied authority. But if a court finds that the shop stewards do have an implied authority within these 'rules' so as to make the union liable, the 1982 Act does not permit the executive committee or the two top officers to save the union by repudiating them. The repudiation provisions apply only to full-time officials and committees to which they report.[349]

As was found in the *Heatons* litigation in 1972, concentration upon the question of legal authority tends to pull the stewards and the members at the grass roots away from the formal institutions of the union and its officers. Despite the persistent, perhaps necessary, tension which exists in Britain between shop stewards and full-time officers in trade unions suffused with direct democracy, it has been noted that this relationship has become increasingly close and the assistance of the former may often be crucial to the work of the latter.[350] The special care which the 1982 legislation displays to encircle the full-time official with a legalistic structure of authority within the (new concept of the) 'rules', bounded by a statutory procedure for repudiation of his acts, is instructive. Wedges will inevitably be driven between stewards and full-time officials, between both of them and the executive and the two top officers, and between all of them (as 'responsible persons') and the membership. The 'union' will increasingly appear to the members as 'they' not 'we'.[351] If the law works the trade union will increasingly assume the character of a policing organization.

It is not difficult to imagine the practical effect of such legal principles. The legal approach in practice would obviously be to expect liability in the union, either if shop stewards with general industrial relations functions were involved in industrial action or if a full-time officer were involved and the executive had not repudiated him, especially if the President or the General Secretary had taken any steps to endorse the action. There is nothing to exclude a finding by the courts that there has been 'implied' endorsement by the executive or by such an officer. Days of legal argument might be spent (while an interim injunction stopped the strike) on whether there had been behaviour inconsistent with the repudiation before or after the repudiation itself, or whether the alleged repudiation did not contain an under-the-counter nod or wink encouraging the members to believe that it was only a legal formality.

The reality of all this is clear. Proceedings for an interlocutory labour injunction, brought at a day's notice, with the evidence all on affidavit, prepared at leisure by the plaintiff, and not subject to cross-examination—that reality makes it highly improbable that the union could establish to the satisfaction of the court in the (theoretically) interim proceedings that it had negotiated successfully the obscure paths set before it by the statutory rules on 'responsible persons'. Where, for example, industrial action erupts against the importation of non-unionists—the very battle against 'free labour' that the trade union movement was fighting at the time of *Taff Vale* at the turn of the century—it will hardly be easy to prove that no persons empowered by the 'rules' approved it, or that every full-time local, district, or even national official who has assisted his members in what has become their illegal fight for trade unionism has been fully and properly repudiated. Meanwhile the union's legal advisers will no doubt do their duty by advising the executive committee to tell the stewards to stand aloof and to repudiate the full-time officers unequivocally, in an effort to protect the union's funds from liability for what (they will have been informed by the employer's lawyers) could amount to damages of a disastrous nature.

If the policy of restriction wishes to endorse severe financial penalties on unions by way of damages, it clearly does not wish to authorize their total destruction. An arbitrary limit has therefore been set on the amounts that can be awarded as damages in any one set of proceedings, on a scale from £250,000 for a union of 100,000 members or more to £10,000 where there are less than 5,000 members.[352] However, awards of damages and costs cannot be executed against 'protected property'. This curious provision includes within that term the political fund and the 'provident benefits fund' of the union.[353] How far a union may switch its general funds in and out of the latter fund to protect its assets from threats of liability is no doubt a matter that will receive further attention.[354]

In the 1982 scheme then, the ordinary doctrine of vicarious liability has been infiltrated with other concepts, mainly because that doctrine does not easily fit trade unions. Certain agents (or 'responsible persons') are appointed by the state, not by the contract in the rule book. The authority of others is to be looked at through a special concept of the 'rules'. But most important in practice, the need to repudiate acts of officials, the roots of which doctrine lie in the penal laws on contempt of court, is insinuated in part to determine the prior question of civil liability; and each repudiation must satisfy the statutory tests. Meanwhile the Act permits the President and the General Secretary to make the union liable by endorsing acts which lie far beyond their authority under the rules, thereby treating them, along with the executive comittee, as the *alter ego* of the union and beyond the democratic control of the members whilst in office.[355] All this is a long way from common law vicarious liability, from the maxim that 'no man can become the agent of another person except by the will of that person', from the rule that the plaintiff must assume the burden of proof to establish any authority which he alleges to exist.[356] The rules of procedure are such that in interlocutory proceedings trade union defendants pleading the trade dispute immunities have always been heavily disadvantaged. The 1982 scheme creates new disabilities. It is an attempt to build a 'command' structure into the trade union, since without one the notion of vicarious liability will not work. The method by which this is done includes an admixture of quasi-criminal tests which will bring to the fore in such proceedings the issue of 'repudiation' of union officials; and to that extent there is a real sense in which trade unions under this legal regime are presumed to be guilty before the litigation begins. As for the age-old problem of trade union 'martyrs', the government did recognize in 1981 that 'the opportunities to seek martyrdom might be reduced but would not be eliminated'.[357] But whenever possible the route back to Tolpuddle from the 1980s is to stop at the bank of Transport House.

The strategy is not, however, confined to strike law. It has also, as we have seen, pared away the positive rights of unions and changed their position by subtle shifts even in 'individual' employment law. Many of the basic principles of individual employment protection have thereby been transformed.[358] We have already noted that the 'joinder' provisions reverse the previous policy, prescribed by Donovan and Kahn-Freund,[359] of confining the industrial tribunals to individual disputes between employee and employer rather than internal trade union and other collective issues. When it intervenes in a case of unfair dismissal of a non-unionist to make the union (by reason of its industrial 'pressure') pay a 'just' share of the compensation awarded, the law crosses a legal and ideological Rubicon. First, the union is made to pay by way of a civil liability (involving vicarious liability) analogous to tort. Secondly, the industrial scene is rearranged by the law, and the individual worker is confronted by twin centres of 'power' apparently in control of his dismissal and his individual destiny: the employer and the trade union. Thirdly, above all, the 'justice' of the collective pressure and the 'equity' of strikes are now to be assessed by the tribunal for the purpose of assessing the causation of the individual unfair dismissal. Here the public is indeed 'told' by the court who is 'right'.[360] And this through the medium of industrial tribunals on which trade unionists are sitting.

Another significance of the 1982 developments lies in the fact that the employer even loses control of the legal procedure. Previously he could at least attempt to balance the desirability of 'joining' the union in an unfair dismissal case against the overall damage this might do to his industrial relations (in which balance the interests of organized workers must have a place). Now 'joinder' is in the hands of the dismissed individual—above all, the non-unionist—whose decision whether or not to 'join' the union may owe nothing (as the government had itself insisted in 1980) to the consideration of any interests other than his own.[361] Indeed, the scheme of the new legislation in effect penalizes the employer who either submits to pressure from, or enters agreements with, his trade unions. If he and his unionized work-force agree to introduce a union membership arrangement, they must abide by the result of a ballot only if those workers who support it can defeat opponents who carry votes weighted against the closed shop by a ratio of four to one.[362] Many employers have been slow to realize—and perhaps some unions have been slow to point out to managers—the manner in which these aspects of the new policy threaten the stability of their industrial relations.

It was therefore in a sense logical for the 1982 legislation to provide for markedly increased compensation payable to non-unionists dismissed from employment covered by a 'closed shop'. And more generally, in the law of redundancy and dismissal, the most recent developments underpin the insistence of the law that the dismissal itself is now a 'given', the product of seemingly immutable economic forces—a feature which was perhaps inadequately sensed by the policy of 'reform'. In redundancy the very definition in the law states as much.[363] In unfair dismissal it may sound paradoxical to say that the dissmisal is a 'given' in order that its 'fairness' can be assessed by the tribunal. However, not only is the approach of the tribunals and courts most nearly consistent with the attitude of management,[364] but, more important, the remedies of reinstatement and re-engagement (though ostensibly primary remedies) are in reality not available to the mass of employees dismissed unfairly. Indeed re-employment has recently been called the 'lost remedy'.[365] Of 28,624 notified cases in 1980, the tribunals ordered re-employment in 78 and conciliation secured that result in 295. The procedure and the remedy (one hears Kahn-Freund reminding us) may be more important than the substantive law—just as the discretionary labour injunction may be of more significance to strikes than the principles of liability. Employment protection in the main gives to an individual worker not a 'right' to his job[366] but an assessment by law of a modest price as compensation for the loss of it.[367] In 1980 the median tribunal award of compensation was £598, a less than princely sum, and nearly three-quarters of the complainants whose cases were heard by tribunals failed to secure any remedy.[368] A legal system like the Italian, which in specific cases actually restores workers to jobs if they are dismissed,[369] is of course generically different from the British system in this respect.

In contrast a privileged position is enjoyed by those categories of specially-protected employees in Britain for whom dismissal is automatically unfair, that is, non-unionists in closed shops and (theoretically)[370] those dismissed for trade union activity. For them the primary remedies are more accessible and the amounts of compensation are increased. It is clear that any alternative 'reform' strategy for labour law must end these privileges of non-unionists (the prized mascots of the policy of 'restriction'), thereby asserting afresh that non-unionism, which among other things directly impedes the process of autonomous collective bargaining, is not based on any parallel to the right to organize in trade unions.[371]

What image of the realities of industrial life and of the role of the law is presented by these legal developments? The trade union, collectively organized labour, is depicted in 1982 as a prime mover in unfair dismissals and as a force against which, if there is a closed shop, the worker or even a person 'seeking' employment needs the protection of the law against 'unreasonable' exclusions or expulsions. Meanwhile no protection is given to the worker 'unreasonably' refused engagement by the employer, even if it happens by reason of a black list of militants; and the collective power of capital leading to investment decisions—and in recent years often to closures and redundancies—which affect the jobs and livelihoods of large numbers of workers is not seen as a force against which the worker needs increased legal protection.

To match its protection of the non-unionist and its assault upon trade union rights in every corner of labour law, 'collective' and 'individual', the policy of restriction has also dismantled those 'props' to collective bargaining and trade unionism favoured by 'reform', the 'auxiliary' laws as Kahn-Freund called them. As we have seen[372] this led to the repeal of the two most important procedures promoting collective bargaining, i.e. the general provision on unilateral arbitration and the more controversial right to bargain with an employer for a union recommended by ACAS. But this was not enough. An EEC Directive of 1977 obliged the Labour government to introduce new laws—which they proposed to do by Regulations—to protect collective bargaining rights, and to transfer workers' rights connected with their employment, when an 'undertaking' is transferred by one employer to another. The Conservative government carefully stripped the earlier administration's 1978 draft of its substance so that now, in the main, the Regulations make 'no difference in practice'[373] to the rights of trade unions.[374] The Regulations, for example, set an absurdly ineffective sanction against an employer who fails in his duty to consult on the transfer with a union: maximum compensation for an employee of two weeks' wages less any compensation for unfair or wrongful dismissal. Even the transfer of workers' rights is incomplete and doubtful.[375] Again, faced with the EEC Commission's proposal for all sizeable undertakings (especially multinationals) to disclose more information over a wide range to their workers, the government's view in 1981 was that legal compulsion in this field would not be appropriate.[376] Even a 'European' commitment cannot overcome the insistence of the new policy that employers must be relieved of responsibility for, and obligations to consult (let alone negotiate) about, the forces of the market. As for industrial training, the new policy's commitment to dismantle large parts of the statutory framework is un-rivalled[377] (and this at a time when there is a pressing need for a concerted effort to make new skills available to workers and to the nation). Futhermore, the major 'auxiliary' rights of trade unions in the 1975 legislation, which depended upon recognition by the employer, are weakened by the Act of 1980. The employer can in fact now remove these legal rights (for example, the right to information) by removing his voluntary recognition of the union.[378] And henceforth, under sections 13 and 14 of the Employment Act 1982, it is illegal for workers to apply industrial pressure to their own employer (no matter what other goals they have) in order to require another employer to recognize, negotiate, or consult with one or more trade unions. Both public and private employers are also forbidden to use commercial pressure to that end.[379]

It is indeed difficult to define the natural boundaries of the new strategy. Why should the legal powers of Wages Councils (other perhaps than the Agricultural Wages Board) survive its logic? Are they sustained by a rationale any stronger than that which failed to salvage the rights of unions to take claims on behalf of the relatively low paid to unilateral arbitration? That provision was after all dismissed by a government spokesman as 'an unnecessary and unwarranted interference in employers' freedom to negotiate their own settlements'.[380] And is the Fair Wages Resolution, protecting the minimum conditions of workers of employers who contract with government departments, saved by any argument other than the demands of ILO Convention No. 94?[381] Are the rights of unions to information from the employer under the 1975 Act retained only because they are largely ineffective?[382] If unions continue to exert influence as they have done for seventy-five years through strong institutional links with the Labour Party, will the 1913 compromise on trade unions' political funds still be sacred? Or will 'contracting-in' (perhaps, in the name of 'individual freedom', contracting-in to any political party nominated by the individual member) replace the present law, thereby reopening the wound inflicted first in 1910 by the Law Lords and again after the General Strike, which few doubted the Donovan Report had finally healed?[383] For Kahn-Freund the institution of the political fund was 'in a sense' one that was 'complementary to the closed shop' and therefore 'taken for granted'; without the closed shop the 1913 arrangements were 'incomprehensible'; the fund and the 'ceremony of "contracting-out" had become part of the pattern of British social life'.[384] If the support of the employer and of the state for joint regulation cannot any longer be taken for granted, will the 1913 compromise perish? If it does, what right has the state to curtail the 'political' activities of trade unions as such, any more than it curtails those of employers and the capital they can use to influence the political process?

Will the restriction strategy lead inevitably to legislation on the maintenance of 'public' or 'essential' services? It should not be forgotten that the public sector in Britain has, since the early acceptance of trade unionism in 1917 by the Whitley Committee, been fortunate in regard to labour law. Public corporations and similar bodies (even local government authorities for the most part) are treated as ordinary employers. Civil servants (or 'Crown' employees), it is true, are a rather special group because it is still not settled whether or how far they have 'contracts' of employment;[385] but their position has been made broadly equivalent to other employees by a mixture of collective agreements and legislation.[386] More important, British labour law has never faced the nightmare experienced by many comparable societies in which the lawyer is obliged to reconcile the historical fact of trade unionism and industrial action by various types of 'public servants' with the legal requirement to jettison his volumes of 'private' labour law and apply to these problems a completely *different* code of 'public' or administrative law—for example the special laws pertinent to the *fonctionnaire* in France, the *Beamte* in Germany, the state or municipal official in Sweden, the public official in Italy, or the federal or state employee in the United States.[387] In most of these countries the law has been forced to bend by granting rights to organize, rights to bargain, and—to some extent—rights to take industrial action. Even now in the United States millions of public employees do not enjoy the right to strike (as the criminal prosecutions of striking air controllers proved in 1981); and academic respectability has been afforded to their industrial subordination by commentators who insist that the 'sovereignty' of the state is at stake, because strikes by public employees can 'skew' the 'normal American political process', and 'work an undesirable change in the distribution of political power in a community' even at municipal level.[388]

In Sweden, also, whose modern system of collective bargaining is generally held to be attractive to the adherents of 'reform' policies, the narrow scope of industrial action which is legitimate for public employees would be regarded by British civil service trade unions as curiously restrictive. In fact the 'body of officials', state and municipal, has been traditionally excluded from ordinary labour law and until the 1930s was subject to penal liability for strikes.[389] Gradually collective rights were conceded; by 1965 rights to organize, to bargain, and (in some measure) to strike were granted; and in 1976 they were extended in regard to statutory rights to negotiate 'joint regulation' agreements along with the private sector. A controversial provision now excludes from legality any 'political' action which is 'intended to influence domestic political matters'—an exception to the normal Swedish principle on the legality of 'political' strikes[390]—though disputes about strikes in that area go by agreement to a special arbitration committee on which the majority are members from the Parliament.[391] After strikes and lock-outs in 1971, an emergency statute (passed in one day) imposed the terms of collective agreements that had expired on the state employees involved. One Swedish authority concluded that, in this area of the public sector, 'a union will scarcely risk going on strike again'.[392]

Although the industrial culture is so very different, the Swedish perspective is useful if only as a corrective to any complacency in Britain about the industrial rights of public service trade unions. In 1927 the legislation that followed the General Strike limited the industrial rights of civil servants; and there is no guarantee that the state will refrain in the eighties from carving similar exceptions out of what remains of the golden formula, to the disadvantage of civil servants and perhaps municipal employees. The policy of restriction will not refrain from invoking the sovereignty of the state or of the 'community' or of the 'national interest' if it is expedient to do so. Such considerations are manifestly not irrelevant; on the contrary labour law must be part of an overall policy for the wider society. But when these phrases are advanced as justifications for law, it is necessary to inquire just how the balance of different interests within the 'community' is likely to be affected. The 1981 Green Paper gave notice of the Conservative government's concern about 'essential services' and protection of 'the community', but with little recognition of the different interests of which the latter is composed. Moreover the judges have reasserted their right to a special discretion to issue injunctions if the harm threatened by industrial action to the 'community' or the 'public' seems to them 'disastrous';[393] and now they have the Secretary of State's Codes to assist them.

Having learned the skills of manipulating 'non-interventionist' institutions in the service of restricting trade union activity, the new policy may have no need for the legislature to introduce new concepts. Parliament has learned from the judges the central technique of 'modifying' the immunities. Special restrictions on the immunities for 'essential' groups of workers might be devised, ready for litigation if employers or other plaintiffs so wish (and perhaps the government if it acquires the necessary *locus standi*). Where the 'national interest' demands it, one can foresee restrictions upon industrial rights in order to protect 'high security' technologies or new powers for the government to use troops. The existing law already affords a little-publicized platform in this respect, ripe for 'gradual' development.[394] And to each individual worker the new structure can be interpreted through the mass media as a vulgarized version of the message that this is after all only a 'step-by-step' modification of the traditional voluntary system, the formal institutions of which remain intact. At each step trade unions would complain—and rightly—of loss of 'fundamental' liberties; but after a few more steps the government could hope they might exhaust their stock of epithets. The same technique could be used on collective bargaining and incomes policy. By 1982 influential voices were once again heard advocating a national wage-fixing system (this time through 'almost compulsory arbitration') to break the 'monopoly' power of trade unions; and arguments were advanced in favour of inhibiting industrial action for pay claims outside the fixed national limits by such sanctions as restriction of social security benefits payable to workers—or more accurately their families—and limitations on the trade union immunities.[395]

In broad terms the policy and its likely developments point to the rejection of the influence of independent trade unions in the market place, whilst attributing to them wherever possible the fault for the ills suffered by individual workers. In a sense that rejection and that attribution would do more than adjust the legal pattern to myths already central to our society. Along with the maintenance of that institution of mystification, the 'free' individual contract of employment, the legend is now to be confirmed by law that the worker has more to fear from just over 100 TUC organizations with declining membership and total assets of £300 million[396] than from the control exercised over his life by any one major transnational enterprise. The courts would not be slow to endorse that confirmation as their social ideal in labour law.

Such a legal system could now emerge from step-by-step modifications of British labour law. It would be a system, though, which could be used to restrict or even suppress the activity of any working-class movement intending to challenge the social system in ways that were seen to threaten the 'public interest' and disturb 'order'. Mass media focus on such dangers would camouflage the increasingly authoritarian tendencies of the state. The values of pluralism (of dispersion of power, toleration, and consent) would indeed be imperilled. And the traditions of democratic struggle of working people would be tested in the way Kahn-Freund feared but could scarcely bring himself to contemplate in Britain.

There is every reason to believe that the rebirth of British society out of its present crisis will need to involve a trans-formation as fundamental as that which industrial capitalism forced upon Britain in the late eighteenth and early nineteenth centuries. It is unlikely, though, that a pluralist democracy can successfully complete such a social transition without the positive support and confidence of working people. Indeed influential commentators have already warned managers in the early eighties that they 'should not believe . . . that employees' more docile attitudes, which have been bred mainly by fear of unemployment, automatically indicate a permanent accep- tance of economic realities or a permanent willingness to co- operate with management decisions'. On the contrary 'the tide that swept the Bullock proposals on industrial democracy into a major issue has not receded for ever' and in future managers must base 'their new found . . . authority' on the 'involvement and support of their employees'.[397]

For those who seek more radical reform policies to meet the challenges of this period of social transition, there has been much discussion of the 'democratic planning and employment of our national resources',[398] and of 'alternative economic strategies'[399] which aim to combine the regeneration of the economy with an increase in the control and participation of working people and the broader community in wide areas of society. Many of these strategies reject a simple return to the approach of 1973–5. This is in part a reflection of the 'over- centralization' of the Social Contract, and in part a response to the forceful articulation of demands which transcend the trad- itional boundaries of the organized labour movement (relating for instance to nuclear weapons, the environment, young people, women, ethnic groups, the disabled, consumer interests). However, central to all these strategies is the argu- ment advanced, for example, in the 1981 policy statement of the TUC-Labour Party Liaison Committee, in favour of 'full trade union participation in the economic and industrial manage- ment of the nation'.[400] The TUC itself, in proposing in 1982 an immediate programme for recovery through a medium-term growth strategy, contrasted the huge concentration of power in the City of London and in multinational companies with the manner in which the views of trade unionists are 'systematically ignored by most employers'. From such an analysis it con- cluded that a new framework of economic and industrial plan- ning should include new 'statutory rights' for employees, for example, rights to information, consultation, and represent- ation. These would allow for 'effective negotiation' and 'permanent and lasting influence' over the 'major activities' of the enterprise, but, consistent with the Bullock formula, they would only come into operation 'as and when the workers and their unions wish to take up these rights'.[401] The demand for more 'statutory rights' of this kind is indeed implicit in many of the radical reform strategies mentioned above. But the function of such labour law rights in the industrial relations system as a whole and their effect on trade unionism itself are likely to depend in great measure upon thinking through the practical consequences of each particular piece of legislation, on the place of such rights in part of a wider strategy, and on the economic and political environment in which they operate.

What then is the general role of industrial relations and labour law in a wider reform strategy? Unlike the policy of 'restriction', whose overriding objective is the weakening of effective trade union organization, such strategies of 'reform' in industrial relations aim to strengthen the collective organization of working people and to extend their influence on work relations and the conduct of the economy (an extension which would itself entail a massive increase in opportunities for education and training). Apart from the principled 'democratic imperative' underlying this approach, greater employee control over basic decisions affecting their working lives is seen as the only realistic way of gaining broad consent for the major changes which may well be required if this period of social transition is to be successfully 'negotiated'. Such a strategy also recognizes that the social power of employers and senior managers in modern capitalist societies is inherently superior to that of the individual employee, and that the democratization of work relations necessarily involves the representation of worker interests through strong collective organizations and collective action. As Kahn-Freund always insisted, 'on the labour side power is collective power',[402] and if the labour movement is to be a motive force in future social progress, then at every point more stress must be laid than in the past upon the collective interests of employees—even in individualized disputes.

If any reform strategy therefore involves an increased emphasis on the collective interests, organization, and action of workers, then it also stresses that collective labour law (the legitimacy of industrial disputes, the making and enforcement of collective agreements, etc.) must be based upon the collective autonomy of organized workers in trade unions. The danger to any conception of pluralist democracy (whether of a 'liberal' or 'socialist' nature) if there is strong state intervention in the central areas of collective labour relations is only too well illustrated by the history of Weimar Germany between 1929 and 1933,[403] and it was his experience of the defeat of Weimar democracy that led Kahn-Freund to stress consistently his commitment to collective autonomy.[404] This commitment was also based on the recognition that the prime source of worker influence is their 'spontaneous' (i.e. independently created) social power. The law may aim to mitigate the inequality of bargaining power inherent in the employment relationship, but success is dependent in the first instance on the strength of worker organization. Again Kahn-Freund clearly illuminated this basic fact of industrial life: 'The law has important functions in labour relations, but they are secondary if compared with the impact of the labour market . . . and with the spontaneous creation of social power on the workers' side to balance that of management. . . . The law does, of course, provide its own sanctions, administrative, penal, and civil, and their impact should not be underestimated, but in labour relations legal norms cannot often be effective unless they are backed up by social sanctions as well, that is by the countervailing power of trade unions and of the organized workers asserted through consultation and negotiation with the employer and ultimately, if this fails, through withholding their labour.'[405]

Nevertheless, even if the collective social relationships of workers to management and the need for more democratic 'power' for trade unions (both internally and externally) are accorded primacy in such a strategy, this does not necessarily imply that 'legal abstention' is, in principle and on all issues, to be given primacy over every kind of state intervention. In fact there are a number of ways, as we have seen in the analysis of the Social Contract labour legislation, in which the law can further the objectives of promoting employment protection and the democratization of work relations.

It may be able to assist in respect of consultation and the disclosure of more (and more meaningful) information. It may also provide more effective methods of extending, by unilateral arbitration, reasonable conditions to the low paid. Moreover, demands for trade unions to be given an 'option' to take up statutory rights have been, as we have seen, a consistent theme in trade union thinking since the debate in the early seventies about 'industrial democracy'. If the 'trigger' for the operation of legally-created machinery is in the possession of workers through their unions, autonomous bargaining, it is felt, can be protected.[406] This device, if used with care, may succeed in its objective. But it is still an open question whether a right of 'representation' (involving a legal duty of 'negotiation' on the employer) can be part of a realistic immediate programme until the difficulties encountered in the 1975 legislation are overcome.[407] It might be preferable for British trade unions (with 300,000 often very experienced shop stewards alongside their full-time officers) to concentrate upon a legal right of 'presence' and 'audience' for trade union representatives; that might be an adequate legal prop in the face of an intransigent employer; a steward could use such a foot in the door to the extent that he felt his support growing—and have the option to step back if he wanted. It may be said that 'multi-unionism' makes such a solution inadequate in Britain. But this is, in a sense, a problem to which the solution is in the unions' own hands (many unions were prepared to experiment with the Joint Representation Committees of the Bullock proposals) and it certainly does not seem to have wrecked the progress of the legally-backed health and safety representatives. Unless an answer can be found to the problems (of obligation, machinery, and remedy) apparent in the 1975 'recognition' provisions, legislation with sharper teeth might well be reserved to create the maximum of discomfort for employers attempting to sabotage systematically the democratic right of workers to collective representation through trade unions.[408] If the moral right to organize collectively stems from the worker's inherent subordination in the employment relationship, why should the law be based upon the presumption that it is right for the employer to reject 'unionization' of his employees? And, indeed, why should it be lawful for the employer to refuse to hire a worker on grounds connected with trade union activity, let alone to circulate a blacklist of militants? Legal intervention in respect of the employer's control of firing was a mark of the previous 'reform' strategy; a more radical 'reform' policy demands that the law should play its part in controlling the right to hire.

In any society there will also remain individuals whose protection cannot be always—or perhaps promptly enough—secured against management abuse, in areas ranging from unfair dismissal to equal pay, and from health and safety at work to (in a more general context) racial and sex discrimin-

ation. The relative importance of statutory regulation compared with the use of voluntary methods in these areas, as well
as the impact of this extended 'floor of rights' on collective
autonomy, are matters which can eventually only be resolved in
practice. For example, it is not inconceivable that trade unions
might under certain circumstances be prepared to support
statutory regulation of working hours and overtime in order to
promote a return to full employment, since this is a prerequisite
for their effective activity. In the past the statutory enforcement
of Wages Councils' orders affecting the low paid has been
backed up by governments, trade unions, and employers, and it
is not beyond the bounds of possibility that statutory measures
to deal with the problem of low pay could in the future achieve
tripartite support. The same applies to the vexed question of
'auxiliary legislation' to provide a statutory 'prop' to promote
joint consultation and negotiation and enhance the realization
of the collective rights and interests of workers. The Social
Contract legislation in this area (obligations on employers to
consult with recognized trade unions on health and safety,
pensions, and redundancy, to disclose information, and to
recognize, bargain, and extend the scope of bargaining with
particular trade unions) had an uneven and chequered career
and has already been examined in some detail.[409] Again,
however, an obligation on employers, supported in the last
resort by legal sanctions, to enable trade unions to represent
their members and ultimately even to subject (if they so
request) a wide range of issues to joint or trilateral regulation
(involving in some cases government, local authorities, the local
community, etc., as well as employers and trade unions) need
not always be totally incompatible with the basic principle of
collective autonomy. Experience shows, however, the care
required in introducing such laws in British conditions.

Those who wish to adopt a reform strategy, whether liberal or
socialist, can surely now approach the place of 'the law'—
whether it be law that imposes sanctions or law that provides
machinery (like ACAS)—at each point of their programme in a
pragmatic fashion, so long as the democratic principle of maintaining effective independent trade unions remains paramount.
If that principle remains as the supreme guide in labour law, it
should be possible to discuss whether to introduce a particular
piece of legislation—and (often even more important) a par-

ticular type of remedy—not as a matter of principle (for or against 'the law') but as a matter of tactics. The question of whether and how to use the law will remain of great importance, but one that can be judged on its merits—a balance into which both the aspirations of the labour movement and the current nature of the legal profession and the judges (into whose hands those laws and those remedies will be put) must of course enter and be weighed. In one sense, therefore, it is inevitable that the boundary between collective autonomy and statutory intervention, whether or not it is seen as 'collective' or 'individual' labour law, will remain in a state of flux, dependent on the wider political, economic, and social climate. And labour law will need to be more firmly based upon the policies chosen to fight those wider issues. Without doubt, however, the prerequisite of any 'alternative strategy' in this period of social transition will be a credible solution both to the plight of those with low incomes and, especially, to mass unemployment. The policy for labour law in the eighties must find its appropriate place in that immediate enterprise. It is on that social base that the new relationship between law and industrial relations must be built.

1. For an interesting parallel analysis of recent employment legislation see R. Lewis and B. Simpson, *Striking a Balance? Employment Law after the 1980 Act*, Oxford, 1981 (hereafter *Lewis and Simpson*).
2. See K. W. Wedderburn, *The Worker and the Law*, Harmondsworth, 2nd. ed. 1971, p. 371. See also O. Kahn-Freund, 'Labour Law', in M. Ginsberg (ed.) *Law and Opinion in England in the 20th Century*, London, 1959, pp. 215–63; O. Kahn-Freund, *Labour and the Law*, London, 2nd ed. 1977; R. Lewis, 'The Historical Development of Labour Law' (1976) 14 *British Journal of Industrial Relations* 1; Lord Wedderburn, 'Industrial Relations and the Courts' (1980) 10 *Industrial Law Journal* 65; *Lewis and Simpson*.
3. Cmnd. 3623, London, 1968.
4. Earl Gowrie, *Parl. Deb.*, H.L., 16 June 1981, col. 528.
5. See O. Kahn-Freund, *Labour and the Law*, London, 1st ed. 1972; R. Simpson and J. Wood, *Industrial Relations and the 1971 Act*, London, 1973; B. Weekes *et al.*, *Industrial Relations and the Limits of Law*, Oxford, 1975; A. Thomson and S. Engelman, *The Industrial Relations Act: A Review and Analysis*, London, 1975; M. Moran, *The Politics of Industrial Relations*, London, 1977.
6. *Fair Deal at Work*, Conservative Political Centre, London, 1968, p. 65 (the main policy document which preceded the 1971 Act).
7. [1973] A.C. 15 (H.L.), where dockers' shop stewards had 'implied authority' to take industrial action for which the union was legally responsible. See also *General Aviation Services (UK) Ltd.* v. *TGWU* [1976] I.R.L.R. 224 (H.L.), where in finding the same union not liable for shop stewards' action at London Airport the Law Lords illustrated the discretion available to the courts by taking a different view of the facts about their 'implied authority'.

8. See below on the 'authority' of shop stewards and union responsibility for their acts, text to n. 318 *et seq*. Almost all unions affiliated to the TUC refused to register, thereby becoming under the Act 'organizations of workers' not trade unions.
9. Industrial Relations Act 1971, Sched. 4, para. 10.
10. Ibid., s. 36(2).
11. Cmnd. 8128, London, 1981, paras. 125, 128, 137. If that happened, 'the problems of deciding when a union was vicariously responsible for the acts of its members would be considerably reduced'. That characteristic strain is often found in the policy of restriction, a belief that the difficult legal problems will disappear because, if only the statute is resolute enough, it will change reality.
12. See Lord Hailsham LC, *Evidence to House of Commons Employment Committee*, 8 April 1981, col. 193, bemoaning the divergence of the 'coherent code of rights and obligations' for incorporated companies (aggregations of capital) and laws on trade unions (associations of workers) since 1800.
13. Cmnd. 3623, para. 122.
14. Ibid., para. 190.
15. Wedderburn, *The Worker and the Law* (1971), p. 25.
16. Industrial Relations Bill: *Consultative Document*, Dept. of Employment, 1970, para. 8.
17. See s. 96, Industrial Relations Act 1971, exposing the unregistered union to liability for any inducement of a breach of contract, invariably an inevitable consequence of industrial action. The liability in the *Heatons* case, n. 7 above, was based upon that section.
18. *Midland Cold Storage* v. *Turner* [1972] I.C.R. 230. Cf. *Churchman* v. *Joint Shop Stewards Committee of the Workers of the Port of London* [1972] I.C.R. 222. See J. A. G. Griffith's comments in *New Statesman*, 24 November 1972, and in *The Politics of the Judiciary*, London, 2nd ed. 1981, Chs. 3 and 8, and pp. 221–42.
19. *Con-Mech (Engineers) Ltd.* v. *AUEW* [1973] I.C.R. 620; (No. 2) [1974] I.C.R. 332. See N. Lewis (1974) 3 *Industrial Law Journal* 201; K. W. Wedderburn (1974) 37 *Modern Law Review* 187.
20. See P. L. Davies (1973) 36 *Modern Law Review*, 78, 89. The point had already been made in the Donovan Report (1968), Appendix 6, which had described the fruitless prosecutions of striking Kent miners at the height of the war in 1941, perhaps the most lucid page of prose in British labour law.
21. Industrial Relations Act 1971, s. 5(1) (b). The right to be a member applied only to the registered union: s. 5(1) (a).
22. Weekes *et al*, *Industrial Relations and the Limits of Law*, p. 63.
23. K. W. Wedderburn, 'Labour Law and Labour Relations in Britain' (1972) 10 *British Journal of Industrial Relations* 270, 282.
24. F. A. Hayek, *1980s Unemployment and the Unions*, London, 1980, p. 55. Prime Minister Margaret Thatcher confirmed that she was a 'great admirer' of Hayek's 'absolutely supreme' works immediately before the budget statement of 10 March 1981: *Parl. Deb.*, H.C., Col. 756. She singled out in particular his *Law, Legislation and Liberty* (London, 1979), where, in Volume 3, Hayek castigates the power of the trade unions, 'which in most countries have been allowed by law or jurisdiction to use coercion to gain support for their policies'. Hayek goes on to suggest that, by preventing other workers from doing what they would wish to do, and by reducing the general productivity of labour, the entire system of trade union power and privilege 'is rapidly destroying the economic order. Trades unions can now put governments in a position in which the only choice they have is to inflate or to be blamed for the unemployment which is caused by the wage policy of the trades unions. . . . This position must before long destroy the whole market order.' (p. 144).

25. J. Gorst, MP, question to Wedderburn, *Evidence to Employment Committee*, House of Commons, 6 May 1981 (drawing a response that immunities are about liability for interference with contracts not for 'sinful' acts), col. 241.

26. W. H. Hutt, *The Theory of Collective Bargaining 1930–1975*, London, 1975, p. 124, a process which he has called 'strike-threat impoverishment'.

27. F. A. Hayek, in *Inflation Causes, Consequences, Cures*, London, 1974, p. 120.

28. Employment Protection (Handling of Redundancies) Variation Order 1979 S.I. 958. The other.1979 Order was the Unfair Dismissal (Variation of Qualifying Period) Order 1979 S.I. 959 (which excluded workers from their rights to compensation for unfair dismissal until they had one year of continuous service instead of twenty-six weeks). This was part of a policy of weakening the law on unfair dismissal generally: see Employment Act 1980, ss. 6 (burden of proof of reasonableness no longer to be on the employer), 8 (exceptions for employees in small firms and fixed-term contracts), 9 (reduction of compensation). See too on the weakening of maternity rights for women employees, ss. 11 and 12. Protection for time off for ante-natal care was, it is true, increased, s. 13; but the rights of non-unionists in respect of unfair dismissal were extensively increased, s. 7. See too s. 15(1) on 'action short of dismissal', *Lewis and Simpson*, Ch. 2.

29. Ss. 11–16; see below, text to n. 297 *et seq.*, and text to n. 407 *et seq.*

30. See above, n. 28. See now also the threat to the Fair Wages Resolution and even to Wages Councils, n. 381 below.

31. See, for example, his last published work, *Labour Relations: Heritage and Adjustment*, Oxford, 1979, p. 81.

32. Some 'interim' orders last for many years; see *Stratford* v. *Lindley* (No. 2) [1969] 1 W.L.R. 1547 (C.A.) (litigation about costs). The 'interim' order made in *Stratford* v. *Lindley* [1965] A.C. 269 (H.L.) was still in force four years later. For an excellent account of the problem see P. Davies and M. Freedland, *Labour Law: Text and Materials*, London, 1979, Ch. 8, Part 3. In *NWL Ltd.* v. *Woods* [1979] 1 W.L.R. 1294, the Law Lords, esp. Lord Diplock, recognized that industrial disputes are unusual in that the 'interim' injunction is nearly always the final remedy sought; but the majority of the judgments in this and other cases also looked forward to extensions of the unions' substantive liabilities: see below, text to n. 214.

33. Despite the provisions of the Trade Union and Labour Relations Act, 1974, s. 17(2), hereafter TULRA. See *NWL Ltd.* v. *Woods* [1979] I.C.R. 867 (noted by R. Simpson (1980) 43 *Modern Law Review* 327); *Express Newspapers Ltd.* v. *McShane* [1980] A.C. 672 (noted by Wedderburn (1980) 43 *Modern Law Review* 319); *Duport Steels Ltd.* v. *Sirs* [1980] I.C.R. 161.

34. See section 17, which is fraught with technical difficulty, esp. in the exceptions to (or 'gateways' through) the prohibition: see Lord Wedderburn, 'Secondary Action and Gateways to Legality: A Note' (1981) 10 *Industrial Law Journal* 113; B. Bercusson, 'Picketing, Secondary Picketing and Secondary Action' (1980) 9 *Industrial Law Journal* 215. For the first example of the remarkable limitations upon all 'blacking' and on the narrow character of the 'gateways' in s. 17 of the Employment Act 1980, see *Marina Shipping Ltd.* v. *Laughton* [1982] I.R.L.R. 20 (C.A.).

35. Ss. 16 and 18 respectively of the 1980 Act. See Clerk and Lindsell on *Torts*, London, 15th ed. 1982, Ch. 15; *Lewis and Simpson*, Chs. 8 and 9.

36. See the argument advanced in *Lewis and Simpson*, pp. 171–5. The Code can create no new liability; but it must be 'taken into account' by a court if 'relevant' to any question: s. 3(8).

37. *Hadmor Productions Ltd.* v. *Hamilton* [1981] I.C.R. 690, 710 *per* Lord Denning MR (emphasis in original) interpreting s. 17(8) of the Act; see Clerk and Lindsell on *Torts* (1982), paras. 15–32, on 'unlawful means' and trade disputes.

38. Now *Hadmor Productions Ltd.* v. *Hamilton* [1982] 2 W.L.R. 322 (H.L.) reversing the Court of Appeal.

39. Where, for example, workers are employed by a subsidiary company and the dispute is with the parent holding company, the former is not in law a 'party' to the dispute.
40. Compare the outstanding criminal liability in s. 5 Conspiracy and Protection of Property Act 1875 (strikes in breach of contract damaging life or property) which is widely assumed to have lapsed into desuetude; but see below, n. 162.
41. *Code of Practice: Closed Shop Agreements and Arrangements*, Dept. of Employment, 1980, para. 54.
42. Ss. 4 and 5 of the 1980 Act. The legal term of art if of course 'union membership agreement' (defined in s. 30, TULRA 1974, as amended); but we have used the term 'closed shop' which is more common among non-lawyers.
43. See s. 10 introducing s. 76A into the Employment Protection (Consolidation) Act 1978, hereafter EPCA. See also ibid for ss. 76B and 76C, introducing 'double joinder', whereby an employer who was under contract with another firm, and who had to dismiss a non-unionist by reason of that firm's insistence that he must perform it with union members only, could obtain an indemnity against the compensation he was made to pay from that firm. The firm could then claim an indemnity or contribution from any union or official whose industrial pressure caused it to insist on that condition of union labour. These provisions have now been overtaken by ss. 7 and 11, Employment Act 1982. See below, n. 54 and text to n. 358 *et seq.*, on the real meaning of 'joinder'. On the more severe ss. 12, 13 and 14 of the 1982 Act see below, text to n. 48 *et seq.* and n. 379.
44. Employment Act 1982, s. 18(2).
45. Ibid., s. 18(5); and see *Stratford* v. *Lindley* [1965] A.C. 269, 326, Viscount Radcliffe; Lord Wright in *Crofter Hand Woven Harris Tweed* v. *Veitch* [1942] A.C. 435, p. 480; Wedderburn, *The Worker and the Law* (1971), p. 329; *Lewis and Simpson*, p. 191.
46. Employment Act 1982, s. 18(6).
47. Ibid., s. 15; see further below, text to n. 330 *et seq.* On the revival of *Taff Vale*, the new law will limit damages that can be claimed for any one claim (e.g. £250,000 for a union of more than 100,000 members). But this is for each case of 'proceedings in tort', s. 16. The political funds and 'provident benefit funds' are, however, 'protected property' and not available for enforcement of damages: s. 17. On the 1971 Act and vicarious liability see above, text to n. 7 *et seq.*
48. Employment Act, 1982, s. 12. A late addition to the Act, section 13, goes further still, see below, n. 379.
49. Ibid. s. 14(2) (3). The consequent inability of TUC-affiliated unions to uphold the agreed boundaries between unions in a multi-union situation against a rogue invading union will become of great importance for any manager interested in orderly industrial relations.
50. 'It could provoke trouble on large sites [in the construction industry] already notorious for their chaotic labour relations', *Financial Times*, 29 January 1982.
51. 'The possibilities for anarchic obstruction are endless', *The Times*, 26 January 1982. The men refused to drive trains if they carried copies of a newspaper which had accused railway drivers of widespread dishonesty. In High Court proceedings the two local officials gave an undertaking, which has the same effect as an injunction, obliging them to withdraw their recommendation. On the parallels with 1972, see above, text to n. 18 *et seq.*
52. O. Kahn-Freund, 'Legal Framework', in A. Flanders and H. A. Clegg (eds.), *The System of Industrial Relations in Great Britain*, Oxford, 1954, pp. 110–11. The labour injunction was excluded by the federal law in the United States by the Norris La Guardia Act 1932.
53. Employment Act 1982, s. 15; see further below, text to n. 344 *et seq.*
54. Ibid., s. 7. The 'joinder' is to be available at any stage of the proceedings (instead of, as before, permitted only before the hearing begins: s. 10, Employment Act

1980) but the tribunal has a discretion to refuse joinder if it is claimed after the hearing has begun: s. 7(2). This can only encourage joinder of the union at the outset. The same machinery for joinder is applied to an employee's unlawful action short of dismissal: s. 11.

55. Ibid., s. 9
56. *Parl. Deb.*, H.C., 17 December 1979, Col. 162 (P. Mayhew, Under Secretary of State for Employment).
57. *Trade Union Immunities* (1981), paras. 34, 93, 342 and 384.
58. Lord Wedderburn, 'Industrial Relations and the Courts' (1980) 9 *Industrial Law Journal* 65.
59. Ibid., p. 93.
60. The Employment Act 1980, s. 15(1) deletes the words 'which is not independent' from the EPCA 1978, s. 23(1)(c): see *Lewis and Simpson*, pp. 66–72. For an everyday situation where management and unions might be affected see *Carlson* v. *Post Office* [1981] I.C.R. 343 (refusal of parking place; unlawful infringement of right not to be penalized for trade union membership; applicant not member of recognized union).
61. Employment Act 1980, s. 7; these conditions remain in Employment Act 1982, s. 3.
62. See now the complex ss. 58(3) and 58A of the 1978 Act added by section 3, Employment Act 1982. Action short of dismissal to enforce union membership is also banned except within the same five-year period: s. 10.
63. See s. 58(1)(c) of the 1978 Act as rewritten by section 3, Employment Act 1982.
64. *Proposals for Industrial Relations Legislation*, Dept. of Employment, November 1981; hereafter *Proposals* (1981).
65. S.2, Employment Act 1982; and Sched. 1 which sets out the scheme. The Secretary of State is not bound by the finding of a tribunal which rejected a claim by such a worker. The losers seem to be non-unionists who were successful in tribunal proceedings, esp. those between 1974 and 1975, because of the upper limits set on the Minister's discretionary payments: see paras. 2(1), 3, 6 and 7 of Sched. 1.
66. Employment Act 1982, ss. 4 and 5. In case of non-compliance with an order for re-instatement when it is practicable to comply, the amounts are £17,000 and 156 weeks' pay, plus £2,000. The minimum may be reduced in cases of misconduct by the employee. The 'special awards' also apply to workers dismissed for trade union membership and for trade union activities; but these were not in the forefront of the government's mind. The figures can be changed by Order.
67. See *Proposals* (1981), paras. 12 and 14 (minima of £14,000 and £17,000). The President of the CBI also said such provision 'could lead to abuse by individuals without a genuine grievance': *Financial Times*, 8 January 1982.
68. See the new ss. 58(1), 73(4A), and 75A of the 1978 Act, as rewritten by s. 3, 4, and 5, Employment Act 1982.
69. See paras. 30(vii) and 42–6, *Closed Shop Code*, urging periodic review of existing closed shops.
70. Employment Act 1980, ss. 4 and 5. After 1982, proceedings pending under these sections give the complainant protection against unfair dismissal in a closed shop; s. 3, Employment Act 1982 (new s. 58(7) of the EPCA 1978).
71. See below, text to n. 230 *et seq.*
72. See S. Dunn, 'The Growth of the Post-Entry Closed Shop in Britain since the 1960s: Some Theoretical Considerations' (1981) 19 *British Journal of Industrial Relations* 275; W. Brown (ed.), *The Changing Contours of British Industrial Relations*, Oxford, 1981, Ch. 4. This study argues that the closed shop is in fact fast becoming an institution of 'joint discipline' (union and management) rather than union solidarity; see esp. p. 59.

73. *System* (1954), p. 45.
74. Most of the 'statutory floor' of rights apply only for the benefit of the employee—someone who works under a contract of 'employment' (i.e. 'service'): EPCA 1978, s. 153(1). For slightly wider definitions for protection from sexual and racial discrimination at work: Sex Discrimination Act 1975, s. 82(1), Race Relations Act 1976, s. 78(1).
75. See M. R. Freedland, *The Contract of Employment*, Oxford, 1976, pp. 3–6. On what follows see too the useful condensed analysis in B. Hepple and P. O'Higgins, *Employment Law*, London, 4th ed. 1981, Ch. 2; and the stimulating analysis in Davies and Freedland, *Labour Law: Text and Materials*, pp. 262–78, 455–83.
76. 'Introduction' to Karl Renner, *The Institutions of Private Law and their Social Functions*, London, 1949, p. 28.
77. See respectively s. 30(1), TULRA 1974; Trade Disputes Act 1906, s. 5(3); Molestation of Workmen Act 1859; Combination Act 1800, ss. 1, 4.
78. For an example where it does, see Equal Pay Act 1970, s. 1.
79. O. Kahn-Freund, 'A Note on Status and Contract' (1967) 30 *Modern Law Review* 635, 641. We lacked for too long the concept of a contract 'voluntarily' entered into but moulded as to its terms by positive law. As to the 'apparent exception' in the Truck Acts 1831 to 1896 see ibid., pp. 641–2.
80. O. Kahn-Freund, 'Blackstone's Neglected Child: The Contract of Employment' (1977) 93 *Law Quarterly Review*, 508, 527; even Blackstone was 'unable to see statute law and common law as a whole', p. 528.
81. On the specialized industrial tribunals see below, text to n. 230 *et seq.*
82. Kahn-Freund, 'Introduction' to *Renner*, p. 28; *Labour* (1977), p. 6. Compare P. S. Atiyah, *The Rise and Fall of Freedom of Contract*, Oxford, 1979, pp. 523–44, who does however recognize collective bargaining as a form of 'freedom of contract' (p. 600).
83. Lord Atkin, *Nokes v. Doncaster Amalgamated Collieries Ltd.* [1940] A.C. 1014, 1026; see Kahn-Freund's note in (1941) 4 *Modern Law Review* 221. The case concerned a merger; see on the automatic transfer of employment contracts when an 'undertaking' is transferred (but not control of a company) the Employment Protection (Transfer of Undertakings) Regulations S.I. No. 1794, 1981, n. 375 below.
84. See O. Kahn-Freund, 'A Note on Status and Contract' (1967) 30 *Modern Law Review* 643; his message here was also that an increase of statutory regulation of the content of employment relations and thereby an increase of 'status' did not imply a move towards an authoritarian direction of labour.
85. A. Fox, *Beyond Contract: Work, Power and Trust Relations*, London, 1974, p. 184.
86. Buckley L. J., *Secretary of State for Employment* v. *ASLEF* (No. 2) [1972] I.C.R. 19, 62. On the terms implied in contracts of employment see Hepple and O'Higgins, *Employment Law* (1981), pp. 115–50; Wedderburn, *The Worker and the Law* (1971), pp. 95–112; Davies and Freedland, *Labour Law: Text and Materials*, pp. 240–9.
87. Davies and Freedland, *Labour Law, Text and Materials*, p. 457.
88. Bramwell, B., *Yewens* v. *Noakes* (1880) 6 Q.B.D. 530, 532–3.
89. For the law today see Winfield and Jolowicz on *Tort*, London, 11th ed. 1979, pp. 551 *et seq.*; and on vicarious liability and trade unions see below, text to n. 332 *et seq.*
90. See W. Houldsworth, *History of English Law*, London, 3rd ed. 1974, Vol. II, pp. 460 *et seq.*, (hereafter *Houldsworth*); B. Putnam, *The Enforcement of the Statute of Labourers 1349–1359*, New York, 1908; J. Riddall, *The Law of Industrial Relations*, London, 1981, Ch. 2.
91. *Houldsworth*, Vol. IV, p. 382.
92. S. F. C. Milsom, *Historical Foundations of the Common Law*, London, 1967, p. 280. Servants might of course be in different categories under such statutes; for

example, domestic servants did not fall under normal rate-fixing, and an Act of 1548, which forbade combination of workmen, required certain groups to be hired by the year: *Houldsworth*, Vol. IV, p. 383.

93. G. Jones, 'Per Quod Servitium Amisit' (1958) 74 *Law Quarterly Review* 39, 54.

94. Conspiracy and Protection of Property Act 1875, s. 17; they were a primary weapon of enforcing employment discipline: see D. Simon, 'Master and Servant', in J. Saville (ed.), *Democracy and the Labour Movement*, London, 1954. The master was subject only to money penalties.

95. *Lumley* v. *Gye* (1853) 2 E & B 216. On these torts see Clerk & Lindsell on *Torts* (1982), Chs. 15 and 16. Houldsworth called *Lumley* v. *Gye* 'an enormous extension' of liability: Vol. IV, p. 384. (The action for loss of *servitium* will be abolished by s. 2, Administration of Justice Act 1982.)

96. *Jones Bros. (Hunstanton)* v. *Stevens* [1955] 1 Q.B. 275, 282, *per* Lord Goddard C. J. *Servitium* comes from the time when 'service was a status': *Admiralty Commissioners* v. *S.S. Americka* [1917] A.C. 38, 60, *per* Lord Sumner.

97. C. H. S. Fifoot, *History and Sources of the Common Law, Tort and Contract*, London, 1949, p. 184; and pp. 185–95 on what follows.

98. See below, text to n. 330 *et seq.*; T. Baty, *Vicarious Liability*, Oxford, 1916; and P. Atiyah, *Vicarious Liability in the Law of Torts*, London, 1967, Chs. 1 and 2. The principle of the 'implied command' can be traced back to *Tuberville* v. *Stamp* (1697) 1 Ld. Raym. 264. Today the master is liable if the employee acts 'within the course of his employment'.

99. *Commentaries on the Laws of England*, 1st ed. 1765, Vol. I, Bk. I, Ch. 14, p. 422.

100. Kahn-Freund, 'Blackstone's Neglected Child: The Contract of Employment', p. 519, where he also discusses the development and function of the 'yearly hiring' and the 'minute contract' of industrial workers. For the social and economic causes which created a need to enforce liability against enterprises in the expanding sector of corporate commercial activity between the seventeenth and nineteenth centuries, see H. Laski, 'The Basis of Vicarious Liability' (1916) 26 *Yale Law Journal* 110, and H. Wigmore, 'Responsibility for Tortious Acts' (1894) 7 *Harvard Law Review*, Part II, pp. 383–405. The vicarious liability doctrine (together with insurance against risk of liability) was ultimately the vehicle for transferring the cost of liability to the consumer: see Laski, ibid., pp. 110–12; W. Friedman, 'Social Insurance and the Principles of Tort Liability' (1949) 63 *Harvard Law Review* 241. For a remarkable comparative assessment see G. F. Mancini, 'Rapporto di lavoro e responsabilita del committente nella Common Law' (1952) *Rivista di diritto del lavoro* 404. See too, P. S. Atiyah, *Accidents, Compensation and the Law*, London, 2nd ed. 1975.

101. *Blake* v. *Lanyon* (1795) 6 T.R. 221, 222, a landmark decision for the supplanting of 'status' by 'contract' in the legal structure: *Houldsworth*, Vol. IV, p. 384.

102. For an excellent account of the effect of the Poor Laws see J. Fulbrook, *Administrative Justice and the Unemployed*, London, 1978, Ch. 5.

103. On other factors, such as the payment of wages, the right to dismiss, etc., see Atiyah, *Vicarious Liability in the Law of Tort*, Ch. 6.

104. Note on *Cassidy* v. *Ministry of Health* [1951] 2 K.B. 343, in (1951) 14 *Modern Law Review* 504, 506.

105. *Mersey Docks and Harbour Board* v. *Coggins and Griffith* [1947] A.C. 1, 20, *per* Lord Simonds. See too *Donovan* v. *Laing* [1893] 1 Q.B. 629 (crane driver; the '*right* of controlling him' was the test used).

106. H. Street, *Law of Torts*, London, 6th ed. 1976, p. 418.

107. *Boson* v. *Sandford* (1691) 2 Salk. 440 (Holt C. J., who was the father of the new 'implied command' principle). Many of Holt's judgments and the later judicial developments were probably bad law on a strict reading of the precedents (Baty (1916), pp.. 20–35), thus illustrating the force of economic and social factors (see Laski (1916), n. 100 above).

108. McCardie, J., *Performing Right Society Ltd.* v. *Mitchell and Booker Ltd.* [1924] 1 K.B. 762, 767.
109. Law Reform (Personal Injuries) Act 1948.
110. *Lister* v. *Romford Ice and Cold Storage Co. Ltd.* [1957] A.C. 555 (H.L.). See G. Williams, 'Vicarious Liability and the Master's Indemnity' (1957) 20 *Modern Law Review* 220, 437.
111. On the subsequent 'gentlemen's agreement' by insurance companies not to enforce this right, the Employers' Liability (Compulsory Insurance) Act 1969, and the Civil Liability (Contribution) Act 1978, see B. Hepple and M. Matthews, *Tort Cases and Materials*, London, 2nd ed. 1980, pp. 673–712.
112. Note on *Cassidy* v. *Ministry of Health* (1951), p. 505. There were of course always problems about certain classes of servants and apprentices; and later there were periods when some problems (like 'common employment') were evaded in certain judgments by the enlargement of the employer's 'personal' liability.
113. Denning L. J., *Stevenson Jordan and Harrison Ltd.* v. *Macdonald and Evans* [1952] 1 T.L.R. 101, 111 (C.A.) (who gives those illustrations); see Atiyah, *Vicarious Liability in the Law of Torts*, pp. 31–9; and C. Drake, 'Wage Slave or Entrepreneur?' (1968) 31 *Modern Law Review* 408.
114. *Withers* v. *Flackwell Heath F.C.* [1981] I.R.L.R. 307; *Ready Mixed Concrete Ltd.* v. *Minister of Pensions* [1968] 2 Q.B. 497. The answer to this, in ordinary language, would clearly be 'No' in respect of many 'self-employed' workers (e.g. building workers 'on the lump').
115. *Cassidy* v. *Ministry of Health* [1951] 2 K.B. 343, 352; *Thames TV* v. *Wallis* [1979] I.R.L.R. 136, 138 (EAT); *Challinor* v. *Taylor* [1972] I.C.R. 129, 134 (NIRC).
116. *Parsons* v. *Albert Parsons Ltd.* [1979] I.C.R. 271 (C.A.).
117. *Young and Woods Ltd.* v. *West* [1980] I.R.L.R. 201 (C.A.), *per* Stephenson L. J. at p. 207; compare *Massey* v. *Crown Life Insurance* [1978] I.C.R. 590; *Ferguson* v. *Dawson* [1976] I.C.R. 346 (C.A.).
118. See R. Upex (1981) 10 *Industrial Law Journal* 124 and (1979) 8 *Industrial Law Journal* 102, for a very useful survey of the cases between 1975 and 1981.
119. *WHPT Housing Association Ltd.* v. *Secretary of State for Social Services* [1981] I.C.R. 737. The echo of the medieval obligation of the servant to 'present himself' for work is an inescapable feature of the judgment.
120. Ibid. at p. 751; and see *Tyne and Clyde Warehouses* v. *Hamerton* [1978] I.C.R. 661 (EAT going behind the parties' intentions).
121. See Hepple and O'Higgins, *Employment Law*, pp. 68–72; Wedderburn, *The Worker and the Law* (1971), pp. 61–7; and the *Committee of Inquiry* under Professor Phelps Brown concerning labour in building and civil engineering, Cmnd. 3714, London, 1968.
122. Finance Act 1971, ss. 29–31, and Finance (No. 2) Act 1975, ss. 68–71.
123. Davies and Freedland, *Labour Law: Text and Materials*, p. 466. On the problems which attend the inadequacy of legal structures for genuine small enterprises see *A New Form of Incorporation for Small Firms*, Cmnd. 8171, London, 1981, esp. Annexe A, Professor L. C. B. Gower. Neither the Companies Act 1980 nor that of 1981, which both benefited large capital concentration, found a place for such provisions.
124. See generally on such workers, Hepple and O'Higgins, *Employment Law*, pp. 70–1; and B. A. Hepple and B. Napier, 'Temporary Workers and the Law' (1978) 7 *Industrial Law Journal* 84, who argue that such workers need to be identified by statute and protected in ways that might require defining a 'legitimate' area of seasonal or other temporary employment.
125. Employment Agencies Act 1973, and the Regulations S.I. 1976 No. 710, 1979 No. 342, and 1981 No. 1481 (on au pair girls). The worker is not normally the 'employee' of the supplier: *Construction Industry Training Board* v. *Labour Force Ltd.* [1970] 3 All E.R. 220.

126. Conduct of Employment Agencies Regulations 1976, No. 715, Reg. 9(6); Social Security (Categorization of Earners) Regulations 1975, No. 528, Reg. 5; and 1976, No. 404.
127. *Wiltshire County Council* v. *Guy* [1980] I.C.R. 455 (C.A.); *Ryan* v. *Shipboard Maintenance Ltd.* [1980] I.C.R. 88.
128. For details see Hepple and O'Higgins, *Employment Law*, p. 69. The classic and exceptional example of 'decasualization' is provided by the registered dock workers' scheme under the Dock Workers (Regulation of Employment) (Amendment) Order 1967 S.I. 1252; see now the Dock Workers Regulation Act 1976, ss. 4, 12.
129. Ibid., p. 72.
130. M. R. Freedland, 'Leaflet Law: The Temporary Short-Time Working Compensation Scheme' (1980) 9 *Industrial Law Journal* 254.
131. (1951) 14 *Modern Law Review*, p. 508.
132. This phenomenon is not confined to Britain. An intense debate has recently developed in France concerning 'la reconstruction de la communauté de travail', which touches upon all the topics discussed above (including 'temporary work'): see J. C. Javillier, *Mise à Jour*, Paris, 1982, to his *Droit du Travail*, Paris, 2nd ed. 1981, p. 81, para. 78. The Socialist government has recently been associated with the objective of re-establishing 'the protective and unifying role of labour law' in respect of employment as a whole, ibid., p. 115, para. 101. Despite the comprehensive legal regulation which divides French from British labour law, the parallels in this debate with regard to the concept of 'employment' are striking. In Italy too, the traditional line between 'il lavoro subordinato' and 'il lavoro autonomo' is blurred (see E. Ghera, *Il diritto del lavoro*, Bari, 1982, pp. 26–51), and the difficult category of 'parasubordinazione' is employed for testing the constitutional trade union rights of certain marginal groups of 'workers' (see G. Ghezzi and U. Romagnoli, *Il diritto sindacale*, Bologna, 1982, pp. 59–61). On the legal consequences of the 'fragmentation' of the labour market, see G. Giugni, *Prospettive del diritto del lavoro per gli anni '80*, Milan, 1982.
133. S. 8(1), Employment Act 1980: see too s. 12; and *Lewis and Simpson*, Ch. 2.
134. See Wedderburn, *The Worker and the Law* (1971), p. 65; see too the Phelps Brown Report, n. 121 above.
135. See below, n. 408.
136. See ss. 17 and 18, Employment Act 1980; Clerk and Lindsell on *Torts* (1982), paras. 15–30 and 15–32. For the problems attending industrial action against labour-only subcontracting even before 1980 see *Emerald Construction* v. *Lowthian* [1966] 1 W.L.R. 691 (C.A.). See also Employment Act 1982, ss. 12, 13, 14, and 18.
137. *System* (1954), p. 127.
138. *BBC* v. *Hearn* [1977] I.C.R. 685 (C.A.).
139. Lord Diplock, *NWL Ltd.* v. *Woods* [1979] 1 W.L.R. 1294, 1304, commenting on *BBC* v. *Hearn*, above; at first instance the judge, Pain J., had held that the union demand was of that nature; see Wedderburn (1978) 41 *Modern Law Review* 80. And see *per* Lord Scarman [1979] 1 W.L.R. at p. 1314. But the majority Law Lords (including Lord Diplock) appeared to reject this way of making a dispute into a 'trade dispute' in *Universe Tankships Inc.* v. *ITF* [1982] 2 W.L.R. 803 (H.L.); see Wedderburn (1982) 45 *Modern Law Review* 556.
140. S. 29(1), TULRA 1974: 'connected with' (in summary): terms and conditions or duties or physical conditions of employment; recruitment, dismissal, suspension of workers; allocation of work; discipline; membership or non-membership of a union; facilities for union officials; and machinery or procedures on those matters including recognition of a union. See the amendments to s. 29 made by s. 18, Employment Act 1982, above, text to n. 44 *et seq.*
141. The 'economic torts' are concerned largely with interference with contracts, at

first (under the 1906 Act) with contracts of employment and later with all types of contract (now mainly in s. 13, TULRA 1974–6). As for the different immunity of the union itself in tort under s. 14(1) of TULRA see above, text to n. 44 *et seq.*, and below, text to n. 328 *et seq.* For details of the modern law see Clerk and Lindsell on *Torts* (1982), Ch. 15; and now Employment Act 1982, ss. 15–19.

142. *Trade Union Immunities* (1981), Ch. 4, pp. 86–91.

143. CBI, *Trade Unions in a Changing World: The Challenge for Management* (discussion document), 1980, p. 22.

144. A. Goodhart, 'The General Strike' (1927) 36 *Yale Law Journal* 464, in *Essays in Jurisprudence and the Common Law*, 1937, p. 234.

145. *Heritage* (1979), pp. 70–88; see also Wedderburn above, text to n. 189 *et seq.*

146. That is why judges sometimes advise 'considerable caution' in using the term 'political strike', arguing that it has no 'precise or accurate definition', and that there is a danger that a judge may use it to condemn 'something of which he subjectively disapproves'. Roskill L. J., *Sherard* v. *AUEW* [1973] I.C.R. 421, 435.

147. See U. Romagnoli in *Commentario della costituzione: rapporti economici* (T. Treu *et al.*, ed. G. Branca, Bologna, 1979) pp. 289–302; and on the complementary Workers Statute 1970, *Lo Statuto dei Lavoratori*, ed. G. Giugni, Varese, 1979, Arts. 15–20, 28. Dismissal for strike action is unlawful.

148. *Public Prosecutor* v. *Antenaci*, 27 December 1974, reported (1978) 1 *International Labour Law Reports*, pp. 51–4.

149. G. Camerlynck and G. Lyon-Caen, *Droit du Travail*, Paris, 10th ed. 1980, p. 755 and p. 752 respectively.

150. *Per* Lord Scarman, *NWL Ltd.* v. *Woods* [1979] 1 W.L.R. 1294, 1312.

151. See s. 17, Employment Act 1980 (which in particular excluded most disputes between workers from protection because they would always involve 'secondary action'). For the meaning of s. 17(8) see *Hadmor Productions Ltd.* v. *Hamilton* [1981] 2 All E.R. 724 (C.A.); [1982] 2 W.L.R. 332 (H.L.).

152. See Employment Act 1982, ss. 15–19.

153. *A Giant's Strength*, 1958, Inns of Court Conservative and Unionist Society, p. 26 (emphasis supplied). By 1968, *Fair Deal at Work* (Conservative Political Centre), the forerunner of the 1971 Act, proposed an amendment of the term 'trade dispute' so as to exclude sympathetic strikes (but this did not include cases where workers had 'a direct and personal interest in the original dispute'), p. 30.

154. Lord Wedderburn, 'Industrial Relations and the Courts' (1980) 9 *Industrial Law Journal* 65, 75.

155. See: Wedderburn, *The Worker and the Law* (1971), Chs. 7 and 8; Davies and Freedland, *Labour Law: Text and Materials*, 1979 and 1980 Supplement, Chs. 8 and 9; *Lewis and Simpson*, Chs. 1 and 9.

156. *Proposals* (1981), para. 37.

157. *The Times*, 7 and 12 December 1981.

158. *Financial Times*, 12 September 1981.

159. As in the case of the strikes on the TUC 'Day of Action' on 14 May 1980 (*Express Newspapers Ltd.* v. *Keys* [1980] I.R.L.R. 247) and the strikes against the Industrial Relations Bill (*Associated Newspapers Group* v. *Flynn* (1970) 10 K.I.R. 17). See too *BBC* v. *Hearn* [1977] I.C.R. 685, n. 138 above.

160. *The Times*, 31 December 1981, Professor J. A. Jolowicz.

161. *Bromley LBC* v. *GLC* [1982] 1 All E.R. 129 (H.L.), without doubt one of the more 'political' judicial decisions of our time, in Professor Griffith's sense: n. 165 below.

162. *Financial Times*, 22 December 1981; Conspiracy and Protection of Property Act 1875, s. 7. The union pointed out that co-ordination of selective action (on which the official was engaged) could be rendered impossible by such judgments. A warning note that the offences under this section, including 'intimidation', would be revived was heard in the Shrewsbury picket case, *R.* v. *Jones* [1974] I.C.R. 310;

but the use made of conspiracy in that case to allow for longer sentences than the section allows was largely prevented by the Criminal Law Act 1977 (though other offences, such as unlawful assembly, may do so: *Lewis and Simpson*, p. 164).

163. *Financial Times*, 23 December 1981; evidence to the government's inquiry into non-industrial civil service pay; *Trade Union Immunities* (1981), Ch. 3, pp. 75–82, esp. para. 337. On the varying approach to the right to strike for public employees see B. Aaron and K. W. Wedderburn (eds.), *Industrial Conflict—A Comparative Legal Survey*, London, 1972, Ch. 6.

164. *NWL Ltd.* v. *Woods* [1979] 1294 at p. 1304; and R. C. Simpson (1980) 43 *Modern Law Review* 336.

165. See Griffith, *The Politics of the Judiciary*, pp. 221–5; and below, text to n. 213 *et seq.*

166. Because, as there is no employer 'party' to the dispute (often a very technical decision), the action must qualify as 'secondary action' under s. 17 of the 1980 Act; see *Lewis and Simpson*, Ch. 9; Clerk and Lindsell on *Torts* (1982), paras. 15.27–15.38. On the difficulty of knowing when the employer is a 'party' to the dispute see *Cory Lighterage Ltd.* v. *TGWU* [1973] I.C.R. 339 (C.A.).

167. Compare: *Health Computing Ltd.* v. *Meek* [1981] I.C.R. 24; *Crazy Prices (Northern Ireland) Ltd.* v. *Hewitt* [1980] I.R.L.R. 396 (Northern Ireland C.A.); and *Hadmor Productions Ltd.* v. *Hamilton* [1981] I.C.R. 690 (C.A.); [1982] 2 W.L.R. 322 (H.L.); R. C. Simpson (1982) 45 *Modern Law Review* 447.

168. See section 18(2) restricting trade disputes to disputes between employers and their own employees which *relate wholly or mainly* to the 'industrial' content. The term 'relates to', used also in the 1971 Act, is more restrictive than 'connected with'.

169. Astbury, J., *National Sailors and Firemans Union of GB* v. *Reed* [1926] Ch. 536, 539–40; and A. L. Goodhart (1927) 36 *Yale Law Journal* 464 (see above, n. 144). On the political roles of Astbury J. and Sir John Simon in 1926 see Griffith, *The Politics of the Judiciary*, pp. 66–9.

170. The government enacted instead the Trade Disputes and Trade Union Act 1927, introducing (amongst other things) new limitations on strikes called against the government, on the rights of civil servants and other public employees, and on union political funds. See G. W. McDonald, Special Study I, in M. Morris, *The General Strike*, Harmondsworth, 1976, pp. 306–12. The government also refused the request to appoint a Royal Commission. The 1927 Act was repealed in 1946.

171. S. 12, Employment Act 1982.

172. Ibid., s. 14. On section 13 see too below, n. 379.

173. *Financial Times*, 29 December 1981. This concession or 'acceptance' by the government is a curious posthumous victory for Kahn-Freund's teaching that the law is a 'secondary force in human affairs, and especially in industrial relations', *Labour* (1977), p. 2.

174. See above, text to n. 73 *et seq.*

175. See S. and B. Webb, *The History of Trade Unionism*, London, 1894, Chs. 1 and 2.

176. *Labour Research*, Vol. 70, July 1981, p. 152 where the very wide variety of union policies is disclosed; a few recruiting unemployed workers, others declaring it to be a matter 'for the TUC', etc. The six unions whose rules forbade membership for persons unemployed were all in the civil service or Post Office.

177. See the Social Security (No. 2) Act 1980, s. 6; Employment Act 1980, s. 16(1), enacting the new s. 15(1)(3) of TULRA 1974 on peaceful picketing; and Employment Act 1982, ss. 9 and 18.

178. *Proposals* (1981), para. 37. Disputes between any workers and an employer have been accepted since 1906 as trade disputes; and 'worker' has for long included an unemployed person who 'normally works or seeks to work', s. 30(1), TULRA 1974 (a definition used even in s. 167(1) of the Industrial Relations Act 1971).

179. See Employment Act 1982, s. 18(6). Unemployed workers can however join

workers who are parties to the dispute and enjoy such immunities as remain for their acts in contemplation or furtherance of a trade dispute: s. 18(7).

180. See *Lewis and Simpson*, pp. 40–4; see also M. Partington, 'Unemployment, Industrial Conflict and Social Security' (1980) 9 *Industrial Law Journal* 243.
181. See Wedderburn above, text to n. 189 *et seq.*
182. Kahn-Freund, *Heritage* (1979), p. 75.
183. *Trade Union Immunities* (1981), p. 82, which gives the authentic flavour of the problem, pp. 75–82.
184. See Employment Act 1982, s. 18, but also ss. 12–15.
185. See above, text to n. 147 *et seq.*
186. K. W. Wedderburn and P. L. Davies, *Employment Grievances and Disputes Procedures in Britain*, Berkeley and Los Angeles, 1969, p. 275.
187. Kahn-Freund, *Ginsberg* (1959), p. 241.
188. O. Kahn-Freund, *Federation News* (General Federation of Trade Unions), Vol. 14, 1964, p. N.41.
189. Griffith, *The Politics of the Judiciary*, p. 235.
190. Published in (1923) 1 *Cambridge Law Journal* 8.
191. For example, Lord Scarman's Report on the Grunwick dispute, Cmnd. 6922, 1977; on which see P. Elias, B. Napier, and P. Wallington, *Labour Law: Cases and Materials*, London, 1980, pp. 29–58.
192. Wedderburn, *The Worker and the Law* (1971), p. 30; and see p. 8.
193. TUC, *Action on Donovan*, London, 1968, p. 28, para. 72.
194. See below, text to n. 263.
195. For accounts see Kahn-Freund, *Labour* (1977), Ch. 1, *Ginsberg* (1959), and *System* (1954); Wedderburn, 'Industrial Relations and the Courts' (1980), p. 65; R. Lewis, 'The Historical Development of Labour Law' (1976).
196. Wedderburn, *The Worker and the Law* (1971), p. 314.
197. Respectively *A Giant's Strength* (1958), p. 11, and *Fair Deal at Work* (1968), p. 30.
198. *Trade Union Immunities* (1981), p. 92.
199. *Express Newspapers Ltd.* v. *McShane* [1979] I.C.R. 210, 218 (emphasis in original); reversed without reference to this point [1980] A.C. 672 (H.L.). Perhaps Lord Scarman is the only judge to have reflected reality in his basic analysis of the law in *NWL Ltd.* v. *Woods* [1979] 1 W.L.R. 1294, 1311–13.
200. One of the primary issues in *Hadmor Productions Ltd.* v. *Hamilton* [1981] I.C.R. 690 (C.A.); [1982] 2 W.L.R. 322 (H.L.) as to the effect of the repeal of s. 13(3), TULRA 1974–6 by s. 17(8), Employment Act 1980; see too *Camellia Tanker SA* v. *ITF* [1976] I.C.R. 274; Clerk and Lindsell on *Torts* (1982) paras, 15–32. On s. 17 see too *Marina Shipping Ltd.* v. *Laughton* [1982] I.R.L.R. 20 (C.A.); but contrast the argument by Wedderburn (1981) 10 *Industrial Law Journal* 113.
201. See above on 'political' strikes and trade disputes, text to n. 137 *et seq.*
202. For example, tenants peacefully picketing an estate agent, *per* Lord Denning MR in *Hubbard* v. *Pitt* [1976] Q.B. 142, 172; but the majority of the Court of Appeal denied any such rights on the highway. See on the police discretion to prosecute for obstruction in such cases, Griffith, *The Politics of the Judiciary*, pp. 94–6, 69–71.
203. *Broome* v. *D.P.P.* [1974] A.C. 587, 597, *per* Lord Reid. See Davies and Freedland, *Labour Law: Text and Materials*, pp. 675–84.
204. See *Labour* (1977), p. 264; contrast the approach in Wedderburn, *The Worker and the Law* (1971), pp. 321–6; and *Lewis and Simpson*, pp. 157–65; see also Wedderburn above, text to n. 150 *et seq.*
205. See, for example, *Hodges* v. *Webb* [1920] 2 Ch. 70 Peterson J.; *White* v. *Riley* [1921] 1 Ch. 1 (C.A., Lord Sterndale MR, Younger LJ and Warrington LJ).
206. *Lyons* v. *Wilkins* [1896] 1 Ch. 811, 825 (*arguendo*); [1899] 1 Ch. 255.
207. See Professor E. Jenks, *A Short History of English Law*, London, 1928, p. 337, commenting esp. on *Quinn* v. *Leathem* [1901] A.C. 495 (H.L.), and *Taff Vale*

Railway Co. v. *Amalgamated Society of Railway Servants* [1901] A.C. 426 (H.L.). See too the judicial denial of lawful political activities to unions in *Amalgamated Society of Railway Servants* v. *Osborne* [1910] A.C. 87 (H.L.); the Trade Union Act 1913 permitted union political funds on condition that any member can 'contract out'; see below, text to n. 383 *et seq.*

208. *Rookes* v. *Barnard* [1964] A.C. 1129, 1177 (emphasis supplied); see too pp. 1192, 1236 (H.L.).

209. See Wedderburn, *The Worker and the Law* (1971), Chs. 1, 7 and 8; Davies and Freedland, *Labour Law: Text and Materials*, Chs. 8 and 9; and Griffith, *The Politics of the Judiciary*, Chs. 3 and 9.

210. See *Crofter Hand Woven Harris Tweed* v. *Veitch* [1942] A.C. 435 (H.L. both); *Reynolds* v. *Shipping Federation* [1924] 1 Ch. 28 (employer and established union).

211. See the discussion by K. Ewing, 'The Golden Formula; Some Recent Developments' (1979) 8 *Industrial Law Journal* 133 (mostly judgments associated with Lord Denning MR).

212. *NWL Ltd.* v. *Woods* [1979] 1 W.L.R. 1294; *Express Newspapers Ltd.* v. *McShane* [1980] A.C. 672; *Duport Steels* v. *Sirs* [1980] 1 All E.R. 529.

213. The *Express* case at p. 687; the *Duport* case at p. 541 (see above, n. 212).

214. [1980] A.C. at p. 690.

215. Griffith, *The Politics of the Judiciary*, p. 225; see too Wedderburn, 'Industrial Relations and the Courts' (1980), p. 65; *Lewis and Simpson*, Ch. 9. See the parallel when, after the Employment Bill 1982 had been launched, the Law Lords decided *Hadmor Productions Ltd.* v. *Hamilton* [1982] 2 W.L.R. 322 (H.L.), reversing the repressive judgment of the Court of Appeal [1981] I.C.R. 690.

216. See *Universe Tankships Inc.* v. *ITF* [1982] 2 W.L.R. 803 (H.L.), and discussion by P. Atiyah (1982) 98 *Law Quarterly Review* 192; Wedderburn (1982) 45 *Modern Law Review* 556. Central to the new liability is pressure which 'overbears the will' of another (something which is also central to the entire process of collective negotiation), leaving the judges a free hand—yet again—to decide what is 'legitimate' pressure and thereby to determine whether one party may claim 'restitution' of money paid to the other.

217. The main exceptions are perhaps Lord Wright in the *Crofter* case, n. 210 above; and Lord Scarman in *UKAPE* v. *ACAS* [1981] A.C. 424.

218. Browne-Wilkinson J., *Powley* v. *ACAS* [1978] I.C.R. 123, at p. 135 (on the statutory powers of ACAS on 'recognition').

219. *Trade Unions in a Changing World: The Challenge for Management*, London, 1980 (discussion document, Steering Group Chairman Sir Alex Jarratt), p. 22.

220. *R.* v. *C.A.C. ex parte B.T.P. Tioxide* [1981] I.C.R. 843 (union 'recognized' within the meaning of the EPA 1975 for limited purposes and therefore entitled to information under s. 17 of the Act only within that limited area).

221. *Post Office* v. *Crouch* [1973] I.C.R. 366, 375; see too *TSA* v. *Post Office* [1974] I.C.R. 97, 104; aff'd. [1974] I.C.R. 658 (H.L.).

222. *UKAPE* v. *ACAS* [1979] I.C.R. 303, 310: 'By which I mean a small union pitted against a giant one'; reversed by the House of Lords [1981] A.C. 424 (one of the cases concerned with the 'obligatory recognition' provisions of the Social Contract legislation discussed below, text to n. 297 *et seq.*).

223. *Donovan Report*, Cmnd. 3623, p. 159 (in Chapter X, a chapter on which Kahn-Freund had great influence).

224. It is believed that Pain J. is the only English judge with trade union experience (as an official of the Fire Brigades Union during the war).

225. Griffith, *The Politics of the Judiciary*, p. 235.

226. 'Industrial Relations and the Law—Retrospect and Prospect' (1969) 7 *British Journal of Industrial Relations* 301, 316.

227. See Trade Union Act 1913, s. 3(2); and now ibid., s. 5A; EPA 1975, s. 88(2)(a)

and Sched. 16, Part IV, para. 2(3); and EPCA 1978, s. 136(2)(a). The EAT acquired appellate jurisdiction when the Certification Officer took over from the Registrar. It is presided over by a High Court judge.

228. G. F. Mancini, 'Politics and the Judges—The European Perspective' (1980) 43 *Modern Law Review* 1, 9–11 (on the *Magistratura Democratica* in Italy, emphasis supplied). On the consequences of courts becoming involved in the question of legitimacy of strikes, see O. Kahn-Freund, *Labour Law and Politics in the Weimar Republic*, Oxford, 1981, pp. 117–24.

229. Griffith, *The Politics of the Judiciary*, p. 241.

230. *The Social Ideal of the Reich Labour Court*, in O. Kahn-Freund, *Labour Law and Politics in the Weimar Republic*, Oxford, 1981, p. 152.

231. The famous remark of Winston Churchill on 30 May 1911; see Kahn-Freund, *Ginsberg* (1959), pp. 232 and 242.

232. *Employment Gazette* (1981), Vol. 89, p. 368. In 1980, 28,624 cases on unfair dismissal were brought, of which compensation was agreed in 9,041 out of 18,587 settled by conciliation, and awarded in 1,994 out of 10,037 decided by the tribunals; £1,000 or more was awarded in only 640 cases and the median award was £598, ibid., p. 539.

233. Industrial Tribunals (England and Wales) Regulations 1965, S.I. No. 1101.

234. K. Wraith and G. Hutchesson, *Administrative Tribunals*, London, 1973, pp. 85–7.

235. R. Whitesides and P. Hawker, *Industrial Tribunals*, London, 1975, p. 2.

236. Minimum notice periods were introduced by the Contracts of Employment Act 1963.

237. Statement of Intent, 17 December 1964; and see K. W. Wedderburn, *The Worker and the Law*, Harmondsworth, 1st ed. 1965, n. to pp. 94–5, for those criticisms.

238. 'Redundancy in Britain', *Ministry of Labour Gazette* (1963), p. 1.; G. Goodman, *Redundancy in the Affluent Society* (Fabian Trust 340), London, 1962.

239. But not actions for breach of the employment contract, to which the jurisdiction of the tribunals still has not been, though it could be, extended: EPCA 1978, s. 131.

240. See, for example, TUC Reports: 1963, p. 219; 1964, p. 144; 1965, p. 144. In 1967 Kahn-Freund said of proposals to introduce legislation on unfair dismissal: 'opinions are divided'; *Labour Law, Old Traditions and New Developments*, Toronto, 1968, p. 52.

241. *Dismissal Procedures*, N.J.A.C. (Ministry of Labour), paras. 194, 195.

242. *In Place of Strife*, Cmnd. 3888, 1969, paras. 103, 104; such provisions were included in the Labour government's Industrial Relations Bill 1970 (which lapsed); see Wedderburn, *The Worker and the Law* (1971), pp. 139–49. The TUC supported the government on the suitability of the tribunals; see TUC Report 1969, pp. 161–70.

243. For the thirty-two separate statutory heads of jurisdiction, see Hepple and O'Higgins, *Employment Law* (1981), pp. 362–4; and ibid., Ch. 22, for the modern law and practice of the tribunals generally.

244. Ministry of Labour, *Written Evidence* to the Royal Commission, etc., London, 1965, pp. 92–3.

245. *Parl. Deb.*, H.C., 26 April 1965, col. 46.

246. Donovan Report, Cmnd. 3623, paras. 568–78. As to the loss of informality and 'legalism' which now afflicts the tribunals—perhaps the only major defeat for civil service policy—see W. Hawes and G. Smith, *Patterns of Representation of the Parties in Unfair Dismissal Cases*, Research Paper No. 22, Dept. of Employment, London, 1981.

247. Wedderburn and Davies, *Employment Grievances and Disputes Procedures in Britain*, p. 245.

248. Hepple and O'Higgins, *Employment Law* (1981), p. 3.

249. See C. Jenkins and J. Mortimer, *The Kind of Laws the Unions Ought to Want*, London, 1968, pp. 80–6 (cases of 'arbitrary dismissal' should first be dealt with by

industrial procedures, and the union should decide whether to take them to 'an industrial court'). See too *Industrial Democracy* (The Labour Party), London, 1967, where proposals for legislation on arbitrary dismissal did not centre on the tribunals.

250. *In Place of Strife* (1969), p. 32.
251. See Wedderburn and Davies, *Employment Grievances and Disputes Procedures in Britain*, Part IV, pp. 243–75.
252. See the full accounts of the current position in Hepple and O'Higgins, *Employment Law* (1981), Ch. 22; Davies and Freedland, *Labour Law: Text and Materials*, pp. 726–54.
253. *Lewis and Simpson*, p. 121.
254. See now ss. 62, 63, EPCA 1978.
255. Ibid., ss. 23, 27, 58, as amended by the Employment Act 1980, ss. 7, 15. It is also noteworthy that in certain cases the trade union must initiate action before the tribunal for protection of members' rights to compensation: s. 99 of the 1975 Act (consultation on proposed redundancies).
256. Employment Act 1980, s. 10.
257. Employment Act 1982, s. 7. See too ibid., s. 11, and the 1980 Act, s. 15(4). For further discussion see above, text to n. 43 *et seq.*, and below, text to n. 358 *et seq.*
258. EPCA 1978, ss. 65, 96; and see Bourn (1979) 8 *Industrial Law Journal* 85.
259. See above, text to n. 73 *et seq.* and to n. 137 *et seq.*
260. See below, text to n. 293 *et seq.*
261. A. Campbell, *The Industrial Relations Act*, London, 1971, p. 29.
262. Industrial Relations Act 1971, s. 111.
263. TUC, *Action on Donovan* (1968), p. 28, para. 72: the TUC proposed they should be called 'Employment Tribunals'.
264. Sir John Donaldson MR, as he now is (President of NIRC 1971–4) 'Lessons from the Industrial Court' (1975) 91 *Law Quarterly Review* 181, 192. For an argument that the 1980 Codes put the courts now into a similar position, see *Lewis and Simpson*, pp. 226–9.
265. *A Giant's Strength* (1958), p. 22. See too below, text to n. 395, on proposals in 1982 by a leading social-democrat economist.
266. TUC Report 1971, pp. 368–70.
267. TUC Report 1972, p. 96.
268. Elias, Napier and Wallington, *Labour Law: Cases and Materials*, p. 25.
269. TUC Report 1969, p. 170; and see below, text to n. 289 *et seq.*
270. TUC Report 1975, pp. 97, 101.
271. Hepple and O'Higgins, *Employment Law* (1980), p. 365; by 1981, also, there were 62 full-time and 113 part-time chairmen compared with 19 and 32 in 1972; and the President had been joined by various regional chairmen.
272. See the full analysis of the 1980 Act in *Lewis and Simpson*, esp. Chs. 4 and 5.
273. *Trade Union Immunities*, Cmnd. 8128.
274. TUC Report 1980, pp. 389, 392 (Mr A. Scargill; but the sentiment was general).
275. TUC Report 1981, p. 82; and Statement of 24 November 1981. The ensuing Bill was also condemned by the TUC on its publication on 19 January 1982.
276. TUC Report 1980, p. 26.
277. TUC Report 1981, pp. 28–9; the body was the Managerial, Professional and Staff Liaison Group.
278. At the special conference of the TUC on 5 April 1982, the following recommendation was unanimously adopted: 'No trade union member of an industrial tribunal or the Employment Appeal Tribunal should serve on cases arising from the application of a union membership agreement or arrangement.'
279. *Traditions* (1968), p. 52; and 'Postscript', ibid., p. 81, where he looked forward to 'labour tribunals with jurisdiction over disputes arising from the contracts of employment'.

280. 'Retrospect and Prospect' (1969), pp. 301, 316.
281. Under what is now s. 131, EPCA 1978.
282. Kahn-Freund, *Labour* (1977), p. 134, n. 65.
283. Kahn-Freund, *Labour Law and Politics*, p. 152, and see on Sinzheimer's view of the function of labour tribunals, ibid., pp. 93–4.
284. His influence on Chapter X of the Donovan Report in this respect is striking; and his influence led to new interest in the French labour courts by English lawyers: see the useful articles by B. Napier (1979) 42 *Modern Law Review* 270; and S. Van Noorden (1980) Vol. 88 *Employment Gazette* 1098.
285. Camerlynck and Lyon-Caen, *Droit du Travail* (1980), pp. 800–4; *Code du Travail*, Art. L. 512–1; (in certain cases of deadlock a *juge d'instance* sits as chairman). On elections see Napier (1979) 42 *Modern Law Review* 270, who also notes that both employers and unions see them as 'tactical aids in a class conflict', p. 284. But W. H. McPherson and F. Meyers, *The French Labour Courts: Judgment by Peers*, Michigan, 1966, pp. 51–5, were struck by the absence of such 'partisanship' in the early sixties.
286. For the relevant literature see L. Dickens, M. Hart, M. Jones, and B. Weekes, *Third Party Intervention in Individual Disputes: A Study of the Industrial Tribunal System and Unfair Dismissal*, Oxford (forthcoming); and on 'legalism' esp. R. Munday, 'Tribunal Lore: Legalism and the Industrial Tribunals' (1981) 10 *Industrial Law Journal* 146; and Hawes and Smith, *Patterns of Representation of the Parties in Unfair Dismissal Cases*.
287. *Labour Law and Politics*, p. 152.
288. Wedderburn, *The Worker and the Law* (1971), p. 481.
289. See J. Clark, H. Hartmann, C. Lau, and D. Winchester, *Trade Unions, National Politics and Economic Management*, London, 1980, pp. 20–4.
290. Esp. the statutory policies in the Prices and Incomes Acts, 1966, 1967 and 1968; and some of the proposals in *In Place of Strife* (1969).
291. See Kahn-Freund, *Labour* (1977); Lord Wedderburn, 'The New Structure of Labour Law in Britain' (1978) 13 *Israel Law Review* 4; also R. Hyman, 'Green Means Danger?: Trade Union Immunities and the Tory Attack', in *Politics and Power 4*, London, 1981, pp. 134–6.
292. Proposals for more employment protection legislation had featured as early as 1967 in a report of a Labour Party working party, chaired significantly by Jack Jones. See *Industrial Democracy* (The Labour Party), 1967.
293. R. Lewis, 'Kahn-Freund and Labour Law' (1979) 8 *Industrial Law Journal* 202, 218–20; 'The Historical Development of Labour Law' (1976); for a rather different view see Kahn-Freund, *Labour* (1977), p. 46; and Wedderburn, 'Industrial Relations and the Courts' (1980), pp. 84–6.
294. Wedderburn, 'The New Structure of Labour Law in Britain' (1978), pp. 435, 445.
295. On the origins of this strange dichotomy see Kahn-Freund, 'Blackstone's Neglected Child: The Contract of Employment' (1977), p. 508; and above, text to n. 80.
296. And one that has clearly had direct impact in practice, see W. Brown (ed.), *Changing Contours*, p. 75; Health and Safety at Work Act 1974, s. 2; Safety Representatives and Safety Committees Regulations 1977, S.I. 500.
297. See above, text to n. 29; and on the judicial approach to ss. 11–16, EPA 1975 (before the conversion of the House of Lords in *UKAPE* v. *ACAS* [1981] A.C. 424), R. Simpson, 'Judicial Control of ACAS' (1979) 9 *Industrial Law Journal* 69; and now *Lewis and Simpson*, pp. 140–7. On the general story see J. Rogaly, *Grunwick*, Harmondsworth, 1977. See also Wedderburn above, n. 138.
298. Wedderburn, 'The New Structure of Labour Law in Britain' (1978), p. 456, but see below, text to n. 407 *et seq.* Kahn-Freund summarized some comparable countries' attempts to 'promote negotiation' in their labour laws in *Labour* (1977), Ch. 4. See too M. Hart, 'Union Recognition in America—The Legislative Snare'

(1978) 7 *Industrial Law Journal* 201 (a comparative view suggesting that 'recognition legislation [can] make it harder, not easier, to bring recalcitrant employers to the bargaining table'); and B. Doyle, 'A Substitute for Collective Bargaining?' (1980) 9 *Industrial Law Journal* 154 (on the C.A.C approach to enforcement, viewing abrogation of the obligation 'with mixed feelings').

299. Davies and Freedland, *Labour Law: Text and Materials*, p. 200; see too pp. 1–32.
300. Hyman, 'Green Means Danger?', p. 136.
301. See W. Brown (ed.), *Changing Contours*, Chs. 3 and 4; esp. pp. 42–50 (showing the mixed causation of legal intervention, union density, and bargaining practices).
302. A Flanders, *Industrial Relations: What is Wrong with the System?*, London, 1965, p. 28; and see the discussion in B. Aaron (ed.), *Dispute Settlement Procedures in Five Western European Countries*, University of California, 1969, by F. Schmidt, pp. 45 *et seq.* and K. W. Wedderburn, pp. 65 *et seq.*
303. See W. Brown (ed.), *Changing Contours* Ch. 3. See too on what follows: Ch. 5 on industrial conflict; and Ch. 7 where the place and weight of legal intervention in the 'conclusions' of the survey is notable. On job evaluation, see pp. 110–15; on employers' associations, pp. 19–25.
304. The base of the statistics on stoppages (contained in the *Department of Employment Gazette* 1974–81) allows for comparison only back to 1973. During this period the proportion of annual stoppages (other than about pay) relating to dismissal, redundancy, and discipline moved from 33.4 per cent in 1973, to 37.8 in 1975, 24.5 in 1977, 39.1 in 1978, and 34.7 in 1980. (The proportion of days lost and workers involved is even less favourable evidence for any such effect.)
305. M. Mellish and N. Collis-Squires, 'Legal and Social Norms in Discipline and Dismissal' (1976) 5 *Industrial Law Journal* 164.
306. Contrast the position of tripartite judicial tribunals, such as the Employment Appeal Tribunal or industrial tribunal, where the influence of the judge or legal chairman is strong and, in the case of disagreement between the lay members, decisive.
307. *Labour* (1977), p. 121. This point is discussed in the final section of this chapter, see below, text to n. 328 *et seq.*
308. See TUC Report 1973, pp. 106–7.
309. Ibid., p. 107. The TUC subsequently rejected the idea of 'two-tier' company boards.
310. *Industrial Democracy*, TUC Pamphlet, January 1977.
311. Ibid., p. 25.
312. *Industrial Democracy* (1977), pp. 33, 34.
313. *Labour Party Manifesto* (October 1974), p. 12. See generally, J. Elliott, *Conflict or Co-operation: The Growth of Industrial Democracy*, London, 1978; and *Report of the Committee of Inquiry on Industrial Democracy* (Bullock Report), Cmnd. 6706, 1977.
314. For a fuller discussion of the industrial democracy debate during this period see R. Lewis and J. Clark, 'The Bullock Report' (1977) 40 *Modern Law Review* 323–38; O. Kahn-Freund, 'Industrial Democracy' (1977) 6 *Industrial Law Journal* 65; P. Davies and Lord Wedderburn, 'The Land of Industrial Democracy' (1977) 6 *Industrial Law Journal* 197 (where the GMWU proposal is set out); and the government's White Paper *Industrial Democracy*, Cmnd. 7231, 1978.
315. TUC, 'Collective Bargaining and the Social Contract', in TUC Report 1974, p. 284.
316. This phrase was used to refer to the 'non-pay' issues in the Social Contract.
317. TUC, 'Collective Bargaining and the Social Contract', p. 284.
318. TUC Report 1975, p. 460 (emphasis supplied).
319. TUC Report 1975, p. 467.
320. See. J. Clark *et al.*, *Trade Unions, National Politics and Economic Management*, pp. 25–42, 62–7, 122–6. See too this analysis supported by Jack Jones in *The Forward*

March of Labour Halted?, eds. M. Jacques and F. Mulhern, London, 1981, pp. 154–7.

321. T. Topham, 'What Gains Have the Unions Made under Labour?', *Workers' Control Bulletin*, No. 35, 1977, p. 7. Obviously such 'standard norms' did not apply in all other Western European countries apart from Britain.

322. In Jacques and Mulhern (eds.), *The Forward March of Labour Halted?*, p. 21.

323. R. Lewis, 'Kahn-Freund and Labour Law' (1979), p. 220.

324. *Labour* (1977), p. 2.

325. See above, text to n. 5 *et seq.*

326. See above, text to n. 137 *et seq.* and to n. 157 *et seq.*

327. For a treatment of this theme in Kahn-Freund's early German writings see *Labour Law and Politics*, esp. pp. 151–5. One of Kahn-Freund's last words—addressed to a German audience—was to warn against the use of the law in Britain to regulate the activity of shop stewards: '. . . shop stewards are today a mainstay of democracy in trade unions, and any attempt to place them on a "legal" footing could be detrimental to this their most crucial function. The German reader of this book, who is acquainted to some extent with the history of Germany over the last half century, will not need to be reminded of the immense significance of the maintenance of internally active trade unions.' Kahn-Freund, 'Labour Law and Industrial Relations in Great Britain and West Germany', Chapter 1 above, p. 7.

328. *Trade Union Immunities* (1981), paras. 104–37.

329. For the current fluctuation of such uncertain liabilities see *Hadmor Productions Ltd.* v. *Hamilton* [1981] 2 All E.R. 724 (C.A.); [1982] 2 W.L.R. 332 (H.L.); *Universe Tankships Inc.* v. *ITF* [1980] I.R.L.R. 363 (C.A.); [1982] 2 W.L.R. 803 (H.L.); *Lonrho Ltd.* v. *Shell Petroleum Ltd.* [1981] 2 All E.R. 456 (H.L.); *Meade* v. *Haringey B.C.* [1979] I.C.R. 494 (C.A.); and on the interplay with weakened immunities, *Marina Shipping Ltd.* v. *Laughton* [1982] I.R.L.R. 20 (C.A.).

330. The issues were discussed in the Green Paper, *Trade Union Immunities* (1981), pp. 30–4.

331. C. Asquith, *Trade Union Law for Laymen*, London, 1927, p. 58; cf. Wedderburn, *The Worker and the Law* (1971), pp. 313–21; s. 4(1), Trade Disputes Act 1906, remedied the decision in *Taff Vale Railway Co.* v. *ASRS* [1901] A.C. 426 (H.L.).

332. See the useful summary in Winfield and Jolowicz on *Tort* (1979), pp. 550–2; and C.H.S. Fifoot, *History and Sources of the Common Law*, London, 1949, Ch. 9. Today the explanations of the 'philosophy' of the doctrine are numerous; see Atiyah, *Vicarious Liability in the Law of Torts*, Chs. 1 and 2.

333. *Lloyd* v. *Grace Smith and Co.* [1912] A.C. 716 ('ostensible' authority). See the narrow interpretation of vicarious liability today, for commercial 'agents' in *Kooragang Ltd.* v. *Richardson and Wrench Ltd.* [1981] 3 All E.R. 65 (P.C., Lord Wilberforce); compare the attitude to liability of a union for its 'agents' in *Heatons Transport Ltd.* v. *TGWU* [1973] A.C. 15 (H.L., Lord Wilberforce).

334. Cmnd. 3623, June 1968, p. 32, para. 122.

335. As the government claimed in its *Proposals* (1981), para. 33.

336. [1973] A.C. 15 (H.L.), see Lord Wilberforce at p. 103; and P. Davies (1973) 36 *Modern Law Review* 78.

337. *General Aviation Services (UK) Ltd.* v. *TGWU* [1976] I.R.L.R. 224 (H.L.). The Law Lords in the majority were clearly determined to bury the 1971 Act, by then repealed.

338. 'The Industrial Relations Act' (1974) 3 *Industrial Law Journal* 186, 188.

339. S. 36(2), Industrial Relations Act 1971.

340. *Howitt Transport Ltd.* v. *TGWU* [1973] I.C.R. 1; K. W. Wedderburn, 'Will the NIRC Expand Vicarious Liability?' (1973) 36 *Modern Law Review* 226.

341. *Heatons Transport Ltd.* v. *TGWU* [1973] A.C. at p. 111; and see *Con-Mech (Engineers) Ltd.* v. *AUEW* [1974] I.C.R. 332; N. Lewis (1974) 3 *Industrial Law Journal* 201;

Wedderburn (1974) 37 *Modern Law Review* 187. 'Withdrawal of authority' arose only after the 'authority' had been found to exist in respect of initial liability: see [1973] A.C. p. 101.

342. See the judgments in the *Heatons'* case above; and on rule books, Weekes *et al.*, *Industrial Relations and the Limits of Law*, Ch. 4; and Davies and Freedland, *Labour Law: Text and Materials*, Ch. 8.

343. *Proposals* (1981), paras. 33, 34.

344. On the economic or 'industrial' torts, see above, n. 141. It is not clear why the statutory code of agency under the Act applies only to these torts (to which section 13, TULRA 1974, affords some defence in trade disputes for the union along with other defendants) while the common law principles on vicarious liability apply to other torts (for example, libel). One set of proceedings could raise issues of union liability for an 'industrial' tort and for a 'non-industrial' tort.

345. Employment Act 1982, s. 15(3); in what follows 'authorizing' includes 'endorsing'. For the definition of terms see s. 15(7). The term 'official' includes both full-time officers and shop stewards; see s. 30(1), TULRA 1974.

346. See Employment Act 1982, s. 15(3)(d)(e),(4),(5),(6). It appears that a repudiation by the executive committee can be nullified by an inconsistent act by the President or the General Secretary.

347. See above, text to n. 33, on the claims of the judiciary to the right to grant interim injunctions in cases where the damage may be 'disastrous'—an indication of the likely attitude of the courts in such cases in practice.

348. S. 15(3)(b).

349. See ibid., s. 15(4). This applies repudiation only to section 15(3) (d) and (e), not to (3)(b), which deals with officials 'empowered by the rules', such as shop stewards. As for the authority of shop stewards it is difficult to think of 'written provisions' incorporated into the union contract, as section 15(7) envisages, other than such documents as a shop steward's credentials.

350. See. E. Batstone, I. Boraston, and S. Frenkel, *Shop Stewards in Action*, Oxford, 1977, pp. 201–11. Also I. Boraston, H. Clegg, and M. Rimmer, *Workplace and Union*, London, 1975.

351. 'The advantages of a union movement with which its members continue to identify, which is "we" to them and not "they", should be obvious to anyone who like myself has consciously lived through the dying days of the Weimar Republic and witnessed the moral and political collapse of the gigantic German unions— which had long since ceased to be a movement capable of moving.' Kahn–Freund, *Heritage* (1979), p. 20.

352. Employment Act 1982, s. 16. The Secretary of State is empowered to increase the limits by Order. No limit is set in actions for damages for personal injury or for breach of duty based on ownership, control, or use of property (a provision which might include a libel suit against a union journal).

353. Ibid., s. 17. The description (which may not be exhaustive) of 'provident benefits' in section 17(3) will cause major legal difficulties. Further, the position of branch funds is obscure, i.e. whether or not a branch is (as it may be in law sometimes) a separate trade union. The Act defines 'political fund' as a fund which falls within s. 3 of the Trade Union Act 1913 *and* is prevented by the rules from being used to finance industrial action. A union's rules may lawfully authorize use of its political fund for that purpose: N. Citrine, *Trade Union Law*, London, 3rd. ed. 1967, p. 423.

354. Compare the Industrial Relations Act 1971, s. 154(4), which was usually interpreted to mean that property escaped execution only if it was held in such funds permanently under 'unalterable' union rules (for the amendment of which TULRA 1974 gave special statutory permission in s. 20).

355. For the *alter ego* doctrine in company law, where for certain purposes directors are

treated as the company (rather than merely as its agents), see L.C.B. Gower, *Modern Company Law*, London, 4th ed. 1979, pp. 205–13. The union rules, however, remain an enforceable contract, for breach of which the President or General Secretary (or possibly the union) may be liable at the suit of a member. The same act which constitutes that breach gives to an outsider a right in damages against the officer *and* the union–an odd case of double jeopardy.

356. See the classic statement of Lord Cranworth in *Pole* v. *Leask* (1862) 33 L.J. Ch. 155, 161–2. See too above, text to n. 88 *et seq*.

357. *Trade Union Immunities* (1981), para. 135.

358. See above, text to n. 28 *et seq*. and n. 43 *et seq*. On the 1980 Act see *Lewis and Simpson*, Chs. 3, 4, and 5.

359. See Donovan Report, 1968, para. 190 and Ch. IX.

360. See above, n. 264.

361. See now ss. 7 and 11, Employment Act 1982. There is a right to have the union 'joined' before the hearing. Once the hearing has begun, the tribunal has a discretion to refuse joinder. No joinder is permitted once an award has been made. In 1980 the government had in fact refused to extend to the dismissed employee power to 'join' the union, its officials, or other workers, on the grounds that this might create a 'running sore' in a plant's industrial relations (Commitee on Employment Bill, *Parl. Deb.*, H.C., 11 March 1980, cols. 1072–3).

362. See ss. 58(3C) and 58A, EPCA 1978, introduced by s. 7, Employment Act 1980; and now s. 3, Employment Act 1982, explained above, text to n. 61 *et seq*.

363. S. 81(2), EPCA 1978; R. Fryer, 'Myths of Redundancy Payments' (1973) 2 *Industrial Law Journal* 1, and (1973) 4 *Industrial Relations Journal* 2.

364. See H. Forest, 'Political Values in Individual Employment Law' (1980) 43 *Modern Law Review* 361; J. Bowers and A. Clarke, 'Unfair Dismissal and Managerial Prerogative' (1981) 10 *Industrial Law Journal* 34; F. Boothman and D. Denham (1981) 12 *Industrial Relations Journal* No. 3, 6; P. Elias, 'Fairness in Unfair Dismissal: Trends and Tensions' (1981) 10 *Industrial Law Journal* 201.

365. L. Dickens, M. Hart, M. Jones, and B. Weekes, 'Re-employment of Unfairly Dismissed Workers: "The Lost Remedy"' (1981) 3 *Industrial Law Journal* 160; P. Lewis, 'Employment Protection' (1981) 12 *Industrial Relations Journal* No. 2, 9; K. Williams and D. Lewis, 'Re-employing the Unemployed' (1981) 89 *Employment Gazette* 357 (proposing 'trial periods' of re-employment to counter management opposition and to wean tribunals from managerial attitudes).

366. See B. Hepple, 'A Right to Work?' (1981) 10 *Industrial Law Journal* 65 for an examination of the various usages of that phrase.

367. The effectiveness of the rights in respect of maternity after the the 1980 Act are even more dubious; see *Lewis and Simpson*, pp. 45–56; R. Upex and A. Morris, 'Maternity Rights—Illusion or Reality' (1981) 10 *Industrial Law Journal* 218.

368. (1981) 89 *Employment Gazette* 539. Just over one-third of notified cases went before the tribunals. But now under the 1982 Act a non-unionist will of course go through the motions of demanding re-employment in order to secure the higher minimum compensation award.

369. Arts. 18 and 28, Workers Statute 1970, Law 300; *Lo Statuto dei Lavoratori*, ed. G. Giugni, 1979, pp. 455–523; *L'uso politico dello Statuto dei Lavoratori*, ed. T. Treu, Bologna, 1975, Vol. I, Chs. I, III; and ibid. (1976), Vol. II, Chs. II, III, IV, on the use made of the statute.

370. In Britain it is well known to be difficult to prove that a dismissal occurs by reason of trade union membership or activity, let alone to achieve a remedy, as the *Beyer* case illustrated: *Birmingham District Council* v. *Beyer* [1977] I.R.L.R. 211. More attention should however be paid to the protection of workers in respect of 'proposed' trade union activity: ss. 23(1), 58(1), EPCA 1978. On the superficial even-handedness of sections 3 to 6 of the 1982 Act offering higher compensation to

those dismissed either for being non-unionists or for trade union activity, see above, text to n. 66 *et seq.*

371. See the Donovan Report, p. 163, para. 600; and now L. Dickens and R. Lewis, 'A Response to the Government's Proposals for Industrial Relations Legislation 1981', Discussion Paper, Industrial Relations Research Unit, University of Warwick, 1982, pp. 1–8.

372. See above, text to n. 30.

373. Under Secretary of State for Employment, *Parl Deb.*, H.C., 7 December 1981, col. 679.

374. Transfer of Undertakings (Protection of Employment) Regulations 1981 S.I. No. 1794; see for an analysis of the differences between the 1978 draft and 1981 Regulations: *Parl. Deb.*, H.L., 10 December 1981, cols. 1482–1501. Such Regulations which must be passed or rejected by Parliament without amendment illustrate the weakening of the powers of each House under the procedure to enact EEC Directives compared with the normal procedures of a Bill.

375. B. Hepple, 'The Transfer of Undertakings (Protection of Employment) Regulations' (1982) 11 *Industrial Law Journal* 29.

376. Evidence of Department of Employment, 'Employee Consultation' 37th Report, House of Lords Select Committee on European Communities (on the so-called 'Vredeling proposals'), p. 2; and see the Report, p. xix: the proposals are 'too detailed and too doctrinaire'; there is a need for no more than 'legally backed minimum standards' with a 'code of practice embodying guidelines' (which would in effect be unenforceable).

377. Employment and Training Act 1981. The government later announced its intention to close sixteen of the twenty-three statutory training boards, *Financial Times*, 16 January 1982.

378. See section 19, Employment Act 1980, repealing sections 11–16 of the EPA 1975, leaving its grant of rights for the union to information (s. 17) or to consultation on redundancies (s. 99) stranded.

379. The new section 13, which confirmed the government's true intentions on union recognition, was added at a late stage of the 1982 Act's passage through Parliament. It renders unlawful as a statutory tort any commercial pressure (by way of refusal to deal, termination of contract, or the like) where *one* of the grounds is that the other person involved 'does not, or is not likely to, recognize, negotiate, or consult' with a trade union (s. 13(2)(3)). As in section 12, both the person directly affected and any person 'who may be adversely affected' may bring a legal action (s. 13(4)(b); on the parallel section 12, see above, text to nn. 48–50). A condition in a commercial contract requiring one party to negotiate, or even to consult with, trade unions is rendered void (s. 13(1)). The use of commercial pressure between businessmen to support bargaining or consultation is thus outlawed, and with it practices such as 'fair lists' or offers to contract with 'trade union firms only'—a common way of avoiding undercutting by 'cowboys' and of maintaining basic terms and conditions in a number of trades, not least among draftsmen and printers.

Industrial action taken or threatened by a union in order to induce someone to act in contravention of the prohibition on commercial dealing of which one purpose is to maintain recognition, negotiation, or consultation with unions, is deprived of the immunities in section 13 of TULRA 1974 (s. 14(1), Employment Act 1982). The late addition of section 13 of the Act ensures that industrial action is also deprived of the TULRA immunities wherever it can 'reasonably be expected' to interfere with a commercial contract, if *one* of the reasons for the action is that a party to the contract (or at any rate a supplier to the worker's own employer) 'does not, or is not likely to, recognise, negotiate, or consult' with a trade union (s. 14(2) and (3)(c)). Thus the new prohibitions go far beyond the issues of union membership agreements, though they were tacked on to the 1982 Act ostensibly as the closing of 'loopholes' in sections 12 and 14 which forbid commercial or industrial pressure to sustain closed shops.

380. *Parl. Deb.*, H.L., 13 June 1980, col. 807.

381. In 1982 the government in fact followed the logic of its policies by making it clear that it intended, as soon as it could rid itself of the relevant international obligations arising under ILO Conventions, to do away with the Fair Wages Resolution (see *Parl. Deb.*, H.C., 26 May 1982, col. 320) and to 'slim down', if not disband, the Wages Councils (see *Parl. Deb.*, H.L., 22 March 1982, col. 892).

382. See *R.* v. *C.A.C. ex parte B.T.P. Tioxide Ltd.* [1981] I.C.R. 843.

383. *Amalgamated Society of Railway Servants* v. *Osborne* [1910] A.C. 87; Trade Union Act 1913, ss. 3–6; Trade Disputes and the Trade Union Act 1927, ss. 3, 4 (repealed by Trade Disputes and Trade Union Act 1946); Donovan Report (1968), paras. 912–27 and Appendix 7.

384. *Labour* (1977), p. 202.

385. Esp. because of the alleged right of the Crown to 'dismiss at pleasure'. See generally B. Hepple and P. O'Higgins, *Public Employee Trade Unionism in the United Kingdom*, Michigan, 1971. Distinctions may need to be drawn between industrial and non-industrial civil servants.

386. See e.g. TULRA 1974, ss. 29(2), 30(1)(2); EPCA 1978, ss. 95, 138; see also, however, some provisions which are enacted 'without prejudice to any exemption or immunity of the Crown' (e.g. s. 99).

387. See Aaron and Wedderburn (eds.), *Industrial Conflict—A Comparative Legal Survey*, pp. 364–77; in each of these countries the sub-divisions of public employees is more complex. See Ch. 6 generally on 'essential services' and strikes.

388. H. Wellington and K. Winter, *The Unions and the Cities*, New York, 1971, pp. 40–1; but see Chs. 8–12 for some ingenious proposals, recognizing that 'the strike ban, wise as it is in theory, will not work in all places at all times' (p. 201).

389. Partly because, like the German *Beamte*, he was regarded as someone holding 'employment for life', F. Schmidt, *Law and Industrial Relations in Sweden*, Stockholm, 1977, p. 15.

390. See F. Schmidt, *Law and Industrial Relations in Sweden*, pp. 197–201; compare the similar Italian solution on 'political' trade disputes, text to n. 146 *et seq.* above.

391. L. Forsebäck, *Industrial Relations and Employment in Sweden*, Stockholm, 1980, p. 48.

392. Stig Jäerskjöld in *An Introduction to Swedish Law*, ed. S. Strömholm, Nordstets, 1981, p. 88. F. Schmidt was more cautious: *Law and Industrial Relations in Sweden*, pp. 196–7.

393. See above, text to n. 33.

394. See C. Whelan, 'Military Intervention in Industrial Disputes' (1979) 8 *Industrial Law Journal* 222; R. Lewis, 'Nuclear Power and Employment Rights' (1978) 7 *Industrial Law Journal* 1; G. Morris, 'The Police and Industrial Emergencies' (1980) 9 *Industrial Law Journal* 1. See too section 5, Conspiracy and Protection of Property Act 1875, which is still a basis for criminal liability where strike action threatens life or property; and section 7 of that Act, on the crimes of 'intimidation', 'watching or besetting', and 'persistent following', text to n. 162 above. Section 4 of the Act, placing criminal sanctions on certain strikes by gas, electricity, and water workers was repealed in 1971.

395. See J. Meade, *Stagflation Vol. 1; Wage Fixing*, London, 1982; Professor Meade is a leading adviser to the Social Democratic Party. The discussion in Chs. VII and VIII of the Donovan Report of 1968 is very relevant to these remarkable proposals, esp. on the question of limiting social security payments.

396. In 1980 the funds of all trade unions amounted to £295 million and their assets (taking no account of liabilities) were £320 million. In 1982 it was calculated that if the train drivers' union ASLEF paid its members on strike £12 a week, its cash

balance would disappear in a week and its entire assets within eight weeks. Since the new social security rules 'deemed' each striker to be in receipt of £13 a week, prospects of a long strike were 'questionable', *Financial Times*, 20 January 1982.

397. *Financial Times*, 30 November 1981, leading article entitled 'Management by Consent'. During the report stage of the Employment Bill in July/August 1982, the House of Lords, on the initiative of the Liberal and Social Democratic Alliance, won a commitment from the government to give legal effect to a requirement on directors to report annually upon their arrangements for 'consultation' with and 'involvement' of employees, and upon the achievement of a 'common awareness' of the company's problems amongst managers and employees. This new initiative on 'employee participation' made no mention at all of trade unions. In amended form it is now section 1 of the 1982 Act.

398. TUC-Labour Party Liaison Committee, *Economic Issues Facing the Next Labour Government*, London, 1981, p. 14.

399. J. Hughes, *Britain in Crisis: De-Industrialisation and How to Fight It*, Nottingham, 1981; F. Cripps, J. Griffith, F. Morrell, J. Reid, P. Townsend, and S. Weir, *Manifesto—A Radical Strategy for Britain's Future*, London, 1981; S. Aaronovitch, *The Road from Thatcherism: The Alternative Economic Strategy*, London, 1981; D. Currie and R. Smith (eds.), *Socialist Economic Review*, London, 1981.

400. *Economic Issues Facing the Next Labour Government*, pp. 14–15.

401. TUC, *Programme for Recovery—Economic Review*, London, 1982, pp. 42–3, paras. 11.5, 11.11. On the relation between economic planning and new statutory rights for workers see TUC-Labour Party Liaison Committee, *Economic Planning and Industrial Democracy: The Framework for Full Employment*, Report to the 1982 TUC Congress and Labour Party Conference.

402. *Labour* (1977), p. 6.

403. See Lewis and Clark, 'Introduction' to *Labour Law and Politics*, pp. 16–36.

404. See Wedderburn above, text to n. 68 *et seq.*

405. *Labour* (1977), pp. 8–9.

406. See *Supplementary Evidence to the 'Bullock Committee'* in *Industrial Democracy* (1977), p. 48, where it was argued that worker representation of 50 per cent was acceptable 'so long as trade unions were under no obligation to take up 50 per cent of the seats on the policy making board'.

407. On ss. 11–16 of the Employment Protection Act, see above, text to n. 297 *et seq.*

408. In the USA the development of such employer hostility to trade unionism has become a veritable industry, and private consultants now advise companies on techniques of preventing or breaking effective worker organization. The euphemistic term for such activity is 'preventive labour relations'. See 'Killing Unions with Kindness', *The Guardian*, 4 January 1982.

409. See above, text to n. 276 *et seq.*

Index